Problems of Trade Policy

Problems
of
Trade Policy

Gerald M. Meier
Professor of International Economics
Stanford University

Oxford University Press
1973

For Jeremy

Preface

I have found the treatment of foreign economic policy-making in a
textbook usually disappointing; not because it is wrong, but because
it is scarcely there. To remedy this, I have used a new approach in
designing three volumes on policy problems in international political economy. This is the first volume; the others are *Problems of
World Monetary Order* and *Problems of Cooperation for Development*. Each volume focuses on a particular set of policy situations,
related to an underlying theme of foreign economic policy-making.

I have attempted to set forth problems of decision-making in the
public sector in a manner that is more realistic and challenging
than that of a textbook or a casebook. I do not think students want
policy problems which are inherently complex and controversial
to be artificially simplified (as in a textbook) or distilled in a highly
structured manner (as in a casebook). This book concentrates on
three specific policy situations that allow students to confront the
problems of policy-making from "within"—in a less mechanical
fashion and with a livelier sense of participation in the resolution
of tangible policy issues. Using a narrative and primary materials,
I have tried to construct each policy problem in a way that reveals
the plot and the tensions—the controversies over alternatives—involved in the actual decision-making situation.

The problems have not, however, been selected simply because of
their immediate interest in the political arena. The need for rele-
vance is greater than that. Instead of considering it essential that the
facts of the problem be current, I have emphasized policy areas with
long-term issues, so that history will not soon overtake their rele-

vance. The particular problems of international trade policy covered in this book involve the significance of the General Agreement on Tariffs and Trade and the Kennedy Round of tariff negotiations, the pressure for United States import quotas on textiles, and the enlargement of the European Economic Community. The particular is used to illuminate the general—and the part embraces the whole.

Various approaches are possible for utilizing these policy problems along with more theoretical readings in international economics. Each problem reconstructs a policy situation to which the student should respond with a critique of the decisions made and with proposals for the future. The problems may serve as a focus for a general discussion of the issues that arise in the process of reaching policy decisions in foreign economic affairs. Or students may want to engage in some specific role-playing as a decision-maker— whether as an official in an international organization, an adviser to a national government, a business executive, or the representative of some "interest organization." A multi-interest group may even actively enter into negotiations over the policy issues, or position papers may be written. Some instructors may want to use these problems in an applied fashion, after the exposition of the pure theory of international trade. Others may want to precede the theory with a discussion of the problems as a means of arousing interest in fundamental theoretical principles. Regardless of the particular pedagogical approach selected, the study of the problems should facilitate the interweaving of theory and application as a basis for policy prescriptions.

My primary debt is to my students at Stanford: they were sufficiently skeptical of the conventional treatment of international economic policy to inspire me to try new approaches in teaching policy matters. I have appreciated their responses to these policy problems.

For ferreting out such information as "parking-lot campaign pledges on textiles"—and much else—I am grateful to Edward Ericson and Alfred Osborne, Jr. And for keeping track of it all—and seeing it through—I owe many thanks to Mrs. Renée Hamerman.

Permission to reprint extracts from the *Financial Times, Manchester Guardian, The New York Times, The Economist* (London), *The New Statesman,* the *Times* (London), and the *Wall Street Journal* is kindly acknowledged.

February 1972   G. M. M.
Stanford, California

To the Student

From a study of the policy problems in this book, I want you to appreciate that economics is still concerned with social betterment; that economic problems cannot be solved in a political vacuum; that qualitative appraisals may be as important as quantitative calculations; and that in public policy formulation, the formal economic principle must usually give way at some point to a value judgment.

These problems do not permit a technocratic approach to policymaking. On the contrary, they emphasize that most policy problems have no natural boundaries and that decision-making is an art as well as a science. Long ago, Keynes observed that economics does not constitute a body of knowledge immediately applicable to policy. Notwithstanding all the advances in the "science" of decision-making, few—if any—economists would yet deny Keynes' dictum. And all who have experienced the complexities of actual decision-making in international economic affairs will appreciate that technical analysis must sooner or later yield to judgment—or to the qualities of imagination and intuition which Keynes believed to be as much a part of economics as logic and fact.

It is essential to realize that the rational approach to decision-making—that is, systematic analysis of effective alternatives and their consequences—must be tempered by the culture of power and politics, by institutional interests, and even by emotional beliefs. Political feasibility as well as economic rationality are essential ingredients in decision-making. In each of the policy problems that you will study, it will also be evident that nonrational factors may influence decisions through the choice of values involved.

The problems in this book relate to international welfare economics; or in the older terminology of political economy, to free trade versus protection. They pose policy issues that stem from the conflicts between nationalist politics and internationalist economics. For while the economics of each of these problems may illustrate that the world is becoming more interdependent, the politics of the problems raise the question as to whether the capability for multinational co-operation in dealing with the economic interdependency has managed to keep apace or instead has suffered a decline.

A word on organization. This book begins with a general expository introduction on economic peacekeeping that recapitulates some basic principles and provides some perspective of the problems that follow. The materials for each policy problem are then set forth in a way that I have thought would best reveal the development of events and the execution of policy decisions. I have tried to unfold the "biography" of each policy situation by presenting an analytical narrative and a set of source materials, so that you might gain a sense of the crucial issues in each situation, the types of international conflict involved, and the modes of resolution and co-operation effected. This normally involves placing the problem in its larger context (Section A), followed by the development of the factual situation and the presentation of the actual decisions (Section B). To allow you to discover the major policy issues in the problem made, I have tried to use to advantage, documents, reports, and other source materials—while providing continuity with a narrative. Some "seasoning" has been added by giving the observations of the actors, observers, or commentators of the time. Finally, I have provided some questions designed to aid you in analyzing and evaluating the specific policy decisions (Section C).

This method of presenting policy problems is intended to encourage your own thinking about these problems. While materials are offered to illuminate the particular policy problem, it is up to you to identify and analyze the major issues; and you must be prepared to adopt and defend your own policy position with respect to the problem's resolution. You need not worry about a "correct" answer to the problem, but you should be very much concerned about the quality of the reasoning behind your own answer—about the "why" of your conclusion. Your specific recommendations are not as important as your understanding of the complexity of the policy problem and your clarity on criteria for judging the merits of alternatives. Each problem has two objectives: to extend your capacity to evaluate the quality of public policy-making and to suggest ways of improving the process in international economic affairs.

In considering each problem, you will therefore have to exercise your own judgment on a set of questions: What were the crucial policy issues in the problem? How were they resolved? Would another course of action have been preferable? What do you now conclude about the desirable future course of action?

Contents

Problems of Trade Policy

Background:
Economic Peacekeeping

This book is concerned with how nations treat each other in matters of international trade. All of its policy problems illustrate the pressing need to develop an allocation of authority and control to maintain a system of order in international trade affairs. The recurrent theme is that trade liberalization has to be deliberately pursued and enforced; free trade is not a natural state of affairs, and trade warfare has to be averted by some form of multilateral surveillance.

Even though the free trade doctrine of comparative advantage demonstrates that the "gains from trade" are mutual—that trade benefits all the trading nations—a single nation is always tempted to improve its own position relative to other countries by imposing trade restrictions. And if successive rounds of retaliatory trade restrictions ensue, then all countries are likely to become worse off, even though each national government initially believes it will improve its own position through a "beggar-my-neighbor" policy. Trade warfare is in essence a zero-sum game: one country's gain is another's loss.[1] And

---

1. Although classic game theory is considerably simpler than the realities of international economics, some conflict situations in international trade may be viewed as games, and a game-theoretic discussion may help highlight some strategies and possible outcomes.

For elaboration of game theory in international affairs, see *International Behavior,*

yet, as long as nation-states remain the main centers of power in the world economy, but are without oligopolistic rationality, it may be possible to reach a stable solution to a situation that is inherently one of conflict only by establishing some international organization that can intervene effectively in the cause of freer trade.[2]

If the real forces of international economic integration are to be allowed to operate and the gains from trade are to be shared among all nations, the escalation toward trade conflicts must be halted and reversed. A strategy of conflict reduction and peacekeeping is as necessary in international economics as in political affairs.

The problems of economic peacekeeping have long been analyzed in terms of international commercial policy. Few, if any, policy issues in economics have a longer intellectual history than that of free trade versus protection. During the last two centuries the basic secular forces in the world economy have been supporting integration and growth of the world economy.[3] Occasionally, however, protectionist commercial policies have come to the fore and have caused disintegration of the world economy. And while the main thrust of the policy implications of international trade theory is in support of freer trade, there are still many arguments for protection that command serious attention.

In the beginning, Adam Smith exposed the fallacies of mercantilism—the system that emphasized the economic power of the State and thought this power could be enhanced by increasing the State treasury and the holding of specie through a "favorable" balance of trade stimulated by export subsidies and import duties.[4]

H. Kelman (ed.) (1965); T. C. Schelling, *The Strategy of Conflict* (1960); Bruce Russett, *Economic Theories of International Politics* (1968); W. H. Ricker, *The Theory of Political Coalitions* (1967); M. Nicholson, *Conflict Resolution* (1970).

2. See T. Scitovsky, "A Reconsideration of the Theory of Tariffs," *Review of Economic Studies*, 1941–42, pp. 89–110; J. Bhagwati, "The Pure Theory of International Trade," *Economic Journal*, March 1964, pp. 1–84.

3. See G. Haberler, "Integration and Growth of the World Economy in Historical Perspective," *American Economic Review*, March 1964, pp. 1–22.

4. Classic discussions of mercantilism are presented by E. F. Heckscher, *Mercantilism* (1935); Jacob Viner, "Power versus Plenty as Objectives of Foreign Policy in the 17th and 18th Centuries," *World Politics*, Oct. 1948, pp. 1–29; Viner, "Mercantilist Thought," *International Encyclopedia of the Social Sciences* (1968), pp. 435–42; Charles Wilson, "'Mercantilism': Some Vicissitudes of an Idea," *Economic History Review*, 1957, pp. 181–88.

To Smith, the objective of trade was to maximize national real income ("to render the annual revenues of society as great as it can be"). By appealing to the principle of absolute advantage, Smith maintained that no country should make at home what would cost more to make than to import: "If a foreign country can supply us with a commodity cheaper than we ourselves can make it, better buy it of them with some part of the produce of our own industry, employed in a way in which we have some advantage . . ." [5]

The intellectual defeat of mercantilism was complete with the enunciation of Hume's self-regulating price-specie-flow mechanism (a "favorable" balance of trade would automatically be removed through the increase in the money supply and rise in prices) and Ricardo's exposition of comparative advantage (there is nothing particularly "favorable" about exports being greater than imports, and what really matters is the principle that a country should specialize in the production of those commodities for which production costs are comparatively low and import those commodities for which production costs are comparatively high). It was Ricardo's accomplishment to demonstrate (in terms of a simple two country-two commodity-one factor of production model) that trade is mutually profitable even when one country is absolutely more—or less —productive in terms of every commodity. The cost of "indirectly producing" a country's imports through specialization in its exports is less than if the country directly produced the importable commodity at home.

The political economy of the Ricardian model of comparative advantage is instructive for problems of international trade policy and welfare. Ricardo did not formulate the theory of comparative advantage out of an intrinsic interest in theory per se, but devised it in response to a real public policy issue—his concern with the repeal of the Corn Laws. Ricardo wanted the import duties on corn (grain) to be removed in order that the cost of living for labor could be lower, and hence wages lower and profits higher, so that there might be greater capital accumulation, more employment, and growth of output. His theory of comparative advantage was therefore not restricted to only positive economic analysis, but also had welfare implications—the policy conclusion that free trade was supe-

5. Adam Smith, *The Wealth of Nations*, (Modern Library Edition), p. 425.

rior to protection and that English society would benefit by free trade.[6]

It is also interesting to note that Ricardo used a labor theory of value, and by expressing the real cost of production in labor-time, he was able to emphasize the subjective costs associated with production—the disutility of labor-time—while emphasizing, on the other side, the gain from trade through "increasing the mass of commodities and therefore sum of enjoyments" per unit of his real value (the disutility of labor-time). Human beings as producers and consumers were not overlooked in Ricardo's formal economics: man was at the very center of the utilitarian calculus.

Finally, Ricardo was well aware that a policy of free trade would alter the distribution of income, making some individuals better off and others worse off. Indeed, he wanted the repeal of the Corn Laws to reduce the rents of landowners and raise the share of profits in national income, because he thought the landowner performed no productive economic function with the rent they received, whereas profit recipients would invest their greater savings, give rise to more employment of labor, and stimulate growth of the economy. In Ricardo's words, "I am of the opinion that the interests of society are best promoted by allowing the free importation of corn, the consequence of which is that the surplus produce from the land in cultivation at home will be divided in proportions more favorable to the farmer and capitalist, and less favorable to the landholder."[7] In this statement, Ricardo undertook no refined weighting of the gains against the losses to different individuals as a result of a change in public policy, but he was willing to make explicit his valuation of which groups should gain or lose in the economy in accordance with his view of what should be the objectives of the economy. He also expressed a judgment on the international distribution of income among the trading nations insofar as he wanted all trading nations to be better off as the result of trade, and he believed that the gains from trade were mutual.

In devising a theory in response to the need to illuminate a pol-

---

6. *Works and Correspondence of David Ricardo*, P. Sraffa (ed.), Vol. I, *On the Principles of Political Economy and Taxation*, chap. VII.

7. *Works and Correspondence of David Ricardo*, P. Sraffa (ed.), Vol. II, *Notes of Malthus*, p. 223.

icy problem, in having the theory possess policy implications, in recognizing that economics is ultimately concerned with the economic welfare of human beings, and in making explicit his value judgments about the distribution of income—in having his model of comparative advantage possess all these qualities, Ricardo incorporated the essential hallmarks of a problem in international political economy. And Ricardo himself acted as an economic reformer—as political economists have now long continued to do in their advocacy of changes in public policy.

The principle of comparative advantage and the policy implications stemming from it have been continually refined since the beginning of systematic economics.[8] The long evolution of thought on this subject may now be summarized. In terms of international welfare economics,[9] free trade is a preferable situation to no trade; restricted trade is also preferable to no trade; free trade is preferable to restricted trade, except that an optimum tariff is preferable to free trade; and an optimum subsidy is preferable to restricted trade.

The arguments for protection, however, die hard. The only first-best argument for tariff protection is that of optimizing the terms of trade. The other arguments have noneconomic objectives, or are for suboptimal policies, or are nonarguments for protection.[10] For example, arguments for protection to promote "national security," or to encourage "industrialization as a modern way of life," or to be "independent of foreigners" are noneconomic arguments insofar as

8. For an elaboration of comparative advantage, see Bhagwati, *op. cit.*

9. The following policy conclusions are developed in J. Bhagwati and V. K. Ramaswami, "Domestic Distortions, Tariffs, and the Theory of Optimum Subsidy," *Journal of Political Economy*, Feb. 1963, pp. 44–50; H. G. Johnson, "Optimal Trade Intervention in the Presence of Domestic Distortions," in R. E. Baldwin *et al.*, *Trade, Growth and the Balance of Payments* (1965), pp. 3–34.

10. H. G. Johnson, "Tariffs and Economic Development: Some Theoretical Issues," *Journal of Development Studies*, Oct. 1964, pp. 3–30. The optimum tariff argument relates to the improvement of a country's terms of trade by taxing imports or exports to the optimum degree. See Scitovsky, *op. cit.*; L. A. Metzler, "Tariffs, the Terms of Trade, and the Distribution of National Income," *Journal of Political Economy*, Feb. 1949, pp. 1–29; J. E. Meade, *A Geometry of International Trade* (1952), pp. 87–90; H. G. Johnson, *International Trade and Economic Growth* (1958), chap. 2.

A "first-best" policy is that policy measure which achieves an objective in the most efficient manner; whereas another policy might also achieve the objective, it would do so with a second-best, third-best, or *n*th-best policy.

their criterion is not the economic criterion of greater real income. Even for the noneconomic arguments, however, it might be noted that the economist can still indicate the "least cost" way of obtaining the noneconomic objective: that is, the least cost policy is a subsidy, so that a subsidy is preferable to a tariff, and a tariff is in turn preferable to a quantitative restriction on trade.[11] Again, when support of a domestic import-competing industry is warranted, a tariff or quota is a suboptimal policy compared with an optimum subsidy.[12]

Among the most common objectives of protection are full employment and improvement in the balance of payments. These objectives are, however, nonarguments for trade restrictions and call for some other superior policy measure. Thus, the advocacy of trade restriction in the interests of full employment should defer to the superior domestic measures of fiscal policy and monetary policy for domestic economic stabilization. The contention that protection would remove a balance-of-payments problem should also defer to superior measures of domestic deflation or devaluation to increase exports and decrease imports, or to an increase in the availability of international liquidity.

These refined distinctions of economic theory have not, however, been honored in the actual political process of making foreign economic policy. Commercial policy has had much more of an ad hoc character, subject to a variety of immediate pressures and yielding to trade restrictions to support the interests of particular groups, promote employment, or meet a balance-of-payments problem.

In the course of history there have been periods of strong movement toward freer trade and other periods of reversion to neomercantilist measures when trade liberalization has been interrupted. The first major movement toward free trade occurred between 1846, with the repeal of the Corn Laws, and the 1880's. After World War I, trade liberalization was again pursued, but the Great De-

11. J. Bhagwati and T. N. Srinivasan, "Optimal Intervention to Achieve Non-Economic Objectives," *Review of Economic Studies*, 1969, pp. 27–38.

12. J. Bhagwati, "The Gains from Trade Once Again," *Oxford Economic Papers*, July 1968, pp. 149–61; M. C. Kemp, "The Gain from International Trade," *Economic Journal*, Dec. 1962, pp. 803–19; W. M. Corden, "Tariffs and Protectionism," *International Encyclopedia of the Social Sciences*, Vol. 8, pp. 113–21.

pression of the 1930's was later to cause the disintegration of the world economy. The height of protectionism in the United States was reached in 1930 with the Smoot-Hawley tariff. In 1934 the first Reciprocal Trade Agreements Act was passed, allowing for bilateral negotiations on a schedule of tariff reductions to be made by each of the negotiating countries. The tariff reductions were treated as a "bargained for" exchange, the principle being that of reciprocity with one country's tariff reductions being "paid for" in theory by reductions on the part of the other negotiating countries. The Reciprocal Trade Agreements Acts during the 1930's did much to further the freeing of trade.

Against the background of these bilateral trade agreements, the General Agreement on Tariffs and Trade (GATT) assumed major significance after World War II. GATT attempted to establish a common code of national conduct in commercial policy, and it tried to facilitate the negotiation of multilateral trade agreements by indicating the rights and obligations of each trading nation and by providing a forum for the discussion and settlement of trade problems. The basic principles, as will be seen in Problem I, are those of reciprocity and nondiscrimination through most-favored-nation treatment by which a member country agrees to levy the same tariff rates on imports from any other GATT member.

It is, however, a striking puzzle of the GATT legal system that the substantive obligations of the Agreement form a long, complex, and carefully drafted instrument which is fairly rigorous in its demands, and at the same time, the GATT's enforcement procedures are highly ambiguous and uncertain. The jurisprudence of GATT has been termed a "diplomat's jurisprudence," insofar as the GATT diplomats attempted to develop an approach toward law which tries to reconcile, on their own terms, the regulatory objectives of a conventional legal system with the turbulent realities of international trade affairs.[13]

The other major developments in commercial policy after World War II were the formation of the European Economic Community (EEC) and the passage of the Trade Expansion Act of 1962 which

13. R. E. Hudec, "The GATT Legal System: A Diplomat's Jurisprudence," *Journal of World Trade Law*, Sept.–Oct. 1970, pp. 615–65.

provided the basis for the Kennedy Round of tariff negotiations, as will be analyzed in Problem I. The prime question now is what is to follow the Kennedy Round.

In recent years there has been an increase in protectionist senti-ment, and many believe that the world confronts another era of neomercantilism with the possibility of trade warfare. As noted by one observer,

> What we are witnessing today is the fundamental clash of na-tional policies which are primarily oriented towards solving do-mestic political and social problems. . . . Multilateral discus-sions are at a standstill. There has been a rise in mercantilist sentiment in most of the world . . .
> This neo-mercantilism is a profoundly disruptive force in in-ternational relations. It takes many forms. . . . In the case of the Common Agricultural Policy (of the EEC), for example, the Europeans have taxed imports, thus reducing import sales while gaining revenues. The revenues are used to push domes-tic surpluses onto world markets, further taxing the exports of competitors by depressing their potential profits elsewhere. All exporters thus end up paying part of the cost of Europe's social program for its rural population. The American textile restric-tion program has a similar effect. It penalizes Asian exporters and American consumers in order to provide special benefits to Southern mills in areas of low wages and high availability of black labor. Neo-mercantilism, sector by sector, whether aimed at industry relief or rural poverty, must inevitably repress the interests of other countries, in particular sectors, in particular regions.[14]

Any reappraisal of commercial policy must now begin with awareness of the emergence of these neomercantilist restrictions. In view of the overriding pursuit of domestic objectives at the expense of other countries and the desire of every country to have a surplus in its balance of trade, how can there be further trade liberaliza-tion? How can nontariff barriers be reduced? How can trade con-flict among regional blocs be avoided?

Through the arduous process of economic diplomacy, the world has established since the 1930's an international trading system of multilateral, reciprocal, nondiscriminatory trading relationships. By

14. Harald B. Malmgren, "Coming Trade Wars?" *Foreign Policy*, Winter 1970–71, pp. 115–43.

what route is this system now to be extended? Can there be another Kennedy Round of tariff negotiations? or sector-by-sector negotiation? or support of the enlargement of the European Economic Community? or support of other multilateral free trade associations? How is future trade conflict to be avoided between the United States and Japan (rapidly rising to a front rank position in the world economy)? between the United States and the EEC (the world's largest trading unit)? These questions are raised by the specific policy problems in this volume.

Consultative machinery and international organization are clearly needed to maintain economic peacekeeping. But there is often a conflict in foreign policy between economic objectives such as maximizing national output, and noneconomic objectives, such as national power or satisfying some interest group. Also, foreign policy objectives and domestic policy objectives are often contradictory, and there must again be some tradeoff. Somehow objectives are sought within a system of international decision-making that involve a spectrum of techniques ranging from co-operation, negotiation, bargaining, and persuasion—economic diplomacy—to the use of power and coercion. It is now clear that there is need for new and improved institutions and consultative arrangements in order to provide intergovernmental co-operation in reconciling national policies. In this pursuit, as will be seen in all the policy problems in this book, the practice of technical decision-making must be supplemented with judgment and a sense of what might be administratively practicable and politically feasible.[15]

15. It would be instructive to pursue a set of readings that would combine three levels of analysis: the more rigorous analysis of the techniques of policy-making, an analysis of the politics of international economics, and an analysis of the role of the technical expert and personal leadership in policy-making. Such a combination might be derived from Y. Dror, *Public Policy-Making Reexamined*, 1968; C. E. Lindblom, *The Policy-Making Process*, 1968; K. W. Deutsch, *The Analysis of International Relations*, 1968; C. P. Kindleberger, *Power and Money*, 1970; Fred Charles Iklé, *How Nations Negotiate*, 1964; R. O. Keohane and J. S. Nye, Jr. (eds,), *Transnational Relations and World Politics, International Organization*, Summer 1971; Raymond Tanter and Richard H. Ullman (eds.), *Theory and Policy in International Relations, World Politics*, Supplement, Spring 1972, esp. pp. 123–50, 229–47.

Problem I
Trade Liberalization:
The Kennedy Round

A. The Context
1. TRADE NEGOTIATIONS

The most extraordinary trade liberalization effort in history was the round of multilateral negotiations held in Geneva from 1963 to 1967 under the auspices of the General Agreement on Tariffs and Trade (GATT). Popularly known as the Kennedy Round, these trade negotiations were unique not only in engaging the energies of forty-six nations for four years, but even more because of their innovations in negotiating rules, their attempt to grapple with exceedingly complex issues of intergovernmental commercial relations, and their eventual attainment of the most extensive tariff concessions in history.

Under a series of Reciprocal Trade Agreements Acts, the United States had concluded bilateral agreements with a number of countries to lower trade barriers between 1934 and 1946. Starting in 1947 the GATT became instrumental in sponsoring a series of multilateral bargaining conferences to reduce trade barriers.[1] The Ken-

---

1. The history of trade policy from 1920–48 is covered by W. A. Brown, *The United States and the Restoration of World Trade* (1950); Clair Wilcox, *A Charter*

nedy Round was the sixth such conference; it was exceptional in having the principal negotiators enter with unprecedented bargaining powers: the European Economic Community (EEC) had become an increasingly strong regional grouping, and the United States Trade Expansion Act of 1962 had granted President Kennedy the most extensive tariff negotiating power in the history of the Trade Agreements program. In essence, the Kennedy Round meant that the principal negotiating parties—the U. S. and the EEC— had to achieve agreement within the institutional and legal framework of the GATT in four principal areas: industrial tariffs, agricultural trade, non-tariff barriers, and the trade of less-developed countries.

It is desirable to begin with some understanding of the GATT framework—particularly the degree to which GATT provides an international code of trading conduct. The Articles of the International Monetary Fund (IMF) and the International Bank for Reconstruction and Development (World Bank) were drafted at the Bretton Woods Conference of 1944. The term "Bretton Woods system" may be used to incorporate the GATT as well as the IMF and World Bank, because the Bretton Woods Conference looked forward to the creation of an ancillary institution that would reduce obstacles to international trade and give effect to the principle of multilateral nondiscriminatory trade. While the IMF was intended to repair the disintegration that had befallen the international monetary system prior to the War and the World Bank was designed to support the flow of foreign capital, which had declined to a small amount, the GATT was intended to reverse the protectionist and discriminatory trade practices that had become widespread during the prewar depression years. In combination, the Fund, Bank, and GATT were designed to help countries achieve the multiple objectives of full employment, stable exchange rates, and freer and expanding trade. As the basis for major negotiations on commercial policy through tariff conferences, the multilateral trade agreement

for World Trade (1949). General histories of the GATT include Gerhard Curzon, *Multilateral Commercial Diplomacy* (1965); Gardiner Patterson, *Discrimination in International Trade* (1966); Karin Kock, *International Trade Policy and the GATT, 1947–1967* (1969); Kenneth W. Dam, *The GATT (1970)*. The Kennedy Round negotiations are discussed by E. H. Preeg, *Traders and Diplomats* (1970); J. W. Evans, *The Kennedy Round in America's Trade Policy* (1971).

embodied in GATT has been prominent in shaping the postwar international economy.

The text of the GATT is highly technical, consisting of thirty-eight articles, ranging from the stipulation of general most-favored-nation treatment in tariff concessions, through details about quotas, subsidies, and other trade policies, to issues of trade and development. Some of the major articles follow.

1.1 THE GENERAL AGREEMENT ON TARIFFS AND TRADE

Article 1
General Most-Favoured-Nation Treatment

1. With respect to customs duties and charges of any kind imposed on or in connection with importation or exportation or imposed on the international transfer of payments for imports or exports, and with respect to the method of levying such duties and charges, and with respect to all rules and formalities in connection with importation and exportation, and with respect to all matters referred to in paragraphs 2 and 4 of Article III, any advantage, favour, privilege or immunity granted by any contracting party to any product originating in or destined for any other country shall be accorded immediately and unconditionally to the like product originating in or destined for the territories of all other contracting parties.

Article VI
Anti-dumping and Countervailing Duties

1. The contracting parties recognize that dumping, by which products of one country are introduced into the commerce of another country at less than the normal value of the products, is to be condemned if it causes or threatens material injury to an established industry in the territory of a contracting party or materially retards the establishment of a domestic industry. For the purposes of this Article, a product is to be considered as being introduced into the commerce of an importing country at less than its normal value, if the price of the product exported from one country to another

  (a) is less than the comparable price, in the ordinary course of trade, for the like product when destined for consumption in the exporting country, or,
  (b) in the absence of such domestic price, is less than either
    (i) the highest comparable price for the like product for export to any third country in the ordinary course of trade, or
    (ii) the cost of production of the product in the country of origin plus a reasonable addition for selling cost and profit.

Due allowance shall be made in each case for differences in conditions and terms of sale, for differences in taxation, and for other differences affecting price comparability.

2. In order to offset or prevent dumping, a contracting party may levy on any dumped product an anti-dumping duty not greater in amount than the margin of dumping in respect of such product. For the purposes of this Article, the margin of dumping is the price difference determined in accordance with the provisions of paragraph 1.

Article XI
General Elimination of Quantitative Restrictions

1. No prohibitions or restrictions other than duties, taxes or other charges, whether made effective through quotas, import or export licenses or other measures, shall be instituted or maintained by any contracting party on the importation of any product of the territory of any other contracting party or on the exportation or sale for export of any product destined for the territory of any other contracting party.

2. The provisions of paragraph 1 of this Article shall not extend to the following:

(a) Export prohibitions or restrictions temporarily applied to prevent or relieve critical shortages of foodstuffs or other products essential to the exporting contracting party;

(b) Import and export prohibitions or restrictions necessary to the application of standards or regulations for the classification, grading or marketing of commodities in international trade;

(c) Import restrictions on any agricultural or fisheries product, imported in any form, necessary to the enforcement of governmental measures which operate:

    (i) to restrict the quantities of the like domestic product permitted to be marketed or produced, or, if there is no substantial domestic production of the like product, of a domestic product for which the imported product can be directly substituted; or

    (ii) to remove a temporary surplus of the like domestic product, or, if there is no substantial domestic production of the like product, of a domestic product for which the imported product can be directly substituted, by making the surplus available to certain groups of domestic consumers free of charge or at prices below the current market level; or

    (iii) to restrict the quantities permitted to be produced of any animal product the production of which is directly dependent, wholly or mainly, on the imported commodity, if the domestic production of that commodity is relatively negligible.

Any contracting party applying restrictions on the importation of any product pursuant to sub-paragraph (c) of this paragraph shall give public notice of the total quantity or value of the product permitted to be imported during a specified future period and of any change in such quantity or value. Moreover, any restrictions applied under (i) above shall not be such as will reduce the total of imports relative to the total of domestic production, as compared with the proportion which might reasonably be expected to rule between the two in the absence of restrictions. In determining this proportion, the contracting party shall pay due regard to the proportion prevailing during a previous representative period and to any special factors which may have affected or may be affecting the trade in the product concerned.

Article XII
Restrictions to Safeguard the Balance of Payments

1. Notwithstanding the provisions of paragraph 1 of Article XI, any contracting party, in order to safeguard its external financial position and its balance of payments, may restrict the quantity or value of merchandise permitted to be imported, subject to the provisions of the following paragraphs of this Article.

2. (a) Import restrictions instituted, maintained or intensified by a contracting party under this Article shall not exceed those necessary:

   (i) to forestall the imminent threat of, or to stop, a serious decline in its monetary reserves, or
   (ii) in the case of a contracting party with very low monetary reserves, to achieve a reasonable rate of increase in its reserves.

Due regard shall be paid in either case to any special factors which may be affecting the reserves of such contracting party or its need for reserves, including, where special external credits or other resources are available to it, the need to provide for the appropriate use of such credits or resources.

   (b) Contracting parties applying restrictions under sub-paragraph (a) of this paragraph shall progressively relax them as such conditions improve, maintaining them only to the extent that the conditions specified in that sub-paragraph still justify their application. They shall eliminate the restrictions when conditions would no longer justify their institution or maintenance under that sub-paragraph.

Article XVI
Subsidies

Section A—Subsidies in General. 1. If any contracting party grants or maintains any subsidy, including any form of income or price support, which operates directly or indirectly to increase exports of any product from, or to reduce imports of any product into, its territory, it shall notify the CONTRACTING PARTIES in writing of the extent and nature of the subsidization, of the estimated effect of the subsidization on the quantity of the affected product or products imported into or exported from its territory and of the circumstances making the subsidization necessary. In any case in which it is determined that serious prejudice to the interests of any other contracting party is caused or threatened by any such subsidization, the contracting party granting the subsidy shall, upon request, discuss with the other contracting party or parties concerned, or with the CONTRACTING PARTIES, the possibility of limiting the subsidization.

Article XVIII
Governmental Assistance to Economic Development

1. The contracting parties recognize that the attainment of the objectives of this Agreement will be facilitated by the progressive development of their economies, particularly of those contracting parties the economies of which can only support low standards of living and are in the early stages of development.

2. The contracting parties recognize further that it may be necessary for those contracting parties, in order to implement programmes and policies of economic development designed to raise the general standard of living of their people, to take protective or other measures affecting imports, and that such measures are justified in so far as they facilitate the attainment of the objectives of this Agreement. They agree, therefore, that those contracting parties should enjoy additional facilities to enable them (a) to maintain sufficient flexibility in their tariff structure to be able to grant the tariff protection required for the establishment of a particular industry and (b) to apply quantitative restrictions for balance of payments purposes in a manner which takes full account of the continued high level of demand for imports likely to be generated by their programmes of economic development.

Article XIX
Emergency Action on Imports of Particular Products

1. (a) If, as a result of unforeseen developments and of the effect of the obligations incurred by a contracting party under this Agreement, including tariff concessions, any product is being imported into the territory of that contracting party in such increased quantities and under such conditions as to cause or threaten serious injury to domestic producers in that territory of like or directly competitive products, the contracting party shall be free, in respect of such product, and to the extent and for such time as may be necessary to prevent or remedy such injury, to suspend the obligation in whole or in part or to withdraw or modify the concession.

(b) If any product, which is the subject of a concession with respect to a preference, is being imported into the territory of a contracting party in the circumstances set forth in sub-paragraph (a) of this paragraph, so as to cause or threaten serious injury to domestic producers of like or directly competitive products in the territory of a contracting party which receives or received such preference, the importing contracting party shall be free, if that other contracting party so requests, to suspend the relevant obligation in whole or in part or to withdraw or modify the concession in respect of the product, to the extent and for such time as may be necessary to prevent or remedy such injury.

2. Before any contracting party shall take action pursuant to the provisions of paragraph 1 of this Article, it shall give notice in writing to the CONTRACTING PARTIES as far in advance as may be practicable and shall afford the CONTRACTING PARTIES and those contracting parties having a substantial interest as exporters of the product concerned an opportunity to consult with it in respect of the proposed action. When such notice is given in relation to a concession with respect to a preference, the notice shall name the contracting party which has requested the action. In critical circumstances, where delay would cause damage which it would be difficult to repair, action under paragraph 1 of this Article may be taken provisionally without prior consultation, on the condition that consultation shall be effected immediately after taking such action.

3. (a) If agreement among the interested contracting parties with respect to the action is not reached, the contracting party which proposes to take or continue the action shall, nevertheless, be free to do so, and if such action is taken or continued, the affected contracting parties shall then be free, not later than ninety days after such action is taken, to suspend, upon the expiration of thirty days from the day on which written notice of such suspension is received by the CONTRACTING PARTIES, the application to the trade of the contracting party taking such action, or, in the case envisaged in paragraph 1 (b) of this Article, to the trade of the contracting party requesting such action, of such substantially equivalent concessions or other obligations under this Agreement the suspension of which the CONTRACTING PARTIES do not disapprove.

Part III

Article XXIV
Territorial Application—Frontier Traffic—
Customs Unions and Free-trade Areas

4. The contracting parties recognize the desirability of increasing freedom of trade by the development, through voluntary agreements, of closer integration between the economies of the countries parties to such agreements. They also recognize that the purpose of a customs union or of a free-trade area should be to facilitate trade between the constituent territories and not to raise barriers to the trade of other contracting parties with such territories.

5. Accordingly, the provisions of this Agreement shall not prevent, as between the territories of contracting parties, the formation of a customs union or of a free-trade area or the adoption of an interim agreement

necessary for the formation of a customs union or of a free-trade area; *Provided* that:

(a) with respect to a customs union, or an interim agreement leading to the formation of a customs union, the duties and other regulations of commerce imposed at the institution of any such union or interim agreement in respect of trade with contracting parties not parties to such union or agreement shall not on the whole be higher or more restrictive than the general incidence of the duties and regulations of commerce applicable in the constituent territories prior to the formation of such union or the adoption of such interim agreement, as the case may be;

(b) with respect to a free-trade area, or an interim agreement leading to the formation of a free-trade area, the duties and other regulations of commerce maintained in each of the constituent territories and applicable at the formation of such free-trade area or the adoption of such interim agreement to the trade of contracting parties not included in such area or not parties to such agreement shall not be higher or more restrictive than the corresponding duties and other regulations of commerce existing in the same constituent territories prior to the formation of the free-trade area, or interim agreement, as the case may be; and

(c) any interim agreement referred to in sub-paragraphs (a) and (b) shall include a plan and schedule for the formation of such a customs union or of such a free-trade area within a reasonable length of time.

Article XXVIII
Modification of Schedules

1. On the first day of each three-year period, the first period beginning on 1 January 1958 (or on the first day of any other period that may be specified by the CONTRACTING PARTIES by two-thirds of the votes cast) a contracting party (hereafter in this Article referred to as the "applicant contracting party") may, by negotiation and agreement with any contracting party with which such concession was initially negotiated and with any other contracting party determined by the CONTRACTING PARTIES to have a principal supplying interest (which two preceding categories of contracting parties, together with the applicant contracting party, are in this Article hereinafter referred to as the "contracting parties primarily concerned"), and subject to consultation with any other contracting party determined by the CONTRACTING PARTIES to have a substantial interest in such concession, modify or withdraw a concession included in the appropriate Schedule annexed to this Agreement.

2. In such negotiations and agreement, which may include provision for compensatory adjustment with respect to other products, the contracting parties concerned shall endeavour to maintain a general level of re-

ciprocal and mutually advantageous concessions not less favourable to trade than that provided for in this Agreement prior to such negotiations.

Article XXVIII bis
Tariff Negotiations

1. The contracting parties recognize that customs duties often constitute serious obstacles to trade; thus negotiations on a reciprocal and mutually advantageous basis, directed to the substantial reduction of the general level of tariffs and other charges on imports and exports and in particular to the reduction of such high tariffs as discourage the importation even of minimum quantities, and conducted with due regard to the objectives of this Agreement and the varying needs of individual contracting parties, are of great importance to the expansion of international trade. The CONTRACTING PARTIES may therefore sponsor such negotiations from time to time.

2. (a) Negotiations under this Article may be carried out on a selective product-by-product basis or by the application of such multilateral procedures as may be accepted by the contracting parties concerned. Such negotiations may be directed towards the reduction of duties, the binding of duties at then existing levels or undertakings that individual duties or the average duties on specified categories of products shall not exceed specified levels. The binding against increase of low duties or of duty-free treatment shall, in principle, be recognized as a concession equivalent in value to the reduction of high duties.

(b) The contracting parties recognize that in general the success of multilateral negotiations would depend on the participation of all contracting parties which conduct a substantial proportion of their external trade with one another.

3. Negotiations shall be conducted on a basis which affords adequate opportunity to take into account:

(a) the needs of individual contracting parties and individual industries;
(b) the needs of less-developed countries for a more flexible use of tariff protection to assist their economic development and the specific needs of these countries to maintain tariffs for revenue purposes; and
(c) all other relevant circumstances, including the fiscal, developmental, strategic and other needs of the contracting parties concerned.

Part IV
Trade and Development

Article XXXVI
Principles and Objectives

1. The contracting parties,

(a) recalling that the basic objectives of this Agreement include the raising of standards of living and the progressive development of the economies of all contracting parties, and considering that the attainment of these objectives is particularly urgent for less-developed contracting parties;

(b) considering that export earnings of the less-developed contracting parties can play a vital part in their economic development and that the extent of this contribution depends on the prices paid by the less-developed contracting parties for essential imports, the volume of their exports, and the prices received for these exports;

(c) noting, that there is a wide gap between standards of living in less-developed countries and in other countries;

(d) recognizing that individual and joint action is essential to further the development of the economies of less-developed contracting parties and to bring about a rapid advance in the standards of living in these countries;

(e) recognizing that international trade as a means of achieving economic and social advancement should be governed by such rules and procedures—and measures in conformity with such rules and procedures—as are consistent with the objectives set forth in this Article;

(f) noting that the CONTRACTING PARTIES may enable less-developed contracting parties to use special measures to promote their trade and development;

agree as follows.

2. There is need for a rapid and sustained expansion of the export earnings of the less-developed contracting parties.

3. There is need for positive efforts designed to ensure that less-developed contracting parties secure a share in the growth in international trade commensurate with the needs of their economic development.

4. Given the continued dependence of many less-developed contracting parties on the exportation of a limited range of primary products, there is need to provide in the largest possible measure more favourable and acceptable conditions of access to world markets for these products, and wherever appropriate to devise measures designed to stabilize and improve conditions of world markets in these products, including in particular measures designed to attain stable, equitable and remunerative prices, thus permitting an expansion of world trade and demand and a dynamic and steady growth of the real export earnings of these countries so as to provide them with expanding resources for their economic development.

5. The rapid expansion of the economies of the less-developed contracting parties will be facilitated by a diversification of the structure of their economies and the avoidance of an excessive dependence on the export of primary products. There is, therefore, need for increased access in the largest possible measure to markets under favourable condi-

tions for processed and manufactured products currently or potentially of particular export interest to less-developed contracting parties.

6. Because of the chronic deficiency in the export proceeds and other foreign exchange earnings of less-developed contracting parties, there are important inter-relationships between trade and financial assistance to development. There is, therefore, need for close and continuing collaboration between the CONTRACTING PARTIES and the international lending agencies so that they can contribute most effectively to alleviating the burdens these less-developed contracting parties assume in the interest of their economic development.

7. There is need for appropriate collaboration between the CONTRACTING PARTIES, other intergovernmental bodies and the organs and agencies of the United Nations system, whose activities relate to the trade and economic development of less-developed countries.

8. The developed contracting parties do not expect reciprocity for commitments made by them in trade negotiations to reduce or remove tariffs and other barriers to the trade of less-developed contracting parties.

9. The adoption of measures to give effect to these principles and objectives shall be a matter of conscious and purposeful effort on the part of the contracting parties both individually and jointly.

In the next selection, the former Director-General of GATT interprets the nature and context of the General Agreement.

1.2 GATT AS AN INTERNATIONAL TRADE ORGANIZATION [2]

Although the General Agreement is a complicated text and is therefore universally regarded as a somewhat impenetrable mystery intelligible only to an élite of specialists and technicians, its broad lines are simple enough. It contains in essence three fundamental principles. The first principle is that trade should be conducted on the basis of non-discrimination. Accordingly, all contracting parties are bound by the most-favoured-nation clause in the application of import and export duties and charges, and in their administration. In addition, insofar as the use of import quotas is permitted under the rules, these are to be administered on a non-discriminatory basis. Any departure from these fundamental rules of non-discrimination is hedged around with conditions and safeguards. Thus, countries may protect themselves against unfair competition through dumping and export subsidization by measures limited to imports from the countries where such dumping or subsidization occurs. But the conditions in which such countermeasures can be taken are strictly limited and defined, so as to prevent abuse. When countries are compelled

2. Eric Wyndham White, *GATT*, Geneva, Aug. 1961, pp. 5–12.

to restrict the volume of imports in order to safeguard reserves of foreign exchange the strict application of the rule of non-discrimination might lead to a greater degree of discrimination than the financial situation in fact requires. Here again—but within narrow limitations, and subject to international consultation—the rule of non-discrimination is relaxed. However, the most-favoured-nation clause is also qualified so as to permit contracting parties to enter into genuine customs unions and free-trade areas, the purpose of which is: "to facilitate trade between the constituent territories and not to raise barriers to the trade of other contracting parties with such territories," and a series of criteria is laid down designed to ensure that the arrangements shall be "trade creating" and not "trade diverting."

The second major principle is that protection shall be afforded to domestic industries exclusively through the customs tariff and not through other commercial measures. Thus the use of import quotas as a means of protection is explicitly condemned. The use of import quotas for other purposes—notably to safeguard the balance of payments—is governed by a formidable series of criteria and conditions coupled with procedures for consultations. There are also numerous provisions designed to prevent the use of administrative techniques as a means of protection additional to the tariff. There are also provisions designed to prevent the use of subsidies as a means of obtaining unfair advantages in export markets or to hamper imports.

The third principle, inherent throughout the General Agreement, is the concept of consultation aimed at avoiding damage to the trading interests of all contracting parties.

This in broad outline is the content of the General Agreement. The sum total of the detailed rules which are built around this basic framework constitutes a code which is voluntarily accepted by GATT contracting parties to govern their trading relationships. The importance of this code can be measured by the fact that it is accepted and applied by forty-two countries whose foreign trade is some eighty-five per cent of the total volume of world trade—countries which are drawn from all parts of the world, having interests as diverse as their geographical location, but which are united in the conviction of the beneficial effects of expanding world trade on an orderly basis.

The General Agreement is a multilateral trade agreement and therefore contractual in nature. It is not merely a set of principles or standards. The parties to the General Agreement have contractual rights and contractual obligations aimed at a balance of mutual advantage. It is these rights and obligations that determine the terms of access of contracting parties to each other's markets.

Important consequences follow from the contractual nature of the General Agreement. In the first place the procedures for enforcement of the terms of the Agreement are set in motion only where initiative is taken by an affected contracting party. The "organization" does not have an independent or autonomous role in enforcement of the rules. This has both advantages and disadvantages. On the positive side it leaves it to the good judgement of each contracting party whether in any particular case there is any advantage in invoking the GATT machinery. The automatic intervention of the "organization" would not always, or in all circumstances, be fruitful or helpful and there are obvious advantages in leaving this judgement in the first instance to the parties most closely concerned. It also means that there is a maximum encouragement to contracting parties to settle differences by consultation and agreement with the possibility of ultimate recourse to the "organization" as a powerful catalyst to reaching a settlement. In practice this situation has led to a large number of settlements "out of court"—in fact these are far more numerous than those which have required the intervention of the CONTRACTING PARTIES. On the negative side it must be recognized that most countries are very reluctant to take the initiative of invoking international complaints procedures and that this reluctance is particularly marked in the case of small countries which have differences with very powerful countries. In practice, however, things have worked out reasonably well in the GATT and a nice balance has been struck between too frequent and vexatious use of the complaints procedure on the one hand, and on the other an overly circumspect approach to bringing differences into court. The record of GATT as an instrument for settlement of trade disputes is a good one and its constructive character is well reflected in the adaptation of terminology used in the GATT. For many years reference was made to the "complaints" procedures; this has now yielded in the light of experience to the more attractive expression, the "conciliation" procedures.

A second consequence of the contractual nature of the Agreement is the relative weakness of the sanctions which may be applied in the event of non-compliance with the rules. In the last resort, where consultation has failed and when the conciliatory intervention of the CONTRACTING PARTIES has also failed, the ultimate remedy which the CONTRACTING PARTIES can offer to the injured party is a release from obligations to the offender, opening the way to retaliation. This is poor comfort to the injured party for whom the only satisfactory solution is the fulfilment of contractual obligations, and in only one case have the CONTRACTING PARTIES proceeded to this last step. The emphasis in all the work of GATT is directed to conciliatory and positive settlements to trade disputes.

A third consequence is that new members can only be admitted on terms to be agreed upon by two thirds of the existing contracting parties. In most international organizations accession of non-members is semi-automatic, when an applicant declares its readiness to accept the basic objectives and principles of the organization and to pay the annual dues. But since accession to GATT entitles the newcomer to all the contractual advantages which the Agreement secures to contracting parties, the latter require that acceding governments negotiate for accession so that there is and shall be a balance of rights and obligations between themselves and the newcomer. This in practice has normally meant that an acceding government has to enter into tariff negotiations in order to pay for the tariff benefits which it receives automatically upon accession from the existing contracting parties. But if there are reasons to doubt whether an acceding government, because of its trading system or fixed policies, is likely to be able to fulfil the numerous obligations contained in the many provisions of the General Agreement, there is also the possibility of the contracting parties agreeing upon special "terms of accession" to ensure the balance of rights and obligations.

2. THE NEGOTIATING PARTIES

The original membership of GATT was 23, but by the end of the Kennedy Round it had increased to 74 full members and 12 provisional or other related members. The process used by these members to negotiate tariff reductions is as follows: The basic feature of the trade negotiations is a "concession"—that is, a promise either to lower the duty on a commodity and keep it at or below that level, or a promise not to raise the duty on that item. Concessions are negotiated usually with the principal supplier and then, in accordance with the most-favored-nation principle, they are generalized to all suppliers. Before each negotiating session, countries prepare lists of their export products on which they seek tariff reductions. After receiving the lists of requests for concessions, each country prepares a list of responses or offers and submits it to the GATT. The contracting parties then meet in a negotiating session in which multilateral bargaining ensues. The multilateral negotiating session concludes with the submission by each country of its revised tariff schedules including all those items on which concessions have been granted. When a concession on a product is granted it is referred to as a "binding," and the duty on that product is said to be "bound." An important principle of the negotiating process has been that of reciprocity. Governments agree to reduce tariffs only in exchange for equally valuable tariff reductions by others, and any subsequent action which upsets the exchange is deemed an injury deserving some compensation equivalent to the value of the concession that is unbound.[3] Such compensation may take the form of either a conces-

3. When Part IV on Trade and Development was added to the GATT, an exception was made to this rule of reciprocity for less-developed countries. See Article XXXVI:8.

sion by the offending party on another item of import or withdrawal by the injured party of the concession granted to the offending party. There is no explicit provision in the General Agreement regarding the value of a concession, but the assumption has been that the value of a concession, or the breach of the concession, on a product is measured roughly by the amount of trade in that product moving to the importing country in a base period multiplied by the change in the rate of duty.

Prior to the Kennedy Round, the economic integration of the six West European nations had created a large internal market, and the EEC had become the world's largest trading bloc, maintaining a common external tariff on imports from nonmember countries, while reducing tariffs among its own members. In response to the European Common Market, seven other countries formed the European Free Trade Association (EFTA) in 1959. Members of EFTA proceeded to reduce internal tariffs while maintaining, under their free trade area arrangement, individual external tariffs.[4]

The United States government anticipated considerable impact on world trade as a result of the formation of the EEC and EFTA. The Kennedy administration was especially fearful that the preferential trading blocs in Europe would divert trade from the United States to other European countries, that the common agricultural policy (CAP) of the EEC would adversely affect agricultural imports from the United States, and that the external tariffs coupled with the wider European market would also unduly stimulate private overseas investment from the United States and hence aggravate the United States balance of payments. On July 31, 1961, the United Kingdom announced its decision to apply for membership in the Common Market. The United States expected the United Kingdom and other EFTA countries to join the EEC, and this made it all the more urgent for the United States to forestall adverse effects upon its trade with Europe by seeking a major revision in United States trade legislation. The Trade Expansion Act of 1962 was therefore strongly promoted as the basis under which the United States could urge GATT to negotiate a major reduction of trade barriers. This became the United States objective in the Kennedy Round.

4. See Problem III, pp. 188–89 below.

3. *TRADE EXPANSION ACT OF 1962*

In his January 1962 State of the Union message, President Kennedy stated, "We need a new law—a wholly new approach—a bold new instrument of American trade policy." Following is the text of President Kennedy's special message to the Congress on foreign trade policy.

3.1 PRESIDENT KENNEDY'S CALL
FOR THE TRADE EXPANSION ACT [5]

To the Congress of the United States:
Twenty-eight years ago our nation embarked upon a new experiment in international relationships—the Reciprocal Trade Agreements Program. Faced with the chaos in world trade that had resulted from the Great Depression, disillusioned by the failure of the promises that high protective tariffs would generate recovery, and impelled by a desperate need to restore our economy, President Roosevelt asked for authority to negotiate reciprocal tariff reductions with other nations of the world in order to spur our exports and aid our economic recovery and growth.

That landmark measure, guided through Congress by Cordell Hull, has been extended eleven times. It has served our country and the free world well over two decades. The application of this program brought growth and order to the free world trading system. Our total exports, averaging less than $2 billion a year in the three years preceding enactment of the law, have now increased to over $20 billion.

On June 30, 1962, the negotiating authority under the last extension of the Trade Agreements Act expires. It must be replaced by a wholly new instrument. A new American trade initiative is needed to meet the challenges and opportunities of a rapidly changing world economy.

In the brief period since this Act was last extended, five fundamentally new and sweeping developments have made obsolete our traditional trade policy:

The growth of the European Common Market—an economy which may soon nearly equal our own, protected by a single external tariff similar to our own—has progressed with such success and momentum that it has surpassed its original timetable, convinced those initially skeptical that there is now no turning back and laid the groundwork for a radical alteration of the economics of the Atlantic Alliance. Almost 90 percent of the free world's industrial production (if the United Kingdom and others successfully complete their negotiations for membership) may soon be con-

---

5. John F. Kennedy's Message to the Congress on Foreign Trade Policy, Jan. 25, 1962. Public Papers of the Presidents, 1962, pp. 68–77.

centrated in two great markets—the United States of America and the expanded European Economic Community. A trade policy adequate to negotiate item by item tariff reductions with a large number of small independent states will no longer be adequate to assure ready access for ourselves—and for our traditional trading partners in Canada, Japan, Latin America and elsewhere—to a market nearly as large as our own, whose negotiators can speak with one voice but whose internal differences make it impossible for them to negotiate item by item.

The growing pressures on our balance of payments position have, in the past few years, turned a new spotlight on the importance of increasing American exports to strengthen the international position of the dollar and prevent a steady drain of our gold reserves. To maintain our defense, assistance and other commitments abroad, while expanding the free flow of goods and capital, we must achieve a reasonable equilibrium in our international accounts by offsetting these dollar outlays with dollar sales.

The need to accelerate our own economic growth, following a lagging period of seven years characterized by three recessions, is more urgent than it has been in years—underlined by the millions of new job opportunities which will have to be found in this decade to provide employment for those already unemployed as well as an increasing flood of younger workers, farm workers seeking new opportunities, and city workers displaced by technological change.

The communist aid and trade offensive has also become more apparent in recent years. Soviet bloc trade with 41 non-communist countries in the less-developed areas of the globe has more than tripled in recent years; and bloc trade missions are busy in nearly every continent attempting to penetrate, encircle and divide the free world.

The need for new markets for Japan and the developing nations has also been accentuated as never before—both by the prospective impact of the EEC's external tariff and by their own need to acquire new outlets for their raw materials and light manufactures.

To meet these new challenges and opportunities, I am today transmitting to the Congress a new and modern instrument of trade negotiation —the Trade Expansion Act of 1962. As I said in my State of the Union Address, its enactment "could well affect the unity of the West, the course of the Cold War and the growth of our nation for a generation or more to come." . . .

Specifically, enactment of this measure will benefit substantially every state of the union, every segment of the American economy, and every basic objective of our domestic and foreign policy.

Our efforts to expand our economy will be importantly affected by our ability to expand our exports—and particularly upon the ability of our farmers and businessmen to sell to the Common Market. There is arising across the Atlantic a single economic community which may soon have a population half again as big as our own, working and competing together with no more barriers to commerce and investment than exist among our

50 states—in an economy which has been growing roughly twice as fast as ours—representing a purchasing power which will someday equal our own and a living standard growing faster than our own. As its consumer incomes grow, its consumer demands are also growing, particularly for the type of goods that we produce best, which are only now beginning to be widely sold or known in the markets of Europe or in the homes of its middle-income families.

Some 30 percent of our exports—more than $4 billion in industrial goods and materials and nearly $2 billion in agricultural products—already goes to the members and prospective members of the EEC. European manufacturers, however, have increased their share of this rapidly expanding market at a far greater rate than American manufacturers. Unless our industry can maintain and increase its share of this attractive market, there will be further temptation to locate additional American-financed plants in Europe in order to get behind the external tariff wall of the EEC. This would enable the American manufacturer to contend for that vast consumer potential on more competitive terms with his European counterparts; but it will also mean a failure on our part to take advantage of this growing market to increase jobs and investment in this country.

A more liberal trade policy will in general benefit our most efficient and expanding industries—industries which have demonstrated their advantage over other world producers by exporting on the average twice as much of their products as we import—industries which have done this while paying highest wages in our country. Increasing investment and employment in these growth industries will make for a more healthy, efficient and expanding economy and a still higher American standard of living. Indeed, freer movement of trade between America and the Common Market would bolster the economy of the entire free world, stimulating each nation to do most what it does best and helping to achieve the OECD target of a 50 percent combined Atlantic Community increase in Gross National Product by 1970.

Our efforts to prevent inflation will be reinforced by expanded trade. Once given a fair and equal opportunity to compete in overseas markets, and once subject to healthy competition from overseas manufacturers for our own markets, American management and labor will have additional reason to maintain competitive costs and prices, modernize their plants and increase their productivity. The discipline of the world market place is an excellent measure of efficiency and a force to stability. To try to shield American industry from the discipline of foreign competition would isolate our domestic price level from world prices, encouraging domestic inflation, reduce our exports still further and invite less desirable Government solutions.

Our efforts to correct our adverse balance of payments have in recent years roughly paralleled our ability to increase our export surplus. It is necessary if we are to maintain our security programs abroad—our own military forces overseas plus our contributions to the security and growth of other free countries—to make substantial dollar outlays abroad. These outlays are being held to the minimum necessary, and we are seeking increased sharing from our allies. But they will continue at substantial rates—and this requires us to enlarge the $5 billion export surplus which we presently enjoy from our favorable balance of trade. If that surplus can be enlarged, as exports under our new program rise faster than imports, we can achieve the equilibrium in our balance of payments which is essential to our economic stability and flexibility. If, on the other hand, our surplus should fail to grow, if our exports should be denied ready access to the EEC and other markets—our overseas position would be endangered. Moreover, if we can lower the external tariff wall of the Common Market through negotiation our manufacturers will be under less pressure to locate their plants behind that wall in order to sell in the European market, thus reducing the export of capital funds to Europe.

Our efforts to promote the strength and unity of the West are thus directly related to the strength and unity of Atlantic trade policies. An expanded export program is necessary to give this Nation both the balance of payments equilibrium and the economic growth we need to sustain our share of Western military security and economic advance. Equally important, a freer flow of trade across the Atlantic will enable the two giant markets on either side of the ocean to impart strength and vigor to each other, and to combine their resources and momentum to undertake the many enterprises which the security of free peoples demands. For the first time, as the world's greatest trading nation, we can welcome a single partner whose trade is even larger than our own—a partner no longer divided and dependent, but strong enough to share with us the responsibilities and initiatives of the free world.

The communist bloc, largely self-contained and isolated, represents an economic power already by some standards larger than that of Western Europe and hoping someday to overtake the United States. But the combined output and purchasing power of the United States and Western Europe—nearly a trillion dollars a year—is more than twice as great as that of the entire Sino-Soviet world. Though we have only half the population, and far less than half the territory, we can pool our resources and resourcefulness in an open trade partnership strong enough to outstrip any challenge, and strong enough to undertake all the many enterprises around the world which the maintenance and progress of freedom require. If we can take this step, Marxist predictions of "capitalist" empires warring over markets and stifling competition would be shattered for all time—Communist hopes for a trade war between these two great economic giants would be frustrated—and Communist efforts to split the West would be doomed to failure.

As members of the Atlantic Community we have concerted our military objectives through the North Atlantic Treaty Organization. We are concerting our monetary and economic policies through the Organization for

Economic Cooperation and Development. It is time now to write a new chapter in the evolution of the Atlantic Community. The success of our foreign policy depends in large measure upon the success of our foreign trade, and our maintenance of Western political unity depends in equally large measure upon the degree of Western economic unity. An integrated Western Europe, joined in trading partnership with the United States, will further shift the world balance of power to the side of freedom.

Our efforts to prove the superiority of free choice will thus be advanced immeasurably. We will prove to the world that we believe in peacefully "tearing down walls" instead of arbitrarily building them. We will be opening new vistas of choice and opportunity to the producers and consumers of the free world. In answer to those who say to the world's poorer countries that economic progress and freedom are no longer compatible, we—who have long boasted about the virtues of the market place and of free competitive enterprise, about our ability to compete and sell in any market, and about our willingness to keep abreast of the times—will have our greatest opportunity since the Marshall Plan to demonstrate vitality of free choice.

Communist bloc nations have negotiated more than 200 trade agreements in recent years. Inevitably the recipient nation finds its economy increasingly dependent upon Soviet goods, services and technicians. But many of these nations have also observed that the economics of free choice provide far greater benefits than the economics of coercion—and the wider we can make the area of economic freedom, the easier we make it for all free peoples to receive the benefits of our innovations and put them into practice.

Our efforts to aid the developing nations of the world and other friends, however, depend upon more than a demonstration of freedom's vitality and benefits. If their economies are to expand, if their new industries are to be successful, if they are to acquire the foreign exchange funds they will need to replace our aid efforts, these nations must find new outlets for their raw materials and new manufactures. We must make certain that any arrangements which we make with the European Economic Community are worked out in such a fashion as to insure nondiscriminatory application to all third countries. Even more important, however, the United States and Europe together have a joint responsibility to all of the less-developed countries of the world—and in this sense we must work together to insure that their legitimate aspirations and requirements are fulfilled. The "open partnership" which this Bill proposes will enable all free nations to share together the reward of a wider economic choice for all.

Our efforts to maintain the leadership of the free world thus rest, in the final analysis, on our success in this undertaking. Economic isolation and political leadership are wholly incompatible. In the next few years, the nations of Western Europe will be fixing basic economic and trading patterns vitally affecting the future of our economy and the hopes of our less-developed friends. Basic political and military decisions of vital inter-

est to our security will be made. Unless we have this authority to negotiate and have it this year—if we are separated from the Common Market
by high tariff barriers on either side of the Atlantic—then we cannot hope
to play an effective part in those basic decisions.

If we are to retain our leadership, the initiative is up to us. The revolu-
tionary changes which are occurring will not wait for us to make up our
minds. The United States has encouraged sweeping changes in Free
World economic patterns in order to strengthen the forces of freedom.
But we cannot ourselves stand still. If we are to lead, we must act. We
must adapt our own economy to the imperatives of a changing world, and
once more assert our leadership.

The American businessman, once the authority granted by this Bill is
exercised, will have a unique opportunity to compete on a more equal
basis in a rich and rapidly expanding market abroad which possesses potentially a purchasing power as large and as varied as our own. He
knows that, once artificial restraints are removed, a vast array of American goods, produced by American know-how with American efficiency,
can compete with any goods in any spot in the world. And almost all
members of the business community, in every state, now participate or
could participate in the production, processing, transporting, or distribution of either exports or imports.

Already we sell to Western Europe alone more machinery, transportation equipment, chemicals and coal than our total imports of these commodities from all regions of the world combined. Western Europe is our
best customer today—and should be an even better one tomorrow. But
as the new external tariff surrounding the Common Market replaces the
internal tariff structure, a German producer—who once competed in the
markets of France on the same terms with our own producers—will
achieve free access to French markets while our own producers face a
tariff. In short, in the absence of authority to bargain down the external
tariff, as the economy of the Common Market expands, our exports will
not expand with it. They may even decline.

The American farmer has a tremendous stake in expanded trade. One
out of every seven farm workers produces for export. The average farmer
depends on foreign markets to sell the crops grown on one out of every
six acres he plants. Sixty percent of our rice, 49 percent of our cotton, 45
percent of our wheat and 42 percent of our soybean production are exported. Agriculture is one of our best sources of foreign exchange.

Our farmers are particularly dependent upon the markets of Western
Europe. Our agricultural trade with that area is four to one in our favor.
The agreements recently reached at Brussels both exhausted our existing
authority to obtain further European concessions, and laid the groundwork for future negotiations on American farm exports to be conducted
once new authority is granted. But new and flexible authority is required
if we are to keep the door of the Common Market open to American agri-

culture, and open it still wider. If the output of our astounding productivity is not to pile up increasingly in our warehouses, our negotiators will need both the special EEC authority and the general 50 percent authority requested in the bill described later in this message.

The American worker will benefit from the expansion of our exports. One out of every three workers engaged in manufacturing is employed in establishments that export. Several hundred times as many workers owe their jobs directly or indirectly to exports as are in the small group— estimated to be less than one half of one percent of all workers—who might be adversely affected by a sharp increase in imports. As the number of job seekers in our labor force expands in the years ahead, increasing our job opportunities will require expanding our markets and economy, and making certain that new United States plants built to serve Common Market consumers are built here, to employ American workers, and not there.

The American consumer benefits most of all from an increase in foreign trade. Imports give him a wider choice of products at competitive prices. They introduce new ideas and new tastes, which often lead to new demands for American production.

Increased imports stimulate our own efforts to increase efficiency, and supplement anti-trust and other efforts to assure competition. Many industries of importance to the American consumer and economy are dependent upon imports for raw materials and other supplies. Thus American-made goods can also be made much less expensively for the American consumers if we lower the tariff on the materials that are necessary to their production.

American imports, in short, have generally strengthened rather than weakened our economy. Their competitive benefits have already been mentioned. But about 60 percent of the goods we import do not compete with the goods we produce—either because they are not produced in this country, or are not produced in any significant quantity. They provide us with products we need but cannot efficiently make or grow (such as bananas or coffee), supplement our own steadily depleting natural resources with items not available here in quantity (such as manganese or chrome ore, 90 percent or more of which must be imported if our steel mills are to operate), and contribute to our industrial efficiency, our economic growth and our high level of consumption. Those imports that do compete are equal to only one or one and one-half percent of our total national production; and even these imports create jobs directly for those engaged in their processing, distribution, or transportation, and indirectly for those employed in both export industries and in those industries dependent upon reasonably priced imported supplies for their own ability to compete.

Moreover, we must reduce our own tariffs if we hope to reduce tariffs abroad and thereby increase our exports and export surplus. There are many more American jobs dependent upon exports than could possibly be adversely affected by increased imports. And those export industries are our strongest, most efficient, highest paying growth industries.

It is obvious, therefore, that the warnings against increased imports based upon the lower level of wages paid in other countries are not telling the whole story. For this fear is refuted by the fact that American industry in general—and America's highest paid industries in particular—export more goods to other markets than any other nation; sell far more abroad to other countries than they sell to us; and command the vast preponderance of our own market here in the United States. There are three reasons for this:

(a) The skill and efficiency of American workers, with the help of our machinery and technology, can produce more units per man hour than any other workers in the world—thus making the competitive cost of our labor for many products far less than it is in countries with lower wages. For example, while a United States coal miner is paid eight times as much per hour as the Japanese miner, he produces fourteen times as much coal—our real cost per ton of coal is thus far smaller—and we sell the Japanese tens of millions of dollars worth of coal each year.

(b) Our best industries also possess other advantages—the adequacy of low cost raw materials or electrical power, for example. Neither wages nor total labor costs is an adequate standard of comparison if used alone.

(c) American products can frequently compete successfully even where foreign prices are somewhat lower—by virtue of their superior quality, style, packaging, servicing or assurance of delivery.

Given this strength, accompanied by increasing productivity and wages in the rest of the world, there is less need to be concerned over the level of wages in the low wage countries. These levels, moreover, are already on the rise, and, we would hope, will continue to narrow the current wage gap, encouraged by appropriate consultations on an international basis.

This philosophy of the free market—the wider economic choice for men and nations—is as old as freedom itself. It is not a partisan philosophy. For many years our trade legislation has enjoyed bi-partisan backing from those members of both parties who recognized how essential trade is to our basic security abroad and our economic health at home. This is even more true today. The Trade Expansion Act of 1962 is designed as the expression of a nation, not of any single faction or section. It is in that spirit that I recommend it to the Congress for prompt and favorable action.

[*The section of the message dealing with the provisions of the bill is omitted.*]

The purpose of this message has been to describe the challenge we face and the tools we need. The decision rests with the Congress. That decision will either mark the beginning of a new chapter in the alliance of free nations—or a threat to the growth of Western unity. The two great Atlantic markets will either grow together or they will grow apart. The meaning and range of free economic choice will either be widened for the benefit of free men everywhere—or confused and constricted by new barriers and delays.

Last year, in enacting a long-term foreign aid program, the Congress made possible a fundamental change in our relations with the developing nations. This bill will make possible a fundamental, far-reaching and unique change in our relations with the other industrialized nations— particularly with the other members of the Atlantic Community. As NATO was unprecedented in military history, this measure is unprecedented in economic history. But its passage will be long-remembered and its benefits widely distributed among those who work for freedom.

At rare moments in the life of this nation an opportunity comes along to fashion out of the confusion of current events a clear and bold action to show the world what it is we stand for. Such an opportunity is before us now. This bill, by enabling us to strike a bargain with the Common Market, will "strike a blow" for freedom.

The major provisions of the Trade Expansion Act dealt with tariff-cutting authority, a change in the structure of executive authority for conducting trade negotiations,[6] and safeguards and adjustment assistance for domestic industries and labor.[7] The tariff-cutting authority was unique in introducing the "linear" technique of reducing tariffs. This means that each participant in the trade negotiations agrees to make a uniform across-the-board percentage cut in import duties. This method of tariff reduction was intended to reduce the time and negotiating effort that had hitherto been needed in bilateral negotiations between countries on an item-by-item basis, and it was also designed to achieve a deeper average tariff cut for the participants. The authority to reduce tariffs was also unprecedented in allowing reductions by the President of up to 50 per cent and having no duties on articles for which the United States and the EEC together accounted for at least 80 per cent of the world's export value. The executive authority to reduce

6. For a full analysis of the Act, see Stanley D. Metzger, *Trade Agreements and the Kennedy Round* (1964). For a legalistic interpretation of this policy problem generally, see Eric Stein and Pater Hay, *Law and Institutions in the Atlantic Area* (1963), chap. 4, sec. B; Carl H. Fulda and Warren F. Schwartz, *Cases and Materials on the Regulation of International Trade and Investment* (1970), chap. 4.

7. For detailed discussion of adjustment assistance, see Problem II, pp. 170–78 below.

tariffs was to be for five years until July 1967. The President also had the authority to "reserve from the negotiations" for tariff reductions various commodities; his authority stemmed from concern for national security, the escape clause of the Act, or the "orderly marketing" section of the Act. It was intended, however, that only a minimum number of commodities would be subject to these exceptions. The Act also allowed for adjustment assistance to domestic industry or groups of workers, adversely affected as a result of tariff reductions. It was specified that a firm or labor union might petition the Tariff Commission to "promptly make an investigation to determine whether, as a result in major part of concessions granted under trade agreements, an article is being imported into the United States in such increased quantities as to cause, or threaten to cause, serious injury to the domestic industry producing an article which is like or directly competitive with the imported article" (Section 301).

The campaign for passage of the Act turned out to be more successful than had been generally anticipated,[8] and the Trade Expansion Act became law on October 11, 1962, granting the President all the major powers he had requested. It should be noted, however, that the law had already been weakened by two prior actions. First, the authority to eliminate tariffs completely on product groups where the United States and the EEC together accounted for at least 80 per cent of the world exports was reduced to little force (restricted to only aircraft and margarine) when France vetoed Britain's entry into the Common Market in January 1963.[9] Second, the GATT Long-Term Arrangement regarding international trade in cotton textiles, to which the United States was a strong subscriber, became effective in October 1962, and limited cotton textile imports.[10]

Shortly after the passage of the Trade Expansion Act, the United

8. For some diverse views during the campaign for passage of the Act, see Preeg, *op. cit.*, pp. 49–53. For extensive testimony on the proposed bill, see U. S. Congress, House Committee on Ways and Means, *Trade Expansion Act of 1962, Hearings before the Committee on Ways and Means*, 87th Congress, Second Session, 1962; U. S. Congress, Senate Committee on Finance, *Hearings on Trade Expansion Act of 1962, Before Committee on Finance*, 87th Congress, Second Session, 1962.

9. For subsequent efforts of the United Kingdom to join the EEC, see Problem III, below.

10. For more analysis of the restrictions on cotton textiles, see Problem II, below.

States recommended to GATT that a Ministerial meeting be convened to establish the basic objectives for the Kennedy Round of negotiations. While many in the United States thought the Trade Expansion Act had been oversold, many in Europe felt the objective was purely commercial—to increase American sales abroad. A broader assessment—which still remains relevant for the persistent problems of economic peacekeeping—has been offered by one of the active participants in the Kennedy Round negotiations.

> The significance of this [Ministerial] meeting was far greater . . . than narrow commercial interests. The Common Market would emerge either as a unifying force for the community of Western nations or perhaps as a new form of inward-looking Europe, regionally rather than nationally oriented. President Kennedy's bold new program, the centerpiece of the 1962 session of Congress, could become a successful diplomatic effort or an embarrassing miscalculation. Most important, the carefully built postwar trading system, a pillar of solidarity among non-Communist countries, would be seriously shaken if a breakdown should occur between its most powerful members. The *New York Times* on the eve of the meeting warned that "behind the tedious tariff schedules dealing with such prosaic subjects as frozen chicken, lie far deeper problems. For this conference will involve such basic Franco-American issues as nationalism versus internationalism, free trade versus protectionism, and rival blocs versus partnerships." [11]

The key position of France at the start of the negotiations is described in the following selection.

3.2 FRANCE AND THE KENNEDY ROUND [12]

The French brief, prepared at several inter-ministerial meetings, was presented to the recent meeting of the EEC Council of Ministers by M. Giscard d'Estaing, who will seek its adoption by his common market partners by May 16th, when the GATT conference opens in Geneva. France expects to be able to gain much from a reduction in American tariffs. Until now, France has sold comparatively little to the United States: only half as much as Germany and hardly more than a third of Britain's exports in a good year. This is a gap that French industrialists would like to see reduced. And experience in recent years has shown them that this is feasible: over a period of three years, in spite of a dra-

---

11. Preeg, *op. cit.*, p. 5.
12. *The Economist*, April 13, 1963, pp. 169, 171.

matic drop in the export of small cars and a decline in sales of steel products, French sales to the United States have increased by 50 per cent.

On the other hand, France is also conscious of the risks of mutual tariff reduction. Not only would a massive incursion of American goods menace several French industries: too radical a reduction in the common external tariff of the Six would jeopardise the cohesion of the common market. Paris has not gone to so much trouble to exclude Britain only to let in the United States by the back door. Wholesale concessions to the United States would also be detrimental to the agricultural policy of the Six, as well as to their relations with Africa; this, in the eyes of Paris, weighs as heavily as the threat to France's metallurgical, chemical, coal and textile industries.

Thus a combination of fear and self-interest explains the care taken by Paris in the preparation of the French case. This is being based on three overriding ideas: clear definition of the area of negotiation; "real" rather than nominal reciprocity of concessions; and prior elimination of non-tariff obstacles and escape clauses that might dilute American concessions.

Paris would have preferred *agricultural products* to have been excluded from the negotiations, to avoid the risk of American foodstuffs flooding Europe at the expense of French peasants. M. Pisani has put so much effort into the construction of "agricultural Europe" and the drawing up of a multiplicity of regulations for each product that he would prefer not to do anything that might compromise his handiwork. But Germany and Belgium have an opposite interest: they may be glad to purchase more agricultural products from the Americans if they can thereby sell them more industrial goods. Moreover, at the time of the previous (Dillon) tariff round the Six undertook not to exclude agricultural products from future negotiations. These products will therefore come up for discussion at Geneva; but Paris will do its utmost to avoid

> any indirect reopening of questions previously settled in Brussels; any bargaining or compensation between tariff reductions on agricultural products and on industrial products. Conversations on this subject are currently being held with the Germans.

Tropical products should in the Paris view be excluded by the Six from the negotiations, at least at the outset. Thus, at the start, only a few marginal products would be subjects for negotiation, though in later stages of the talks matters will doubtless have to be taken further; but in that event, Paris considers that the Six must

> abide by the concessions laid down in the Agreement of Association between the Six and the eighteen African states; have prior consultations with the Eighteen, as is provided by that agreement.

There can be no question, as Paris sees it, of extending the tariff reductions agreed between the United States and the Six to *"third" countries* through application of the most-favoured-nation clause in the absence of reciprocal concessions. But it has not yet been decided which of the two possible methods of getting round the difficulty should be adopted:

> to limit the application of MFN to the detriment of third countries; or
> to include them in the common effort to reduce tariffs by holding the usual international negotiations product by product with those third countries who are big exporters in each case.

A particular problem is constituted by countries with a low average wage level and by countries behind the Iron Curtain. In the absence of special arrangements, Paris will insist on the exclusion from the negotiations of products originating in low-wage countries, and the maintenance of quotas for trade with the communist bloc. But it is expected that discussion of these exceptions and the principles and limits to be applied to them will be difficult.

It is considered in Paris that the Americans are not in a position to negotiate with the Six as freely as was first believed. Their offers are notably less interesting to the Six than appeared at first sight. The trouble lies in the considerable disparity between the American tariff and the common external tariff of the Six. In certain cases (chemicals, for instance) the American tariff is three times the European; in numerous other cases it is double. Evidently, a proportional reduction in these tariffs would hardly be of interest to the Six. Thus, Paris is to propose to the common market countries that the following distinctions be made:

> For more or less comparable duties in the American and European tariff schedule, France will suggest applying the normal "linear" method of reduction (an annual reduction of one-tenth or one-fifth, of the duty, for example).
> For extremely disparate duties (in Paris the word "prohibitive" is used to describe the highest American tariffs) America will be asked to accept a procedure of "levelling" (*écrêtement*); that is to say, a more radical decrease in the higher duties, so that in a few years' time tariffs have become more or less comparable on both sides. Thus reductions of one-fifth or one-quarter might be made in the higher duty, whereas the lowest duty would decrease by only one-tenth at each stage. This would apply, in particular, to the American duties on chemicals.

Some French observers—though the French government does not really consider their point of view to be tenable—would even go so far as to stipulate a preliminary reduction of the higher tariff, before the lower European tariff begins to be reduced.

In any case—and this is considered a fundamental point in Paris

—it will be necessary to agree in advance on the customs value to which the new tariff will apply. The American calculations of this value are considered in Paris to be both uncertain and arbitrary.

Concern for true reciprocity is the real imperative in Paris, on the eve of the negotiations. Sometimes this is put rather violently in official circles: "Yes we agree to negotiate with Kennedy; but on the basis of 'an eye for an eye and a tooth for a tooth.'"

The future negotiations with the United States are, moreover, not the only ones to which this rule is being applied; it is already operating in relation to the other members of the common market, to whom the French have made it plain that they would not participate in the Kennedy round unless the other member countries proceeded with the establishment of "agricultural Europe," which has suffered a check since the break with Britain. This warning produced results at the last meeting of the Council of Ministers of the Six; its effect on the Americans remains to be seen.

At all events, a list has been drawn up in Paris of the "non-tariff" obstacles which it is intended that America should give up. The French government considers this a fundamental question because, in the past, the following obstacles have unfairly prevented or limited European sales to the United States.

> Quotas of a protectionist nature, still maintained by Washington to restrict the quantities of certain imports.
>
> The "Buy American" Act, which gives a strong preference to American firms (6 per cent of the price, in general, but 12 per cent for certain small undertakings or for security reasons) tendering for public contracts. Over and above this rule, which is still more severe in certain states, there is the problem of the American administration's habit of omitting to consult, or of not taking into account, foreign tenders. (An American might be forgiven for asking when the French government last invited a foreign firm to tender for an official contract at all.)
>
> Hygiene regulations, originating in a legitimate desire to protect the consumer, which can be used for protective ends.
>
> Anti-dumping duties, seen in Paris as a surcharge that should be abolished.
>
> Anti-trust legislation which also obstructs the sale of European goods in the United States on the pretext of understandings between European exporters.
>
> Finally, the "tariff adjustment" measures which, on the basis of escape clauses, reimpose duties previously reduced.

France has therefore already put two proposals to the Six:

> —to include in the Kennedy round safeguard clauses for the benefit of the Six;

—to compel Washington to set up an international court of arbitration, charged with interpreting the law ("*dire le droit*") in the event of either party having recourse to such clauses in circumstances considered by the other to infringe the agreement.

These two points seem to have been adopted by the Six.

Finally, it must be pointed out that French industrialists go even further than the Government and that in their view a straightforward application of the same rules to the enormous American trusts and to even the largest European undertakings resembles a struggle between a mouse and an elephant (*pot de terre contre pot de fer*). "How can there be real competition with General Motors," M. Villiers, president of the French employers, recently asked "so long as its enormous powers, its fabulous capital resources, its considerable profits, enable it to have recourse to a range of marketing and publicity techniques unattainable in Europe?" According to the industrialists, true equality would therefore demand concessions from the United States double or treble those required of Europe.

B. The Issues

4. KENNEDY ROUND NEGOTIATIONS

In announcing agreement for the Ministerial meeting in May 1963, the Director-General of GATT stated that there is a "good prospect that ministers would be able to set sights on a target of 50 per cent across-the-board reductions on a wide variety of goods." [13] The chief American negotiator urged the ministers to "reach agreement that the maximum liberalization of trade can best be achieved by a negotiation which begins with across-the-board, equal percentage linear cuts, with limited and narrowly defined exceptions." The American delegation suggested 50 per cent cuts as a good working hypothesis and stated that "any formula based on unequal linear cuts imposes a serious limitation on the amount by which the average tariff will be reduced . . . [and] it is almost sure to create inequalities which will increase the difficulties of the final negotiations." [14]

The EEC countries, however, adopted a strong stand against linear tariff cuts. Their argument was that whereas Common Market tariffs were almost all in the medium 10–20 per cent range, United

13. *Ibid.*, p. 55.
14. *Ibid.*, pp. 6–7.

States tariffs were widely dispersed, with some tariffs being low, but a large number being at high levels ranging from 30 to 50 per cent, and even a few being over 100 per cent. The Common Market countries argued that, unless special attention was given to these peaks in tariff rates, the Common Market's external tariffs after a 50 per cent cut would be uniformly low and relatively ineffective, while high tariffs in the United States would continue to afford significant protection for certain industries. The EEC commission proposed an alternate plan of tariff harmonization by which tariffs would be lowered halfway from their present levels to target levels, tentatively established as 10 per cent for manufactures, 5 per cent for semimanufactures, and 0 per cent for raw materials. The American negotiator contended that this would at most result in an average reduction of only 10–12 per cent and that moderate tariffs would be subject to little or no reduction under the EEC plan, whereas high tariffs which often were related to the domestically most sensitive industries would be subject to disproportionately large cuts. It was also argued that the EEC under its plan would undergo less tariff cutting than the other major countries. This problem of tariff dispersion—with the United States insisting that all tariffs, with a minimum of exceptions, should be cut in half over a five-year period—became a major issue at the start of the negotiations, and it threatened to undermine the entire basis of the Kennedy Round.

Another major issue, related to the procedural implications of across-the-board tariff reductions, was that of reciprocity. Under the previous item-by-item approach to tariff reductions, reciprocity implied some balance of benefits among the negotiating pairs of countries. No formula for reciprocity could be agreed upon, and the participating countries merely stated that they expected a general across-the-board balance between concessions granted and received. The balance of concessions was to be determined through some process of adjustment after the extent of the linear reductions became known.

Another major impasse was over agricultural products. The high support prices and variable import levies that were being proposed for the Common Agricultural Policy of the EEC threatened to reduce agricultural exports from the United States.[15] The United

15. The Common Agricultural Policy is explained in Problem III, below.

States insisted that it would not enter into negotiations on industrial products without some assurance of the maintenance and expansion of markets for its own agricultural exports. The EEC had not yet, however, been able to settle upon the form and timing of its own Common Agricultural Policy, and it was therefore reluctant to engage in negotiations on agricultural products. At the most, the EEC was only willing to establish two ad hoc groups to explore the possibility of arriving at some sort of global "arrangement" in cereals and meats, with the possibility of similar groups to be formed later to consider other agricultural sectors.

In trying to establish the procedures and standards to be used for linear tariff reductions, the Ministerial meeting considered a number of proposals and counterproposals chiefly between the United States and the EEC. Finally, a compromise on tariff-cutting rules was reached, and the Ministerial meeting was able to adopt a set of objectives for the Kennedy Round. Following is the text of the conclusions and resolutions adopted at the Ministerial meeting of GATT on May 21, 1963.

4.1 KENNEDY ROUND OBJECTIVES ESTABLISHED [16]

Measures for the Expansion of Trade of Developing Countries as a Means of Furthering Their Economic Development

Conclusions Adopted on 21 May 1963
on Item 1 of the Agenda

1. The Ministers during their meeting from 16 to 21 May 1963, discussed the question of measures for the expansion of trade of developing countries as a means of furthering their economic development. The Ministers had before them the reports of Committee III and of the Special Group on Trade in Tropical Products, and considered the following *Programme of Action* which had previously been examined in Committee III [of GATT];

(*i*) *Standstill Provision.* No new tariff or non-tariff barriers should be erected by industrialized countries against the export trade of any less-developed country in the products identified as of particular interest to the less-developed countries. In this connexion the less-developed countries would particularly mention barriers of a discriminatory nature.

(*ii*) *Elimination of Quantitative Restrictions.* Quantitative restrictions on imports from less-developed countries which are inconsistent with the provisions of the GATT shall be eliminated within a period of one year.

16. Press Release No. 794, GATT, May 29, 1963.

Where, on consultation between the industrialized and the less-developed countries concerned, it is established that there are special problems which prevent action being taken within this period, the restriction on such items would be progressively reduced and eliminated by 31 December 1965.

(*iii*) *Duty-Free Entry for Tropical Products.* Duty-free entry into the industrialized countries shall be granted to tropical products by 31 December 1963.

(*iv*) *Elimination of Tariffs on Primary Products.* Industrialized countries shall agree to the elimination of customs tariffs on the primary products important in the trade of less-developed countries.

(*v*) *Reduction and Elimination of Tariff Barriers to Exports of Semi-processed and Processed Products from Less-Developed Countries.* Industrialized countries should also prepare urgently a schedule for the reduction and elimination of tariff barriers to exports of semi-processed and processed products from less-developed countries, providing for a reduction of at least 50 per cent of the present duties over the next three years.

(*vi*) *Progressive Reduction of Internal Fiscal Charges and Revenue Duties.* Industrialized countries shall progressively reduce internal charges and revenue duties on products wholly or mainly produced in less-developed countries with a view to their elimination by 31 December 1965.

(*vii*) *Reporting Procedures.* Industrialized countries maintaining the above-mentioned barriers shall report to the GATT secretariat in July of each year on the steps taken by them during the preceding year to implement these decisions and on the measures which they propose to take over the next twelve months to provide larger access for the products of less-developed countries.

(*viii*) *Other Measures.* Contracting parties should also give urgent consideration to the adoption of other appropriate measures which would facilitate the efforts of less-developed countries to diversify their economies, strengthen their export capacity, and increase their earnings from overseas sales.

2. The Ministers of all industrialized countries, with the exception of the Ministers of the member States of the European Economic Community, agreed to the above Programme of Action subject to the understandings set out in paragraphs 3 and 4. The Ministers of the member States of the European Economic Community endorsed, in principle, the general objectives of the Programme of Action and declared themselves ready to contribute, for their part, to the fullest extent possible, towards the development of the developing countries. With respect to the most appropriate methods of achieving the objectives mentioned above, the position of the Ministers of the member States of the European Economic Community is contained in paragraph 6.

3. It was agreed by the Ministers of the industrialized countries, other than those of the EEC, that, in the first instance, the above Programme of

Action relates to the products indentified by Committee III, it being understood that the Programme of Action might subsequently be extended to an enlarged list of products to be agreed upon. It was also recognized that acceptance of the Programme was without prejudice to the rights and obligations of contracting parties under the provisions of the General Agreement, under arrangements negotiated within the framework of the GATT or covered by international commodity arrangements. Further, it should be understood that, where action under the Programme would affect the interest of third countries, as under preferential arrangements, countries granting such preferences would need to take into account the interests of the trade partners concerned. As regards tariffs on primary products, these Ministers indicated that their governments would work towards the elimination or, where this was not possible, at least towards the substantial reduction of tariffs on these products. In respect of tariffs on semi-processed and processed products of substantial interest to the developing countries, these Ministers indicated that their governments would work towards a substantial reduction of the tariffs on these products. Action in connexion with the reduction of tariffs on primary, semi-processed and processed products from less-developed countries would be taken within the framework of the GATT trade negotiations, and while not precluding action in advance of the trade negotiations, these Ministers proposed to ensure, as far as possible, that these products would be included in their offer lists in the negotiations and not be excepted therefrom in accordance with the principles agreed on for the negotiations.

4. Ministers of industrialized countries, other than those of the EEC, stated that they would conform to the standstill provision except where special and compelling circumstances rendered departure from it unavoidable, in which case adequate opportunity for consultation would be afforded to the developing countries mainly interested in the products concerned. Such consultation would occur prior to the introduction of measures constituting a departure from the standstill unless this were impossible or impracticable. . . .

With respect to tariff reductions, the United States Minister pointed out that United States legislation required such reductions to be staged over a period of five years.

5. The Ministers of a small number of countries, mainly dependent for their export earnings on a narrow range of primary products, welcomed the Action Programme and undertook to give effect to it to the best of their ability. However, since they, like many less-developed countries, were in the process of diversifying their economies through industrial development, they would have difficulty in accepting inflexible tariff commitments for certain products.

6. Addressing themselves to the Action Programme, the Ministers of the European Economic Community and the States associated with the EEC stated that, while they recognized that some of the points contained in the Programme could be regarded as objectives to which, to the fullest

extent possible, concrete policies should be adapted, the first seven points of the Programme referred only to measures for the elimination of barriers to trade, whereas, in their view, more positive measures were required to achieve the marked and rapid increase in the export earnings of the developing countries as a whole, which was the fundamental objective. Accordingly, these Ministers urged:

(a) that international action should, in particular, be directed to a deliberate effort to organize international trade in products of interest to the less-developed countries. Such an effort would have to take into account economic inequalities between the less-developed countries themselves and the fact that certain less-developed countries cannot at present, without a transitional phase, face competition from the countries which have already achieved a certain degree of development or from the long-industrialized countries without suffering damage;

(b) that an effort should therefore be made to ensure increasing exports at remunerative, equitable and stable prices for the less-developed countries producing primary products. In this respect any desirable arrangement made at the world level could be inspired by arrangements already tried out on a regional, bilateral or even national level. As regards processed and semi-processed products, a study should be made to determine the selective measures, specially conceived to meet the needs of developing countries, which could assure these countries the necessary markets for the products in question. In this connexion various relaxations of present rules regarding non-discrimination might be considered (in particular the suggestions made at the ministerial meeting by Mr. Brasseur, Minister for Foreign Trade and Technical Assistance of Belgium). A rapid study of them by a special group should enable decisions to be taken without delay.

In the view of the Ministers of the EEC, the decisions which would be taken following the report by such a group could eliminate many of the reasons which have prevented or still prevent the effective implementation, in a manner beneficial to all, of the Programme of Action set forth in paragraph 1.

7. In the opinion of certain Ministers, the same special group could, as a matter of urgency, analyze the possibility and conditions for establishing within the framework of GATT a centre for trade information and market research with a view to the expansion of exports of the less-developed countries.

8. The Ministers finally emphasized that further measures and more ambitious goals should not stand in the way of, or serve as an excuse for not implementing as quickly and as fully as possible, the present Programme of Action which would represent a positive contribution which the industrialized countries could make to the development of the trade

of the less-developed countries within the field in which GATT was specially competent.

9. The Ministers of the less-developed countries sponsoring and supporting the Programme of Action, expressed disappointment with the understandings and positions as set out by some industrialized countries and found them to be unhelpful. They emphasized that the eight point Programme of Action fell far short of the minimum conditions necessary to enable the less-developed countries to make their full contribution to the expansion of international commerce and represented a practical compromise between the difficulties stated by some industrialized countries and their responsibilities under the GATT. In particular, attention was drawn to the fact that all contracting parties are committed to carry out their obligations in respect of quantitative restrictions, without any qualifications. The Ministers of these less-developed countries therefore urged that the Programme of Action should be implemented in full, within the time-table proposed therein, in the interest of the accelerated economic development of their countries. They trusted that industrialized countries would be able to make substantial tariff concessions on primary, semi-processed and processed products, exported by less-developed countries in advance of the forthcoming trade negotiations. They also expressed the hope that products of interest to the less-developed countries should not be excluded from offer lists during negotiations.

Arrangements for the Reduction or Elimination of Tariffs
and Other Barriers to Trade, and Related Matters
and
Measures for Access to Markets for
Agricultural and Other Primary Products
Resolution Adopted on 21 May 1963
on Items II and III of the Agenda

A. Principles

1. That a significant liberalization of world trade is desirable, and that, for this purpose, comprehensive trade negotiations, to be conducted on a most-favoured-nation basis and on the principle of reciprocity, shall begin at Geneva on 4 May 1964, with the widest possible participation.

2. That the trade negotiations shall cover all classes of products, industrial and non-industrial, including agricultural and primary products.

3. That the trade negotiations shall deal not only with tariffs but also with non-tariff barriers.

4. That, in view of the limited results obtained in recent years from item-by-item negotiations, the tariff negotiations, subject to the provisions of paragraph B3, shall be based upon a plan of substantial linear tariff reductions with a bare minimum of exception which shall be subject to confrontation and justification. The linear reductions shall be equal. In those

cases where there are significant disparities in tariff levels, the tariff reductions will be based upon special rules of general and automatic application.

5. That in the trade negotiations it shall be open to each country to request additional trade concessions or to modify its own offers where this
is necessary to obtain a balance of advantages between it and the other
participating countries. It shall be a matter of joint endeavour by all participating countries to negotiate for a sufficient basis of reciprocity to
maintain the fullest measure of trade concessions.

6. That during the trade negotiations a problem of reciprocity could
arise in the case of countries the general incidence of whose tariffs is
unquestionably lower than that of other participating countries.

7. That, in view of the importance of agriculture in world trade, the
trade negotiations shall provide for acceptable conditions of access to
world markets for agricultural products.

8. That in the trade negotiations every effort shall be made to reduce
barriers to exports of the less-developed countries, but that the developed countries cannot expect to receive reciprocity from the less-developed countries.

B. Procedures

1. That a Trade Negotiations Committee, composed of representatives
of all participating countries, shall be set up, and that it shall be the function of the Trade Negotiations Committee, directly or through committees

(a) To elaborate a trade negotiating plan in the light of the principles in
    paragraphs A1–8 above, with a view to reaching agreement on the
    details of the plan of tariff reductions referred to in paragraph A4
    above by 1 August 1963, and to completing the remainder of the task
    by the date of the beginning of the twenty-first session of the Con-
    tracting Parties.
(b) To supervise the conduct of the trade negotiations.

2. That the trade negotiating plan will have to take into account the issues raised by the Ministers, and that the acceptability of the trade negotiating plan, from the point of view of individual countries, will depend
upon the degree to which it succeeds in dealing with such issues.

3. That the Trade Negotiations Committee in elaborating the trade negotiating plan, shall deal *inter alia* with the following issues and special
situations:

(a) The depth of the tariff reductions, and the rules for exceptions.
(b) The criteria for determining significant disparities in tariff levels and
    the special rules applicable for tariff reductions in these cases.
(c) The problem for certain countries with a very low average level of
    tariffs or with a special economic or trade structure such that equal

linear tariff reductions may not provide an adequate balance of advantages.

Note: The Chairman offered paragraph B3(c) as an amendment to paragraph B3(c) in the U.S. proposal. In presenting this amendment, the Chairman established the following interpretation for the record:

"Under this language, the Trade Negotiations Committee will consider the case of certain countries where it is established that their very low average level of tariffs or their economic or trade structure is such that the general application of equal linear tariff reductions would not be appropriate to achieve an adequate balance of advantages. For such countries the objective shall be the negotiation of a balance of advantages based on trade concessions by them of equivalent value, not excluding equal linear reductions where appropriate."

In response to a question by the Australian Delegation, the Chairman established the following additional interpretation for the record:

"The reference to 'special trade structure' includes countries whose exports consist predominantly of agricultural or other primary products, and this is accepted by the Conference." U. S. Department of State, Bulletin, June 24, 1963.

(d) The rules to govern, and the methods to be employed in, the creation of acceptable conditions of access to world markets for agricultural products in furtherance of a significant development and expansion of world trade in such products. Since cereals and meats are amongst the commodities for which general arrangements may be required, the Special Groups on Cereals and Meats shall convene at early dates to negotiate appropriate arrangements. For similar reasons a special group on dairy products shall also be established.

(e) The rules to govern and the methods to be employed in the treatment of non-tariff barriers, including *inter-alia* discriminatory treatment applied to products of certain countries and the means of assuring that the value of tariff reductions will not be impaired or nullified by non-tariff barriers. Consideration shall be given to the possible need to review the application of certain provisions of the General Agreement, in particular Articles XIX and XXVIII, or the procedures thereunder, with a view to maintaining, to the largest extent possible, trade liberalization and the stability of tariff concessions.

With this agreement on objectives, the Kennedy Round surmounted initial disagreements and established the foundation for the subsequent four years of hard negotiations on reduction of trade barriers. It is an interesting commentary on international economic negotiations that the "objectives established during the Ministerial meeting in May 1963 would largely endure the four years of discussion, delay and maneuver, and the substance of the final agreement would be essentially in accord with the foregoing statement adopted at the Ministerial meeting." [17]

The actual negotiations were beset with numerous technical problems as well as bargaining maneuvers. During the first year of preparatory talks the tariff disparities problem was dominant, but the United States and the EEC were unable to agree upon a workable rule for disparities. Settlement of the disparities problem was to be delayed for another three years. Progress was made, however, in the submission of exceptions lists establishing those items that each negotiating country wanted excepted from across-the-board tariff cuts for reasons of "overriding national interest." The differences in the length of initial exceptions lists created obvious difficulties, but negotiation and compromise eventually overcame these—especially in view of the scheduled expiration of the Trade Expansion Act by June 1967.

The other major negotiating problems involved efforts to reduce barriers to exports of less-developed countries, reduction of nontariff barriers (NTB's), and liberalization of agricultural trade.

The May 1963 Ministerial resolution had already affirmed that "the developed countries cannot expect to receive reciprocity from the less-developed countries," and the newly added Part IV to GATT, on Trade and Development, was to absolve less-developed countries from the obligation of reciprocity.

The problems of the developing countries also were to receive much more attention at the first United Nations Conference on Trade and Development (UNCTAD) in Geneva in 1964, and the demands of the "Group of 77"—the LDCs in UNCTAD—were to dominate over the Kennedy talks.

On NTB's, the American selling price (ASP) system played a critical role in the final Kennedy Round bargaining. Negotiations on chemicals, a major sector in the total negotiations, were delayed by the demand that the ASP system be abolished.

The discussions on agricultural products were stalemated until it finally was agreed that proposals for a world cereals arrangement would be presented for negotiation in the spring of 1965, and that specific offers on other agricultural products would be made by the

17. Preeg, *op. cit.*, p. 11.

autumn of 1965. The complexity of negotiations on agricultural products continued to be compounded, however, by the internal debate within the EEC on the common agricultural policy.[18] Until the final days of the negotiation, the United States and EEC remained far apart on the nature and scope of concessions in agriculture—the United States unequivocally maintaining that no general agreement would be signed until adequate concessions were offered on farm products.

Aside from the imprecision of any statistical measure of the "balance" of offers, these negotiation issues made it extremely complicated to establish agreement on what exactly constituted "reciprocity" or "balance of advantages." A number of measures were finally adopted to represent the constituent elements of reciprocity: average depth of tariff reduction, the balance-of-trade volume subject to tariff concession, the loss of duties collectable, and the impact of tariff and other concessions on future trade.[19] The United States continued to insist, however, that progress in negotiating offers on industrial products should be linked to parallel progress in offers on specific agricultural products. Progress for concessions on other agricultural products was, in turn, dependent upon progress toward an arrangement for grains.

A summary appraisal of how the negotiations were faring in the spring of 1964 is presented in the following.

4.2 GRAND DESIGN FRAYED [20]

Although the American Congress passed Mr. Kennedy's Trade Expansion Act less than two years ago, the ensuing "Kennedy round" of tariff talks has played many parts in its brief lifetime. The objective has always been the same: nothing less than to fit the European common market into the world or, more exactly, to wrap the world a little more comfortably round the new and rapidly growing common market. But the implications have changed with changing times. The very name "Kennedy round" now has a ring from another and more hopeful age. When it was launched in 1962, the Trade Expansion Act was, to be sure, America's attempt to safeguard its stake in the European market, just as the European Free Trade Area was Britain's attempt six years earlier. But, unlike the free trade area, its motives were romantic as well as mer-

18. See Problem III, below.
19. For elaboration, see Preeg, *op. cit.*, pp. 130–34.
20. *The Economist*, March 14, 1964, pp. 970, 972.

cantile. It was also to be a part of the grand design for a partnership between America and a uniting Europe that would pull the West together and change the world.

What remained after General de Gaulle's veto on British entry into the common market two Januaries ago was a sense that the Kennedy round was a test of European intentions. If France's common market partners failed to fight for it, they could be assumed to be disappearing behind the general's prison bars. A mixture of political fears and commercial interest, again rather like the mixture that stirred British passions over the free trade area, led the American negotiators into angry tactics. The outcome was the dogfight with the Six at the meeting of the General Agreement on Tariffs and Trade (GATT) in Geneva last May. On the whole, the Six came out of that mêlée slightly on top.

Since then, the emotion has slowly faded out of the Kennedy round, which has come to be seen more and more as a straight business deal. The passing months have proved that France's common market partners do not share, for the present anyway, General de Gaulle's third-force ambitions. Whenever the Germans have been free to choose, as in the NATO mixed-manned nuclear force, they have chosen to act with the United States, not France. The Kennedy round has stopped being a symbol of political attitudes.

To that extent its deflation from political to economic significance has been genuine. But it has also been tactical. For it has gradually dawned upon the negotiators that, within the strictly commercial field, the interests of the Six may be more truly united than one would guess from their divergent public statements. During the crisis among the Six in the Brussels negotiations at Christmas, the Germans made much play with the need for guarantees on the Kennedy round as the price for progress on the agricultural common market, assumed to be essentially a French demand. But in the upshot the appetite of the Dutch and Italians for access to the German food market, and of the German farmers for a maximum of protection, played a much greater part than generalised love of free trade. The debate on agriculture produced a concrete bargain; that on the Kennedy round, perhaps inevitably since it had not got fully under way, produced only generalised declarations of intent. It has become that much harder to believe in the pressure the Five may bring to bear on the French should General de Gaulle decide in his wisdom that the Kennedy round is a snare and a delusion for the Europe of the Europeans. There seems little doubt that the cautious tactics now being pursued by the Americans are a way of adjusting to these more modest hopes.

The Americans seem to be determined to avoid the mistakes, real and reputed, of the British in their dealings with the Six. In essence, their tactics consist of assuming that some part of a loaf is better than no bread. An instance is their attitude on the vexed question of "disparities." The latest position of the Six is that they may reduce their tariffs only 25 per cent (instead of the 50 per cent the Americans want) on that fifth of their dutiable imports where their tariffs are half, or less, of the American and British ones. The Americans have not exploded angrily as they did last year, or suggested another formula. They have not even pointed out, like the British, that the Six's proposal might easily set off a vicious spiral in which more and more countries will limit their tariff-cutting. Instead they have suggested simple amendments that would eliminate two-thirds of the trade to be dealt with in this way. Detailed bargaining can start at last.

Even on agriculture, where the official positions of the common market and the United States are poles apart, no one but the American Department of Agriculture really believes food exporters can obtain guarantees from the Six. Given the social and political pressures from the farms of the common market, where 600,000 people are leaving the land annually though nearly 20 per cent of the working population are still left there, it is not very realistic to expect the old trade channels to survive. The European Commissioners who were in Washington on March 5th and 6th left little room for illusion on this score. And to some extent the paradoxical buoyancy of the common market's food imports, however temporary, has reduced the tension. It is harder to see $1,200 million of American agricultural exports to the common market as a matter of desperate concern when a mere five years ago the Americans were selling only $800 million worth.

The best that can be hoped for is some kind of review procedure if exports show signs of falling off. Even Britain, for all its expressions of liberal intent, is not about to give such guarantees on food imports into Britain as would make much of a precedent for asking great things of the Six. Here, too, the emphasis seems to be moving towards the discussion of world agreements sought by the Six and amended as much as possible to suit outsiders.

This modest, pragmatic approach at least has the virtue of keeping the atmosphere calm. It now seems likely that, despite floods of French scepticism in recent months, the Kennedy round conference will open formally in Geneva on May 4th. This is purely symbolic, for in reality the negotiators have been at it hammer and tongs since the autumn. And even after May 4th the way is strewn with elephant traps for the overly hopeful. The American list of "exceptions" to tariff-cutting is bound to be large. If others follow suit, these could, with disparities, make present hopes even of a 35 per cent cut in industrial duties (acceptable both in Brussels and Washington) seem optimistic. Then there are the non-tariff barriers about which philosophers can wrangle till the Day of Judgment. Last but not least there is agriculture, a vexed kingdom in itself.

The agenda is painfully long. Even though there seems to be general agreement that by the end of the year one ought to know whether a deal is possible or not, neither the French nor the Americans are in a great hurry. The French will not agree to parts of the package before they can judge of the whole (which is reasonable enough but raises horrid memories of the free trade area). And the Americans, though wanting agreement soon on disparities, prefer a package home opinion can judge as a whole to a series of parts some of which may be modest.

All this implies that outside the common market the tendency is to put first things first and to see that tariff reductions by the Six, who have after all nearly doubled their imports between 1958 and 1963, are of more interest than a war of religion on commercial doctrine. But the final attitude of the Six themselves is more mysterious. What interest has General de Gaulle in the successful conclusion of the Kennedy round? Politically, the general's obsession with independence can hardly take kindly to tighter trading links across the Atlantic. In agriculture, a deal can only tend to reduce, however marginally, French preferences in Europe. In industry it is hard now that inflation is sapping the competitive advantages France derived from the 1958 devaluation of the franc to expect French industry to welcome a challenge from America, Britain and Japan as well as that painfully sustained from Germany.

In vague terms, General de Gaulle has indeed told Herr Erhard and the Italian president, Signor Segni, that he favours the Kennedy round. It is not a black-and-white issue like Britain's entry into Europe. Success in trade negotiations can be wan or (more rarely) vivid. But the latest statements of, for instance, the French minister of finance, suggesting that ministers might not attend the formal opening of the Kennedy round on May 4th, have an ominous ring. And what ought to be the ultimate restraint on the general—the determined Altantic spirit of France's common market partners—may, in the very nature of the success of the common market itself, be less effective than it should be.

For three years the negotiations proceeded—with the future of a large part of world trade awaiting settlement of the outstanding issues between the United States and the EEC. In the spring of 1967, before the final negotiating period, the situation was described as follows.

4.3 KENNEDY ROUND AND THE SIX [21]

The Kennedy round of tariff negotiations, launched by President Kennedy in 1961 to prevent United States exports being shut out of the emerging European common market, may yet founder on the common market rock. Largely because of French tactics, the Six have not yet been able to give their negotiator, M. Jean Rey, a viable mandate. M.

21. *Ibid.*, April 22, 1967, pp. 366, 368.

Rey, with his natural tendency to excessive optimism, has made matters worse by failing to make clear in Brussels how badly things are going in Geneva. The other major negotiating countries still hope to shock, cajole or, in the wiser counsel of Switzerland, persuade the Six into concessions at the last possible moment—the Whitsun weekend in mid-May; while the Six, holding firm on the tariff cuts and improvements already offered, hope to come through with their present bargaining position intact. Some senior negotiators in Geneva believe success will be reached, if at all, only after unofficial emissaries from Paris have arrived at the eleventh hour to bail the Six out of the fix into which Paris has got them by a frenzy of last-minute effort.

Mr. Eric Wyndham White, secretary general of the General Agreement on Tariffs and Trade (GATT) and the only committee chairman trusted completely by all the negotiators, suggested on Friday evening last week that all the participants present their "positive offers" of tariff cuts to match the current negotiation position as each of them sees it. As he must have known would happen, the negotiators to a man have leaped at the idea as a means of tabling lists which amount to threats against the common market—either because large areas of trade are excluded from the offers, or because the tariff cuts suggested are small. In the present pessimistic mood in Geneva, the irony of the positive offers is that they are potentially anything but positive. They could turn out much more negative than all the exceptions-lists and withdrawal threats with which the Kennedy round has been living for years.

This reaction has something of the nature of a combined anti-common market front. It was to warn M. Rey of the possibility of such an anti-Six conspiracy, in which they would have had to take part, that the two chiefs of the United States negotiating team, President Johnson's special ambassador, Mr. William Roth and the main executive negotiator Mr. Michael Blumenthal, flew to Brussels with due publicity last Monday night.

Timing now dictates the pattern of this crescendo of in-fighting. Few of the delegations are equipped to present full offer lists by the end of this weekend, so that the common market ministers' meeting planned for Monday and Tuesday will either be postponed or will have little to get its teeth into. The crucial Brussels meeting, when the Six will have to emerge from their lulled belief that all is mostly well with the Kennedy round, will thus take place in the week after next. Heads of agreement will have to be agreed just under a fortnight after that: this time finally, as the American Trade Expansion Act only empowers the President to sign detailed schedules of tariff cuts, not an incomplete document. As the Act expires on June 30th, barely enough time will be left to translate heads of agreement into detailed (let alone agreed) schedules.

The two major issues outstanding between the biggest protagonists, the common market and the United States, remain the question of a new world cereals agreement linked with a food aid programme and the abo-

lition of the American selling price system in the chemical sector. The
United States, Canada and Australia are the largest exporters of hard
grains in the world, and together they have been trying to achieve a 40
cents increase to $1.85 a bushel in the minimum world price for hard
winter wheat. The Australians think even this too low, first because it is
below the Australian cost of production (it is even further below the
American) and second because the suggested new price is only 20 cents
above the prevailing average market price for wheat, which rarely falls
to the present International Wheat Agreement minimum. The common
market, whose own internal wheat price is the highest in the world, has
apparently stuck at $1.72 for the minimum world price, or barely more
than the present market price. The British are aiming lower still, and
the Japanese, for whom the Kennedy round is turning out in a particularly disappointing way, are against any rise in the minimum price at all.
The less developed countries too do not want to have to pay a higher
price for imported wheat, if there is no compensating food aid agreement. The Americans have given private indications that they would
take a lower price than the Australians and Canadians, but Australia's
trade minister, Mr. McEwen, seems in no mood for compromise.

The discussions on cereals have been complicated by the American
request for an agreement on food aid, as an additional outlet for the
wheat exporters, and as a way of spreading the burden of food aid now
carried by the United States virtually alone. Agreement on food aid has
now become yet another pre-condition for success in the Kennedy
round. The United States is willing to carry 40 per cent of the cost of any
eventual agreement. The common market has made great steps, considering its own highly complicated agricultural structure, in agreeing
to a food aid programme at all. But it was significant of the gulf between
the two sides that while there were celebrations in Brussels last week
when the commission persuaded the ministers to accept food aid, the
Americans were (and continue to be) in despair at the modest 3 million
ton programme (worth $250 million) to which the Six agreed. The
Europeans are also very definitely implying that their contributions will
not be in cash, but in agricultural commodities of which they themselves
have surpluses. When they realise this fully, the Americans and the British could be angrier still. With an eye cocked to congressional lobbies in
Washington, the Americans are also trying to get some concession on
such individual items as canned peaches, where the common market's
offer appears to be particularly nefarious (the offer is to lower variable
levies on imports, but at the same time tax the sugar content of canned
fruit, thus effectively raising the total duty above the present level).

Irritations like this reach a peak when the two sides get on to chemicals. The importance of the American selling price (ASP) rule, which
bases the tariff on certain chemical imports on the domestic selling price
rather than the price of the imports and so makes the effective tariff ab-
surdly high, is still disputed by the Americans, who say ASP affects only

5 per cent of total chemical imports. All the other countries, the Six and Britain foremost among them, argue that the benzenoid chemical imports affected are kept low precisely because of ASP: benzenoids make up 40 per cent of American synthetic organic production, and are a potential boom market for British, Swiss and German exporters if ASP can be removed. Still, the negotiations have come some way. The Six are now offering a full 50 per cent cut on their already low chemical tariffs against an original offer of 20 per cent, and the Americans are ready to make a far larger cut which would bring their tariff ceiling to 20 per cent. The British ceiling would come down from its present 33 per cent to something under 15 per cent. The trouble is that separate Congressional approval is needed to abolish ASP. The Six are pressing for an immediate promise of its abolition as part of a single chemicals package. By doing so they hand Congress the chance to undo the whole Kennedy round, but argue that the tariff-cutting offers made by the rest of the world would be the best way of persuading Congress to get rid of ASP. Alternative American and British schemes involve a partial unconditional tariff cut followed by further cuts when the abolition of ASP has been got through Congress.

If the negotiators could get away from the hysteria that fogs these arguments, it would probably be seen that the Six should give way on their single chemicals package, and the Americans on objecting to a modest food aid programme which could always be improved upon in later years. The danger of escalation into withdrawing tariff cuts agreed in the rest of the industrial sector would be reduced, and the likelihood of similar negative-positive offers lists and subsequent withdrawals by the British (who remain profoundly dissatisfied with the Six over steel as well as with some recently introduced fine print in the American steel offers) could be contained.

M. Rey, who would like to succeed Dr. Hallstein as president of the common market commission, knows that his career stands or falls by success in the Kennedy round. But he is having to conduct two negotiations at once, in Geneva and in Brussels. His achievements in Brussels, in getting agreement at all on a food aid programme, and resisting so far Belgian and Dutch demands for withdrawals against the Nordic countries, are rightly represented as a triumph for the common market idea in its present distressingly introspective form. The tragedy is that a triumph for common market togetherness simply does not add up to a successful Kennedy round. The Americans too are involved with a double set of negotiations, with a Congress behind their backs that is in a very different mood to 1962, when the Trade Expansion Act was passed.

Final negotiations began on May 4, 1967, and just as the objectives of the Kennedy Round were established during the six days of the Ministerial meeting back in 1963, so too were the key issues to be settled in the next six days after the final negotiating period began. The delegates faced a now-or-never situation of resolving the stalemated issues involving chemicals, steel, grain, other EEC agricultural offers, exceptions, and residual disparities. Confronting a final deadline that was now only a few days away, the negotiators entered into a "marathon" all-night negotiating session.[22]

The marathon session was itself unsuccessful, but the Director-General of GATT was able to secure agreement for an extension of the final deadline to May 14. In a press release he stated, "The major trading nations participating in the Kennedy Round negotiations have engaged in intensive bilateral and multilateral talks over the last four days with a view to reaching by today an agreement in principle on the major outstanding issues of the negotiations. While some progress has been made, it has not proved possible to reach such an overall agreement. . . . It has therefore been agreed that the discussions will continue throughout this week with a final concluding date of Sunday, May 14. All are agreed that it will not be possible to prolong the negotiating schedule any further and that failure to come to a general agreement by May 14 would necessarily lead to the joint conclusion that the Kennedy Round cannot be successfully concluded at all." [23]

As it turned out, the clock was actually stopped Sunday at midnight, and talks were allowed to go on into Monday. At noon, the Director-General of GATT finally circulated a set of compromise proposals on each of the three key issues:

   1. *Chemicals.* There were some additional concessions granted to the United States. The Americans would cut only 20 per cent on

---

22. Of interest in this connection is the observation by Bernard Béguin of the *Journal de Genève*, who said of the marathon negotiating session: "After four years of discussion on a familiar theme, one wonders how qualified officials can reach a point where the success or failure of their work depends on one night's seance, or a weekend of the last chance. . . . It is a fact, however—regrettable but incontestable fact—that the history of reciprocally advantageous negotiations is marked by these absurd suspenses which allow delegations to claim later before restive opinion that they did not concede except to save the essential. . . . The situation is that the negotiation has become more and more difficult through the years . . . and that it is really necessary to have a last minute strenuous effort to pull it through." Quoted in Preeg, *op. cit.*, p. 192, n. 20.

23. *Ibid.*, pp. 192–93.

low duties in the Kennedy Round; the Europeans would cut 30 per cent instead of 20 per cent on high duties; Switzerland and Japan would maintain their full chemical offers regardless of the American selling price problem. Under these circumstances, the United States was to accept a solution for chemicals by splitting tariff reductions on chemicals into two parts, one conditional on elimination of the American selling price and the other unconditional.

2. *Agriculture.* The EEC would make additional tariff cut offers on certain priority requests of the United States.

3. *Steel.* The British would make a general 20 per cent cut in steel rates in conjunction with the matched rate offers of the United States and the EEC.

The submission of this "package deal" provided the basis for a final take-it-or-leave-it agreement which could result in average tariff cuts of more than one-third on four-fifths of the world's trade and a government food aid commitment of 4½ million tons of wheat per year. In addition, it could be politically significant in displaying unity within the Atlantic community, especially between the United States and the EEC. The reaction to the final package deal has been described by a negotiator:

> There was a flurry of activity to calculate the precise meaning of the proposals. A late afternoon meeting at Wyndham White's office [the Director-General of GATT] confirmed general agreement on the package but firm commitments were withheld. Another meeting was scheduled for 10 o'clock that night.
>
> At 9:25, Ambassador Roth [Chief American negotiator], napping in his room at the Hotel Richmond, was awakened by a telephone call from Jean Rey [Chief EEC negotiator]. Rey requested an informal meeting which Roth gladly accepted and, with Michael Blumenthal [Assistant American negotiator], they met in the hotel room. Within ten minutes the package was agreed essentially as proposed by Wyndham White. The Kennedy Round, after four long and harrowing years, was at last clearly bound for a successful conclusion.
>
> By 10 o'clock all major participants had accepted the final compromise proposals. Le Bocage [GATT headquarters] was adorned with the familiar crowd of press stalwarts but the gathering was otherwise very different. Instead of the few official cars furtively delivering a handful of serious, statistic-laden delegates, a line of vehicles backed up bumper to bumper, and delegates by the dozen poured into the villa. Flashbulbs, handshakes, light-hearted banter—it was all over, and the sponta-

neous relief as the delegates gathered was in perfect harmony
with Wyndham White's opening words: "The essential elements
of the Kennedy Round have now been successfully negotiated." [24]

The Economist summarized the importance of what happened in
Geneva as follows.

4.4 AGREEMENT REACHED [25]

So the Kennedy round of tariff cuts has come off after all. To realise
the importance of what happened in Geneva at midnight on Monday, it
is necessary to remember the hopes of the men who set out to reshape
the trading habits of the capitalist world after 1945. They looked forward to an era of universal near-free trade on a scale unknown since
1914, in a world economy made buoyant by international Keynesian policies of which the pre-1914 world knew nothing. The Kennedy round
takes us a long way to their objective. This is a remarkable achievement
for negotiations over which the shadow of failure has hung so obsti-
nately for four years. It carries the postwar movement for the freeing of
trade between industrial powers close to its logical conclusion. Tariffs
are no longer the dominant problem of world trade among the rich; they
have been reduced to a minor obstacle, even though some other obstacles still abound.

Just how each country's trade will be affected is still being worked
out. But, by previous standards, the result turns all the major industrial
powers into low-tariff areas. In particular, a first quick look suggests that
when the cuts are made the European common market will be far more
like an enlargement of the relatively free trading Germany of Professor
Erhard than it will be like the protectionist France or Italy of pre-com-
mon market days. This alone would justify the negotiators' years of
angry argument.

But will the anxieties and hard feelings of the past four years leave a
permanent mark? Certainly experience has shown, once again, that negotiating with the common market is a formidable proposition. The belief that economic relations between Europe and America are an ill-tem-
pered competitive business has been imprinted in the minds of officials
and the public. It has played its part in an unnecessary process of partial estrangement between the two great western centres of power. Yet
the apparent corollary that they must give up the hope of pursuing a
common interest has been invalidated. The upshot of the great haggle is
to show that when industrial powers of the elephantine size of the
United States and the European community do finally move in unison
they can achieve major reforms of universal benefit.

24. *Ibid.*, p. 195.
25. *The Economist,* May 20, 1967, p. 767.

General de Gaulle could have broken the Kennedy round, and he did not. Why? Perhaps it is simply that he believes French industry must be forced to face competition in order to avoid a repetition of France's economic weakness in the early twentieth century. Such thoughts must have been reinforced by Bonn's hints that German subsidies for French farm surpluses in the common market might be withheld if France sabotaged Germany's hopes of access to a bigger world market. General de Gaulle has to make some concessions to the Germans if he is to keep Britain out of the common market. Even he can only afford to veto some of the people some of the time.

Yet, by a paradox, the success of the Kennedy round should reinforce Britain's European policy. It makes Britain's only plausible alternative to Europe—the idea of a North Atlantic Free Trade Area—virtually irrelevant. The only circumstances in which the Americans might have entertained the notion of a North Atlantic trading area would have been the frustration of their hopes for the Kennedy round. If the common market countries had destroyed the hope of a general lowering of tariffs, the United States might have reconciled itself to leading some of the outsiders into a permanent rival trading group. It is unlikely to do so after the success at Geneva—although a short-term monetary struggle, designed to persuade the French to accept reasonable international liquidity arrangements, could be another matter.

But the other reason why the French may have accepted the Kennedy round could be the most significant of all for the future of the international economy. Tariffs are ceasing to be the central issue in world trade. The great new issues—competition between science-based industries, the problems of agriculture, and the tricky business of trade with communist states and the poor nations—all call for joint policies by governments, in which free trade is at most only one element. This is true even for the poor nations of the world, who need wholly free access to the great industrial markets of the rich.

As a result, the Kennedy round looks like closing one era in world trade policies, and ushering in a new one. The negotiators have been as unenterprising in dealing with the new issues confronting the world as they have been successful on tariffs themselves. The poor seem to have been left begging on the doorstep. As for agriculture, a grains agreement was dropped at the last minute in favour of mere renewal of the international wheat agreement, with commitments from the industrial powers to provide food aid thrown in. The postwar trade negotiators have repaired the follies of the protectionist 1930s more fully than any optimist expected in 1947. But they have not begun to tackle the problems of the 1970s.

Although the foregoing constitutes a highly abbreviated account of the complex and prolonged negotiations of the Kennedy Round, certain features of the negotiating process do stand out. It is clear that the process depended as much on the imponderables and vagaries of commercial diplomacy and political power—and on the personality, acumen, and persistence of the negotiators—as it did on the knowledge of the technical expert and the quantitative data presented by the computer.

5. KENNEDY ROUND OUTCOME

With the signing of the final protocols, there was general satisfaction—except among the LDCs—that the sixth round of GATT negotiations constituted an extremely significant accomplishment in trade liberalization. Aspects of the agreement are summarized in the following Department of State announcement.

5.1 KENNEDY ROUND AGREEMENTS SIGNED AT GENEVA [26]

The Office of the Special Representative for Trade Negotiations announced at Washington on June 29 that, by direction of the President, W. Michael Blumenthal, Deputy Special Representative for Trade Negotiations, would sign the multilateral agreements negotiated in the Sixth Round of Trade Negotiations at Geneva June 30.

The signing ceremony concluded the most comprehensive assault on barriers to international trade that has ever taken place. . . .

The important elements of the Kennedy Round package are:

Tariff cuts of 50 percent on a very broad range of industrial goods and cuts in the 30 to 50 percent range on many more.

Agricultural concessions to which the United States attaches great value because they create new trading opportunities for our farmers and because they support our contention that international negotiation on trade in farm products can accomplish something.

A world grains arrangement guaranteeing higher minimum trading prices and establishing a program under which other nations will share with us in the vital but burdensome task of supplying food aid to the undernourished people in the less developed countries.

Nontariff barrier (NTB) liberalization including a very significant accord on antidumping procedures as well as European NTB modifications in the American Selling Price (ASP) package.

Useful, if limited, progress on the complex and sensitive problems in the steel, aluminum, pulp and paper, and textile sectors, including a 3-year extension of the Long-Term Cotton Textile Arrangement (LTA).

An agreement on the treatment of chemical products that deals with

---

26. Department of State Bulletin, July 24, 1967, pp. 95–101.

the American Selling Price issue in a manner that provides major chemical traders with mutually advantageous concessions in the main Kennedy Round agreement and a separate and balanced package that makes additional concessions available to the United States if it abandons the American Selling Price system.

Significant assistance to the less developed countries through permitting their participation in the negotiations without requiring reciprocal contributions from them, through special concessions on products of particular interest to them, and through the food aid provisions of the grains arrangement.

U. S. participation was made possible through authority granted the President by the Congress through the Trade Expansion Act of 1962. The late Christian A. Herter directed U. S. participation as the Special Representative for Trade Negotiations until his death in late 1966. He was succeeded by William M. Roth, who continues to serve as Special Representative.

The agreements signed June 30 comprise:

1. A Final Act, which authenticates the texts of the agreements described in paragraphs 2–5 below and which expresses the intention of all the signatories to take appropriate steps, subject to their constitutional procedures, to put these agreements into effect.

2. The Geneva (1967) Protocol to the General Agreement on Tariffs and Trade, which embodies most of the tariff and other concessions exchanged in the negotiations.

3. An agreement relating primarily to chemicals, which provides for the elimination of the American Selling Price system.

4. A memorandum of agreement on basic elements for a world grains arrangement.

5. An agreement on implementation of article VI of the GATT, in the form of a code of antidumping practices.

The negotiations were concluded in all essential respects in May at a series of high-level meetings in Geneva. Since that time, the negotiators have been putting the details of their concessions and understandings into the final conference documents.

It is estimated that the agreements will apply to about $40 billion of world trade. In industry, the United States and the other countries have agreed on cuts averaging about 35 percent. In agriculture, the average cut is less, but the United States has obtained important concessions covering a substantial volume of trade.

U. S. tariff reductions will not enter into force until proclaimed by the President. It is expected that their effective date will be January 1, 1968. In accordance with the requirements of the Trade Expansion Act, most U. S. duty reductions will be made in five equal annual stages starting January 1.

In overall trade terms, covering both industrial and agricultural products, the tariff cuts made by the United States are in balance with those of the other industrialized countries. In terms of 1966 trade the United States is giving tariff cuts on about $7½ billion to $8 billion of industrial and agricultural imports and is obtaining tariff concessions on about the same amount of U. S. exports.

Import duties are being cut in half on a broad range of industrial products in international trade. Cuts in the 35 to 50 percent range are being made on many more products. Categories of products on which the principal negotiating countries, including the United States, have made cuts that in the aggregate average over 35 percent include: machinery, both electrical and nonelectrical; photographic equipment and supplies; automobile and other transport equipment; optical, scientific, and professional instruments and equipments; paper and paper products; books and other printed material; fabricated metal products; and lumber and wood products, including furniture.

Negotiations on steel were conducted against a background of tariff rates where U. S. duties are generally lower than those of other participants. These negotiations, held bilaterally and multilaterally, resulted in closer harmonization of tariffs among the major steel producing countries. Virtually all the peaks in these countries' tariffs were eliminated, so that almost all rates will be no higher than 15 percent and most will be well below 10 percent.

Except for U. S. rates, most steel tariffs have not heretofore been bound. In the final negotiating package, however, almost all rates of other countries were bound and many were reduced.

The international harmonization of steel tariffs should also reduce the tendency for exports to be deflected to the U. S. market in instances where U. S. tariffs were much lower than those of other countries. Although the United States is primarily an importer rather than an exporter of steelmill products, lower tariffs abroad will also provide opportunities for U. S. exporters.

The Community offer consisted of a binding of a 130,000-ton annual quota at 5 percent. The EEC had previously bound in the GATT a 9 percent rate of duty on ingot aluminum. Some imports were allowed entry annually under a tariff quota at 5 percent, but neither the amount of the quota nor the lower rate had been bound. The United States is making a 20 percent cut on ingot aluminum, of benefit primarily to Canada and Norway.

On unwrought aluminum (further advanced than ingot), tariff cuts by the United States averaged less than 30 percent. The EEC average cut was about one-third, while the tariff cuts by the U. K. and Canada were larger than those of the EEC. Other EFTA [European Free Trade Association] countries and Japan also made substantial cuts in the aluminum sector.

The chemical sector negotiations were centered on the American Selling Price issue. European countries maintained from the start that any more than token reductions in their chemical tariffs were conditional on U. S. elimination of the ASP valuation system. Since elimination of ASP would require congressional action, U. S. negotiators insisted that chemical concessions be implemented in two packages: first, a balanced settlement in the Kennedy Round; second, reciprocal concessions by other countries in return for abolition of ASP.

The pattern and volume of chemical trade is such that the outcome of negotiations in this sector inevitably played a major role in the outcome of the entire Kennedy Round. U. S. dutiable chemical imports from countries with a major stake in world chemical trade (EEC, United Kingdom, Japan, Switzerland) were $325 million in 1964; these countries' dutiable chemical imports from the United States totaled nearly $900 million.

In the end, all major Kennedy Round participants made concessions in the chemical sector. Many concessions have been agreed on unconditionally, while certain other concessions are conditional on United States elimination of the American Selling Price valuation system.

The concessions on chemicals are, therefore, in two parts: first, the Kennedy Round chemical package, and second, the ASP package.

The Kennedy Round Chemical Package. Unconditional obligations undertaken in the Kennedy Round are as follows:

1. The United States agreed to duty reductions on products accounting for nearly all (95 percent) of U. S. dutiable chemical imports. Tariffs will be reduced 50 percent on most items with rates above 8 percent; 20 percent on items 8 percent and below.

2. The European Economic Community agreed to duty reductions on tariff items accounting for 98 percent of its dutiable chemical imports from the United States. Most duties will be reduced by 20 percent. Certain items, however, will be subject to reductions of 30 percent and 35 percent, while some others will be reduced less than 20 percent.

3. The United Kingdom agreed to duty reductions on virtually all chemical imports from the United States except certain plastics. Most British plastics duties are currently 10 percent, a level considerably lower than other major trading countries. The United Kingdom has agreed to reduce tariffs at rates of 25 percent and above by 30 percent, and rates below 25 percent by 20 percent.

4. Japan agreed to tariff reductions which on a weighted average basis amount to 44 percent on dutiable chemical imports from the United States.

5. Switzerland agreed to tariff reductions which on a weighted average basis amount to 49 percent on $45 million of chemical imports from the United States.

6. Other participants, notably Canada and the Scandinavian countries, agreed to reductions in their chemical tariffs as part of their Kennedy Round concessions.

The ASP Package. The following concessions are contingent on U. S. elimination of the ASP valuation system:

1. The United States would eliminate ASP and replace rates currently based on ASP with rates that have been proposed by the Tariff Commission to be applied on the valuation as normally calculated for other U. S. imports and yielding the same revenue as the previous rates. These "converted" rates would be reduced by stages, generally by 50 percent or to an ad valorem equivalent of 20 percent, whichever is lower.

2. The European Economic Community would reduce its chemical tariffs by an additional amount so as to achieve a combined Kennedy Round-ASP package reduction of 46 percent on $460 million of chemical imports from the United States. Virtually all EEC chemical tariffs would be at rates of 12½ percent or below. Belgium, France, and Italy would also modify road-use taxes so as to eliminate discrimination against American-made automobiles.

3. The United Kingdom would reduce most of its chemical tariffs according to the following formula: Items at present dutiable at 25 percent and above would be reduced to a level of 12½ percent, for a 62 percent combined Kennedy Round and ASP package reduction. Tariff items with duties of less than 25 percent would generally be reduced by the amount necessary to achieve a combined reduction of 50 percent in the two packages. U. K. plastics tariffs which would be above the reduced EEC rate on the same item would be cut to that level and bound.

Most importing countries reduced tariffs on cotton, manmade, and wool textiles less than their average reduction in other industrial products as a whole. The United States agreed to tariff reductions which, on a weighted trade basis, averaged approximately 14 percent for the three fibers. Cotton textiles were reduced 21 percent; manmade textiles, 15 percent; and wool textiles, 2 percent.

Negotiations on cotton textiles involved three elements: the extension of the Long-Term Cotton Textile Arrangement, more liberal access to import markets protected by the LTA, and tariff reductions. The principal concessions by exporting countries of interest to importing countries was the extension of the LTA in its present form until September 30, 1970. In return, importing countries agreed to enlarged quotas under LTA provisions and to tariff reductions.

Within the context of the LTA, the United States negotiated bilateral agreements with its main supplying countries. These agreements typically provided for a 5 percent annual increase in LTA quotas, a one-time bonus for LTA extension, and certain other administrative improvements.

The United States agreed to cotton textile tariff reductions that amounted to a weighted average reduction of 21 percent. Reductions on apparel items averaged 17 percent; fabrics tariffs were reduced 24 percent; and yarn, 28 percent.

The EEC reduced cotton textile tariffs by about 20 percent. It also reached bilateral understandings with major suppliers providing for improved access to the EEC market. Noting that it already accorded liberal access for imports from Hong Kong, India, and other Commonwealth sources, the United Kingdom made token cotton textile tariff reductions toward other suppliers.

The United States agreed to a weighted average tariff reduction of 15 percent on imports of manmade-fiber textiles, excluding fibers. Manmade-fiber apparel duties were reduced by an average of approximately 6 percent; fabrics, by 18 percent; yarn, by 37 percent. Other countries made significant reductions on these textiles.

The United States agreed to tariff reductions on very few wool textiles. The weighted average duty reduction on wool fabric was about 1 percent; on wool apparel, about 2 percent. On total wool textile imports the average duty reduction was 2 percent. Other countries made considerably greater reductions on wool textiles.

A major accomplishment in the field of nontariff barriers was the negotiation of an antidumping code. In addition to the United States, the major participants in this negotiation were the United Kingdom, the European Economic Community, Japan, Canada, and the Scandinavian countries.

The antidumping code supplements the provisions of article VI of the GATT with rules and procedures to be followed in antidumping actions. U. S. legislation and administrative regulations contain detailed provisions relating to the determination of sales at less than fair value and injury, but most countries' procedures lack such specificity.

The principal advantages of the antidumping code to the United States will be the adoption by other countries of fair and open procedures along the lines of present U. S. practices. The code will provide both an opportunity and a basis for U. S. exporters to defend their interests in foreign antidumping actions. In particular, the new common antidumping regulations that are being developed by the European Economic Community will conform with the code.

Of special benefit to the United States will be the adoption by Canada of an injury requirement in its antidumping legislation. The lack of such a requirement has impeded U. S. exports for many years.

The United States originally set as a goal in the agricultural negotiations the same broad trade coverage and depth of tariff cuts as achieved for industrial products. This did not prove negotiable, however. The European Economic Community, when the negotiations got underway, was still in the process of developing its Common Agricultural Policy. It was reluctant to make substantial cuts in the level of protection at the same time it was formulating a Common Agricultural Policy among the six members. The results of the agricultural negotiations with the Community are therefore considerably more modest than the results achieved in industry. Nevertheless, progress was made in the negotiations in reducing barriers to agricultural trade.

The United States was able to obtain significant agricultural concessions from Japan, Canada, and the U. K., the Nordic countries, and Switzerland. The EEC made tariff cuts on agricultural items of trade value to the United States of over $200 million.

No progress was made in negotiating down the trade restrictive effects of the variable-levy system of the EEC. Offers made by the Community on the basis of this system were not accepted.

The agricultural negotiations were divided into so-called commodity groups and nongroup or tariff items. The commodity groups included meats, dairy products, and grains. Of the commodity groups only grains yielded positive results.

A new grains arrangement was negotiated that establishes a minimum price for U. S. No. 2 hard red winter ordinary wheat f.o.b. Gulf ports at $1.73 per bushel. This represents an increase of about 21.5 cents per bushel over the equivalent minimum price for U. S. hard red winter ordinary under the present International Wheat Agreement. There will be a comparable increase in the minimum price of other grades and qualities of wheat under the new arrangements.

Participating countries have agreed to contribute 4½ million tons of cereals to a multilateral food aid program. The U. S. share of this program will be 42 percent of the total, or slightly less than 2 million tons. Importing countries as a whole will contribute about 2 million tons of the total. The grains arrangement thus represents further progress toward one of the United States' key objectives of foreign aid, the multilateral sharing of the food burden.

The United States negotiated with the developing countries on the basis of the plan adopted by the Trade Negotiations Committee, the steering committee of the Sixth Round. One of the objectives of the negotiations, that of reducing barriers to exports of developing countries to the maximum extent possible, was taken into account in the plan. The plan also took into account the ministerial decisions to the effect that developed countries could not expect to receive full reciprocity from the developing countries in trade negotiations and that the contributions of developing countries should be considered in the light of the development, trade, and financial needs of those countries.

Accordingly, the United States made concessions of benefit to developing countries, including nonparticipants, which cover over $900 million of their exports. Included in these concessions will be the complete elimination of the duty on more than $325 million of imports from these countries. Moreover, the elimination of duties on $45 million of these products does not need to be staged over a 4-year period and thus meets one of the more important *desiderata* of the developing countries. Since many of the concessions on tropical products were negotiated in the context of joint action by industrialized countries, the total benefits which developing countries will receive were further increased.

Ten developing countries made concessions benefiting the United States.

At the final signing ceremony the Director-General of GATT gave perspective to the accomplishments of the negotiations.

5.2 DIRECTOR-GENERAL'S CLOSING OF THE KENNEDY ROUND [27]

It is now nearly twenty years ago that here in this same Assembly Hall the original contracting parties set their signature to the General Agreement on Tariffs and Trade. The event did not attract much attention. It was nevertheless momentous. It set in motion—and on a scale hitherto unseen—the process of tariff disarmament which has reached its apogee in the negotiations which we are today formally concluding.

We are gathered here today to set our signature to the results of the most far-reaching international trade negotiation of all times. May I briefly summarize the results.

The industrialized countries participating in the Kennedy Round made duty reductions on 70 per cent of their dutiable imports, excluding cereals, meat and dairy products. Moreover, two thirds of these cuts were of 50 per cent or more. Around another fifth were between 25 and 50 per cent. Of the total dutiable imports on which no tariff cuts have been negotiated (31 per cent of the total), one third are subject to duties of 5 per cent ad valorem or less. All this can be stated in another way. Of the imports by the participating industrialized countries (other than cereals, meat and dairy products) 66 per cent are either duty-free or are to be subject to cuts of 50 per cent or more; on another 15 per cent there are to be cuts of less than 50 per cent and 19 per cent remain unaffected. As for cereals, meat and dairy products, the aim, as you know, was the negotiation of general arrangements. In the case of cereals, agreement relating to prices and food aid has been reached. Some bilateral agreements have been concluded on meat. Very little has been obtained in the negotiations on dairy products. On scores of other agricultural products, significant duty reductions were made.

The duty reductions affected various sectors differently, being most extensive in the field of chemicals, pulp and paper, machinery, transport equipment and precision instruments, raw materials other than fuels and agricultural raw materials, base metals and miscellaneous manufactures. Both the depth of cuts and the range of items affected were below the average in the case of agricultural products, textiles and clothing, iron and steel, tropical products and fuels.

In addition to these tariff cuts, agreements were also reached on chemical products and on anti-dumping policies which will contribute in an important way to the reduction of non-tariff barriers to trade.

The results of the Kennedy Round for the developing countries are less impressive. If the appraisal is made on the basis of those products which

27. The text of the statement by Eric Wyndham White, Director-General of the General Agreement on Tariffs and Trade, at the meeting of the Trade Negotiations Committee at Geneva on June 30, 1967. Press Release No. 993, GATT, June 30, 1967.

were designated by the developing countries as of interest to them, a list which, quite properly, included both goods presently exported and those of potential export interest, the results are, in general, as favourable as the overall results just cited. This should be no cause for surprise, because the developing countries regard as of potential interest to them a range and variety of goods very similar to the range and variety of goods traded among the developed countries. If, however, one bases an appraisal on the goods for which the developing countries presently have significant exports, the results show that of their manufactured exports subjected to duties, some 51 per cent will benefit from tariff cuts by the industrialized countries of 50 per cent or more, and some 25 per cent by tariff cuts of less than 50 per cent. We have not yet been able to complete our calculation of the results for the developing countries with respect to their agricultural exports but it is known that, as for farm products generally, the results were not impressive.

Despite their limitations—and we must recognize that there were failures in some cases—these results are impressive and will, I hope, especially if shortly followed by improvements in the international monetary framework, provide the basis for continued steady expansion of international trade.

But the success of the negotiations may also, I hope, be construed as a reaffirmation of support by governments for the world-wide multilateral trading system of which GATT is the symbol and the expression. Some observers have recently seen a threat to this system from the appearance of powerful regional, economic groupings. If fact, however, and our meeting here today is eloquent proof of this, never has the momentum of world-wide trade liberalization been so marked, and it is reasonable to say that the formation of large economic groupings has provided stimulus to the movement toward this liberalization.

It is for this reason that it is appropriate today that, whilst recording with satisfaction what we have achieved in these last few years, we should also be looking ahead. In the course of the Kennedy Round we have learned a great deal. To some problems we have only been able to bring partial solution. But the discussion and analysis of these questions in detailed negotiations has more clearly revealed their basic characteristics, and suggested the lines along which more radical solutions should be sought. Much has been said and more will be said of the limitations of the results in the field of agriculture. These results should not be underestimated and are certainly greater than anything that has gone before. But perhaps more importantly this difficult sector of economic activity is clearly now within the field of international negotiation and it can no longer be doubted that these negotiations go beyond tariffs and other commercial devices and embrace all aspects of national policies, production, prices, and supports. This is an area in which the GATT has great possibilities and opportunities in the future. In the negotiations we also made a valuable beginning in limiting the restrictive effects of non-tariff barriers to trade. Again this is only a beginning and the question increases in importance with the reduction of tariff barriers. In passing, I would note that differences in tariff nomenclatures gave rise to difficulties in the negotiations and clearly demonstrate the desirability of those who have not done so adopting the Brussels Nomenclature. While there was some progress in the negotiations on problems connected with valuation for customs purposes, other difficulties remain in this area and we should consider setting up machinery within the GATT to deal more effectively with them. Finally, in certain major sectors of modern industry we have now achieved such modest rates of tariff protection that the question arises whether, by working together on new and broader measures of international negotiation and co-operation, including the new elements resulting from technological advances, we cannot remove the various structural obstacles that may still obstruct the path to free trade.

We have made a significant advance in dealing with trade relationships between countries with different economic systems, through the agreement on the terms of accession of Poland to the General Agreement.

I now come to the trade problems of the less-developed countries. This is an area in which GATT has been a pioneer, and I am particularly glad that the importance of this problem has now been universally recognized internationally through the establishment of UNCTAD with which we in the GATT are developing an increasingly close partnership. The GATT secretariat will certainly regard as one of its most important tasks in the next few months to contribute what it can to assisting in the preparation of the second UNCTAD Conference in New Delhi.

In the meantime, it will be our urgent task in the competent organs of GATT to analyze in depth the contribution which the Kennedy Round has made to alleviating the trade problems of the less-developed countries, to assess what remains to be done, to complete unfinished tasks, and to initiate as soon as possible early positive action within the scope and possibilities of the organization.

From the data we have at hand it is clear that the less-developed countries will derive substantial advantages from the Kennedy Round, and equally clear that all their legitimate desires and aspirations are not fully achieved. Those—and there are many—which are heavily dependent upon exports of agricultural products suffer from the general modicity of the results in the agricultural field. We failed to achieve free trade for tropical products, though here the major, if not the only, problem is the difficult one of reconciling the desire of some for larger markets in all developed countries with the reluctance of beneficiaries of existing preferences to surrender these in exchange for free and open competition on open markets. It is also significant—and regrettable—that in a major area of manufactures where some less-developed countries have a clear competitive advantage—and despite their concurrence in the extension of the Cotton Textiles Agreement—tariff reductions fell far short of the 50

per cent target and in some important cases are only granted condition-
ally.

On looking ahead, however, a large place will have to be found in the
future programme of GATT—in partnership with the other international
organizations—for a determined and concerted attack on the formidable
obstacles which lie in the path of the less-developed countries in their
struggle for the economic advancement of their peoples. This is not their
problem alone, it is a clear responsibility for the international community
as a whole.

I will conclude on a mixed tone of optimism and caution. The General
Agreement of 1967 extends and consolidates the impressive achievements of twenty years of international trade co-operation. It points the
way ahead to further achievement. At the same time the structure is
fragile and constantly subject to attack. So far it has not been tested by
periods of economic stress and recession. We cannot confidently say
whether it would take the strain. If national economic policies are managed without sufficient awareness of the economic interdependence of
nations, there is always the risk that governments may feel impelled to re-
vert to policies of external restriction. The happily brief episode of the
United Kingdom surcharge is warning of what could happen. In recent
days too, we have seen carefully negotiated agreements—of vital interest
to the parties concerned—frustrated by powerful sectoral pressures. In
the course of the negotiations we have also seen a great economic power
withhold from negotiations a whole sector of production—alas again in
the field of agriculture—even though this action frustrated any hope of
co-operative action by other participants to develop more liberal policies.
The price of economic liberalization—as of liberty—is eternal vigilance.

No precise evaluation of the outcome of the Kennedy Round can
be given. Although the major accomplishment was clearly the reduction of tariff levels on nonagricultural products, it is not possible
to summarize in simply quantitative terms the impact of these reductions. Not only is there the problem of assessing "average tariff
levels" in order to determine the percentage cut in the Kennedy
Round, but there is also the need to consider the entire tariff
structure—or the tariff differentials at different stages of production
—in order to determine the "effective" as contrasted with the "nominal" tariff rate.[28] Moreover, the future impact of a tariff reduction
will depend on future changes in the elasticities of demand and
supply of not only the dutiable products but also complements and

28. See W. M. Corden, *The Theory of Protection* (1971), with extensive bibliogra-
phy.

Table I. United States Tariff Levels for Nonagricultural Products (Other than Mineral Fuels), before and after Kennedy Round Cuts[a]

| | Dutiable imports, before cuts | | Average tariff on dutiable imports, as percentage of c.i.f. value | | Percent cut in Kennedy Round |
| | As percentage of total imports[b] | As percentage of total dutiable imports | Before cuts | After cuts | |
Category	(1)	(2)	(3)	(4)	(5)
Mineral products	18(17)	1.9	9.9	7.5	24
Chemical products	59(58)	5.7	17.8	9.3	48[c]
Rubber products	25	1.0	11.3	6.0	47
Hides, furs, leather products	47	2.0	16.2	10.4	36
Raw hides, skins, fur	8(7)	0.2	4.1	3.6	54
Articles of leather, fur	100	1.8	17.5	11.2	36
Wood and cork products	86(36)	7.7	6.8	7.1	49
Wood, natural cork	58(30)	0.7	0.9	0.3	89
Articles of wood, cork	90(37)	7.0	7.4	7.9	49
Pulp and paper	6	1.0	10.9	5.5	50
Pulp	0	—	free	free	—
Paper	9	1.0	10.9	5.5	50
Textiles	85(72)	15.8	21.4	20.1	20
Natural fiber and waste	52(50)	2.3	18.3	15.9	16
Yarn and basic fabrics	100(68)	7.2	19.1	21.8	24
Special fabrics, apparel, other	90	6.3	25.0	20.6	18
Footwear and headwear	100	2.2	16.1	12.1	25
Stone, ceramic, and glass products	100(99)	3.2	21.0	15.0	29
Base metals and metal products	93(83)	23.4	8.5	6.3	34
Unwrought, pig iron, scrap	84(58)	8.1	5.2	5.0	35
Basic shapes and forms	100(99)	11.0	8.5	6.4	25
Steel	100	9.4	6.5	5.7	12
Other	100(95)	1.6	19.6	10.4	47
Articles of base metal, misc.	97(95)	4.3	14.7	7.7	48
Nonelectrical machinery	75(74)	7.9	11.9	6.0	50
Electrical machinery	100	5.0	13.6	7.1	48
Transportation equipment	96	11.4	7.1	3.5	51
Precision instruments	100	4.9	21.1	13.1	38
Miscellaneous	52	6.9	19.5	11.5	41
Total	68(61)	100.0	13.5	9.6	36
Manufactures[d]	—	86.8	14.3	9.9	36

SOURCE: E. H. Preeg, *Traders and Diplomats* (1970), p. 208.

[a] Based on c.i.f. value (converted from f.o.b. or American selling price value), 1964 imports.

[b] Figures in parentheses are post-Kennedy Round percentages of total imports that are the result of duty eliminations. It should be noted that where the share of imports dutiable has declined as a result of duty elimination, the post-Kennedy Round tariff level is higher than the pre-Kennedy Round level reduced by the percent cut in column 5.

[c] Includes cuts conditional on acceptance of the separate agreement on American selling price; the reduction would otherwise be about 45 percent.

[d] Includes all categories except mineral products; raw hides, skins, fur; wood, natural cork; pulp; natural fiber and waste; unwrought, pig iron, scrap.

Table II. European Economic Community Tariff Levels for Nonagricultural Products (Other than Mineral Fuels), before and after Kennedy Round Cuts[a]

| | Dutiable imports, before cuts | | Average tariff on dutiable imports, as percentage of c.i.f. value | | Percent cut in Kennedy Round |
| | As percentage of total imports[b] (1) | As percentage of total dutiable imports (2) | Before cuts (3) | After cuts (4) | |
Category					(5)
Mineral products	2	0.2	9.4	5.5	42
Chemical products	91	13.1	14.3	7.6	47[c]
Rubber products	26	1.2	15.0	7.8	48
Hides, furs, leather products	22	1.1	9.2	5.7	38
Raw hides, skins, fur	0	—	free	free	—
Articles of leather, fur	22	1.1	9.2	5.7	38
Wood and cork products	17(12)	1.8	10.9	8.8	41
Wood, natural cork	9(3)	0.7	6.5	4.0	75
Articles of wood, cork	100(99)	1.1	13.8	9.5	31
Pulp and paper	92	10.9	10.7	7.5	30
Pulp	83	4.8	6.0	3.0	50
Paper	100	6.1	14.4	11.1	23
Textiles	37	9.9	16.0	12.6	21
Natural fiber and waste	5	0.6	3.0	3.0	0
Yarn and basic fabrics	97	4.7	13.0	11.4	12
Special fabrics, apparel, other	93	4.6	20.7	14.9	28
Footwear and headwear	100	0.6	17.8	12.4	30
Stone, ceramic and glass products	100	2.1	14.1	8.0	43
Base metals and metal products	60	13.6	9.9	7.0	29
Unwrought, pig iron, scrap	30	3.8	7.4	6.8	8
Basic shapes and forms	100	6.1	9.7	7.0	28
Steel	100	5.2	9.4	6.7	29
Other	99	0.9	11.4	8.8	23
Articles of base metal, misc.	98	3.7	12.8	7.2	44
Nonelectrical machinery	100	21.7	11.1	6.4	42
Electrical machinery	100	7.0	14.2	9.1	36
Transportation equipment	94	8.3	15.4	9.9	36
Precision instruments	100	6.1	13.3	8.4	37
Miscellaneous	24	2.4	16.5	9.8	41
Total	60	100.0	12.8	8.1	37
Manufactures[d]	—	89.9	13.5	8.6	36

SOURCE: E. H. Preeg, *Traders and Diplomats* (1970), p. 209.

[a] Based on c.i.f. value, 1964 imports; excludes trade within EEC and imports from associated countries.

[b] Figures in parentheses are post-Kennedy Round percentages of total imports that are the result of duty eliminations. It should be noted that where the share of imports dutiable has declined as a result of duty elimination, the post-Kennedy Round tariff level is higher than the pre-Kennedy Round level reduced by the percent cut in column 5.

[c] Includes cuts conditional on acceptance of the separate agreement on American selling price; the reduction would otherwise be about 20 percent.

substitutes. Short of full-scale econometric investigations, an economist would be unwilling to offer any general evaluation.[29]

For illustrative purposes, however, it is of interest to note some of the tariff levels before and after the Kennedy Round cuts for the United States and EEC, as in Tables I and II. Table III indicates the change in tariff dispersion (the frequency distribution of individual tariff rates) of the principal Kennedy Round participants. In more general and qualitative terms, the outcome of the Ken-

Table III. Distribution of Dutiable Nonagricultural Products
(Other than Mineral Fuels) by Tariff Level, before and after Kennedy Round Cuts[a]

Tariff level[b]	Percentage of product categories									
	Before cuts				After cuts					
	U.S.	EEC	U.K.	Japan	U.S.	EEC	U.K.	Japan	Sweden	Switzerland
0.1– 2.5	1.3	0.5	0.1	0.1	3.7	3.0	1.6	1.6	7.5	41.1
2.6– 5.0	3.2	2.9	0.2	1.7	21.3	18.3	13.1	7.5	46.9	22.3
5.1– 7.5	6.8	6.7	1.2	0.8	25.3	35.2	14.1	29.2	16.3	16.2
7.6–10.0	14.7	18.2	16.2	7.7	17.7	26.8	34.3	27.8	18.9	8.3
10.1–12.5	15.8	17.4	4.4	3.7	9.5	8.3	14.2	12.7	3.5	5.6
12.6–15.0	11.8	25.8	15.6	32.4	7.7	5.0	7.4	10.1	6.0	2.9
15.1–17.5	11.8	13.6	13.7	10.7	5.5	2.4	7.1	4.0	0.9	1.7
17.6–20.0	7.3	10.6	19.7	21.0	2.8	0.8	6.1	4.3	—	0.7
20.1–25.0	11.0	4.0	15.2	12.3	4.2	0.1	2.1	2.4	—	0.7
25.1–30.0	8.8	0.1	6.7	5.9	1.5	—	—	0.4	—	0.5
30.1–40.0	4.7	0.1	6.7	3.3	0.5	—	—	—	—	—
Over 40.0	2.8	0.1	0.3	0.4	0.3	0.1	—	—	—	—
Cumulative										
0.1– 5.0	4.5	3.4	0.3	1.8	25.0	21.3	14.7	9.1	54.4	63.4
0.1–10.0	26.0	28.3	17.7	10.3	68.0	83.3	63.1	66.1	89.6	87.9
0.1–15.0	53.6	71.5	37.7	46.4	85.2	96.6	84.7	88.9	99.1	96.4
0.1–20.0	72.7	95.7	71.1	78.1	93.5	99.8	97.9	97.2	100.0	98.8
0.1–30.0	92.5	99.8	93.0	96.3	99.2	99.9	100.0	100.0	100.0	100.0

SOURCE: E. H. Preeg, *Traders and Diplomats* (1970), p. 214.
[a] Based on four-digit Brussels Tariff Nomenclature categories.
[b] Percentage rate based on c.i.f. value, 1964 imports; U.S. rates are converted from f.o.b. or American selling price.

29. Although not subject to a refined econometric analysis, a comprehensive summary of the results of the negotiations—by individual country and commodity groups —is presented in Office of the Special Representative for Trade Negotiations, *Report on United States Negotiations, op. cit.*

nedy Round is evaluated in the following statement offered at a
Congressional Hearing on the Future of United States Foreign
Trade Policy.

5.3 FUTURE OF U. S. FOREIGN TRADE POLICY [30]

The subcommittee met at 10 a.m, pursuant to notice, in room 1202,
New Senate Office Building, Hon. Hale Boggs (chairman of the subcom-
mittee) presiding. . . .
Chairman Boggs: Mr. Diebold, may we hear from you first?

Statement of William Diebold, Jr.,
Council on Foreign Relations

Mr. Diebold. Thank you, Mr. Chairman.
Success seems to me to bring problems rather than a surcease of effort. The Kennedy Round is the culmination of a generation of progress
under American leadership to remove barriers to world trade. If it and its
predecessors had accomplished less, I think we would be talking here
today, as we did at intervals of 3 or 4 years over 30-odd years, about the
wisdom of giving the President the power to reduce tariffs, and under what
conditions. I think that remains a problem. But it is only a part of the
larger problem that we have to deal with. I think trade policy is no longer
solely, perhaps not even mainly, a matter of tariff policy. It has broadened.
There are two kinds of problems we face now: Those that were left relatively untouched by the Kennedy Round and those that were opened up
in new ways by the Kennedy Round, so that they can only be dealt with
by bringing into play matters which have ordinarily not been thought of
as being in the forefront of trade policy.
The remaining tariffs on trade in manufactured goods among industrial
countries fall into three categories. First, those that have been substantially cut and, for the most part, are lower than they have been in this
century. We must ask ourselves: How important are these? Can we conceivably ignore some of them, or is there some way of clearing the
ground by perhaps some kind of formula or acceptance of a principle or
rule for reducing these tariffs other than by another Kennedy Round,
which hardly seems called for at this point?
A second category of tariffs includes those which have been left relatively untouched by the Kennedy Round precisely because it has been
difficult for one country, or many of them, to make cuts. And there I think
we face some of our hardest problems, which will require new kinds of
initiative, perhaps along the lines suggested by Eric Wyndham White, the

30. Hearings before the Subcommittee on Foreign Economic Policy, Joint Economic Committee, 90th Congress, First Session, July 19, 1967, pp. 219–23.

Director-General of GATT of negotiation industry by industry, looking not just to tariffs, but at a range of trade barriers.

In the third category are tariffs which would have been cut if the pattern of bargaining had been somewhat different, that is to say, a country was prepared to cut them if it got an adequate concession in return. I think there is not much to say about them except that they are among the chips for the next round in the card game.

It is now generally accepted that as the tariffs have fallen away, nontariff barriers have become more important than ever. They are nothing new. We spent a lot of time at the end of the war working on problems of quotas and the direct controls associated with exchange controls.

But with those largely out of the way, I think we are now facing a highly variegated array of restrictions of new kinds that do not fall into easily understood patterns.

Negotiating about these will raise several problems. They are too varied, in my opinion, to be covered by any kind of simple rule or comprehensive agreement of the sort that we have over the years evolved to deal with tariffs and quotas. It may be that they are susceptible of an approach that seeks to set up some sort of complaint procedure. Certain of the barriers, either types or individual barriers, can probably be dealt with by agreements, and by establishing something like a code of behavior or rules about them. However, barriers are of differing importance for different countries, so that the logic of approaching them barrier by barrier does not stand up too well to the realities of negotiation and the need to bargain with whatever one has to bargain with. Nor is it likely that negotiation about nontariff barriers can be separated from negotiation about remaining tariffs. The complex pull between the logic of separate treatment and the requirements of more collective treatment will, I think, influence our approach to these things, and have some bearing on where and how we try to deal with them. For the United States I think there are additional problems, in that the nontariff barriers do not fall under any simple legislative arrangement, and the problem of how to negotiate, what kinds of powers the President will have to have, will remain, I think, a troublesome one.

Not the least of the problems in negotiating about nontariff barriers is a lack of agreement as to what, in fact, are barriers. Some are more or less covert trade barriers and have that as their main objective. But there are others in which the trade barrier effect is incidental to the pursuit of some other objective perhaps. Such a matter as health or safety. We are now seeing international discussions about the automobile safety arrangements which have to be adopted in this country, because they cause problems for foreign producers.

Price rules, and domestic business practice arrangements, all begin to come into the picture. And so all manner of things are drawn into what used to be simple trade negotiations about tariffs and quotas. Not the least of the problems are those surrounding border taxes which raise very complex issues and which are now, I think, only beginning to be properly analyzed.

All this need for getting into new, more complex fields has been the result of success in removing the traditional barriers to trade. And oddly, in a field where there has been much less success, perhaps even retrogression, that is, in agriculture, I find that a somewhat similar conclusion is indicated.

Far more clearly than before we are now made to see that a large part of the structure of trade barriers in agriculture, ours as well as those of the rest of the world, derive from domestic agricultural policies. And therefore, if we want to do something about these barriers, I think we have to be willing to talk internationally about the policies themselves, about such matters as prices, production controls, surplus disposal. There was a start on that in the Kennedy Round, but it failed to come to a successful conclusion, in my opinion, with the exception of the partial success in the grains agreement on surplus disposal.

Now, I do not suggest that it is easy for us or for any other country to undertake this kind of a negotiation, to talk internationally about things which are already difficult domestically. We may not be willing or able, or others may not be, to carry on the negotiations on that basis. In that case it looks as if we must accept the fact that we are facing an impasse of the sort that we have lived with for 20 years or more, but with the important difference that our exports, American exports, will be more seriously affected this time than in the past.

Once again, the problem I mentioned in regard to nontariff barriers arises. For in spite of the logic of treating agriculture separately, that may not work because it is not of equal importance as a trade matter to every country.

With regard to trade with less-developed countries, I think I shall leave the intricacies to others, with perhaps one comment. There is something of a paradox here. It seems to me that more novel ideas are being discussed with regard to LDC trade, in such matters as preferences and commodity agreements than in the other fields where I have said we need new approaches. And yet, in my opinion, some of this discussion of novelties conceals a very old-fashioned and simple problem. And that is the willingness of the developed countries to accept competition from the less-developed ones. If they are not willing to do that, then I think that any of the array of devices that are being talked about will turn out to be rather disappointing to all concerned. However, I do not exclude the possibility that precisely through the discussion of such matters as preferences—which in my opinion should have been treated as the second question, not the first—we might arrive at the basic issue. That is to say, preferences may prove to be the road to providing freer access.

With regard to East-West trade, it seems to me that we are presently in a situation in which we have very little flexibility and that we have gained very little from imposing that loss of flexibility on ourselves. If we are to undertake some change in our policies about East-West trade, the potential gains we should seek are less in commercial or economic matters than in the ability to add trade to the things we can negotiate about with the Communist countries. And this is a quite different matter if one is talking about trade with the Soviet Union than it is with regard to the trade of the Eastern European countries. And yet I think in its different way it is true of both cases. When we are talking about East-West trade we must recognize frankly that there are no proven satisfactory arrangements for organizing trade between state trading countries and market economies. But there are some possibilities. I think that therefore we have to maintain an experimental attitude. And that means as a practical matter, to be able to alter agreements over relatively short periods. I think we should understand that such approaches as bringing more of the Communist countries into GATT are not solutions to problems, but provide ways of discussing the problems perhaps in a better framework than what we have had before.

Now, in these remarks I have tended to break up the trade problem into several different ones, to speak of East-West trade, LDC trade, and trade among the industrialized countries separately. This is right, and at the same time it is wrong. It is right because I think the problems are somewhat different, and require somewhat different approaches. What is wrong about it, a slightly more subtle point, is that there is always a risk of losing sight of the fact that we are talking about a world trading system, not simply a series of pieces. Always in the postwar period, it has been an important part of American trade policy that we have had a picture in mind of what kind of world trading system we were working toward. There have been exceptions that did not fit the picture. East-West trade is one, but it has been a relatively minor thing. But I think we are now at a period when the exceptions are decreasing. Japan, which was always a special problem, still poses certain issues that do not arise otherwise, but is very far along the road toward being a full member of the trading system. It is true that we shall probably work out something with regard to the special problems of the less-developed countries which will make them exceptions to many rules. But I think we shall find that we can no longer deal with a blanket concept of "less-developed countries." We are going to have to look at the more developed and among the less-developed because they have quite different trading interests and require quite different trading arrangements. That will make it important to have some concept of a road along which developing countries might move as they become better able to make their way in the world trading system.

I think, finally, that the definition, or the depiction, of the world trading system we want cannot probably, be very different from what it has been. It is a system in which there is a means of reducing trade barriers, and in which the basic objective is equal treatment in international trade. This may seem banal. I think it is not so when we recall that conception of this objective has been somewhat blurred or even absent from many discussions in recent years. Many arguments are being made and forces are at work to reduce the scope for equal treatment. Often, I think, people respond to these ideas and pressures without adequate attention to what the alternatives are, or the position this country would be in the kind of trading world we would have if we abandoned equal treatment.

This may seem an old-fashioned sentiment. But I am glad to stand on it, provided you remember, from what I said at the beginning, that the content of trade policy is going to be quite different in the next 10 years from what it has been in the last 30.

Thank you.

Chairman Boggs. Thank you very much, Mr. Diebold.

The final assessment may be left to Ambassador William M. Roth, the President's Special Representative for Trade Negotiations, who stated on behalf of his negotiating staff, "I think many of us who worked in this [the Kennedy Round] have felt that one of the great advantages of a successful Kennedy Round was that we averted something quite terrible—that is, a failure. If there had been a failure, I feel—and I think all of us who worked in this felt —that it would have set back the growth of a liberal world trade policy many years. And therefore we are grateful that it was, in the final analysis, possible to put such an agreement together." [31]

Two years later, Ambassador Roth presented a comprehensive report to the President on future United States foreign trade policy. Against the background of the Kennedy Round and in anticipation of the next two policy problems, it is instructive to note some sections from that report.

5.4 TRADE PROBLEMS IN A CHANGING WORLD [32]

For the past 34 years the trading nations of the world, under U. S. leadership, have pursued a policy of trade liberalization on a reciprocal basis. That policy has, on the whole, served our country well—and it has served the world well. In the United States, it has been pressed forward under Administrations of both parties, with support from both sides of the aisle in the Congress. Its most recent achievement was the successful conclusion of the Kennedy Round in June of 1967.

31. Statement of Honorable William M. Roth, in Joint Economic Committee, *The Future of U. S. Foreign Trade Policy* (1967), p. 18.

32. *Future United States Foreign Trade Policy, Report to the President* submitted by the Special Representative for Trade Negotiations, William M. Roth, Washington, D. C., Jan. 14, 1969, pp. 76–78, 89–95.

At the same time that these long and arduous negotiations were being pursued, new forces were already affecting the currents of world trade. Indeed, in the latter part of 1967, concern was growing throughout the world over problems in domestic economies and in changing international commercial relationships—including the declining U. S. trade surplus.

Both at home and abroad, these problems raised the specter of economic nationalism and a return to the divisive trade policies of the past.

When World War II ended, the economies of Europe and Japan were paralyzed, and the international trading system had broken down. Two actions were urgently necessary. First, national economies had to be made viable. Second, new international institutions had to be created to facilitate an increasing exchange of goods. Only one country was in a position to take the initiative—the United States.

Through the Marshall Plan and other aid programs, the United States assisted in the rebirth of European and Japanese industry and agriculture. It also initiated negotiations leading to the establishment of the General Agreement on Tariffs and Trade (GATT), the International Monetary Fund (IMF), and the International Bank for Reconstruction and Development (World Bank).

Underlying these actions was the belief that a strong international trading community was not possible without strong national economies. On the other hand, without the existence of strong international institutions to assure the freer flow of trade and a viable international monetary system, strong national economies could not be attained. The requirements of nations and the requirements of an international order were inextricably linked. They are today.

American initiatives and the responses of its trading partners were successful. World trade increased from less than $60 billion in 1948 to more than $200 billion in 1967. The institutions that established the rules of international trade and payments became accepted instruments for furthering national interests.

But success itself, of necessity, creates change and thereby problems. The very fact that our foreign economic policy succeeded made it inevitable that Europe and Japan would regain their competitive strength. Today, they offer the United States a serious challenge in world markets.

In the same manner, the dynamic economic progress throughout the world, made possible in part by the GATT and the IMF, began to press upon the institutions themselves. Rigidities in some of the international rules led major trading nations to resort to ad hoc trade measures to cope with balance-of-payments problems. It is ironic that governments leaned heavily on trade measures to shore up a monetary system created primarily to further a smooth and expanding flow of trade.

The problems that both this country and others face today in trade and monetary policy are the result, in part, of expanding international economic activity and changed competitive relationships. Improvements are needed—both domestically and internationally—but they are refinements, not new directions.

In Europe, success had another dimension. The GATT was written to exempt customs unions and free trade areas from the rule of nondiscrimination. This was a logical extension of one of the central themes of U. S. policy after the war—that the economic strength and political unity of Europe were essential to world peace.

In the years following, the European Economic Community (EEC) and the European Free Trade Association (EFTA) were formed. Each has resulted in a substantial increase in trade, not only among its members but also with other countries. But, because the EEC was under the necessity of adopting a common external commercial policy, the need to compromise conflicting national interests made it difficult to give full weight to the international repercussions of some of its policies.

This has been particularly true in agriculture. Under its common agricultural policy, which is being progressively extended over wider areas of products, the EEC uses high support prices to maintain farm incomes. In order to make this policy effective, the EEC has adopted variable import levies and export subsidies, which restrict imports and compete unfairly with foreign exports in third markets. The danger of a major confrontation between agricultural exporters and the EEC is very real.

The impetus toward regional trading has not been limited to Europe. Regional African and Latin American associations have also been formed, designed to evolve into customs unions or free trade areas. They are far from reaching that goal. Their impact on world trade is not yet serious, but they too pose problems for our future trade policy.

The growth of regional trading blocs has provided one of the incentives for the development of yet another important agent of change—the multinational corporation. Challenged by growing markets abroad, particularly in Europe, American companies have become international. Europeans welcome the benefits that well-capitalized, highly efficient, and technologically equipped enterprises bring to their economies. They worry, however, about a possible American take-over in important industrial sectors. Some Americans, on the other hand, fear that U. S. manufacture abroad is displacing domestic employment by decreasing exports and increasing imports.

In principle, an expanding world economy requires the freest possible movement not only of trade but also of capital and technical and managerial resources. In practice, however, the specific effects of the multinational corporation on employment and trade are unclear. Such considerations as the balance of payments and the relative immobility of labor can raise problems that require solutions. These must be solved without unnecessarily restricting the most efficient allocation of resources.

One of the most difficult problems in trade policy is the need of the less-developed countries to expand their foreign commerce. Most of them have not shared fully in the general increase in international trade that has taken place since the end of the war. Most of them are dependent for export earnings on a narrow range of primary products, which, in many cases, are characterized by inelastic demand and unpredictable price fluctuations.

The primary responsibility for economic development and diversification rests with the less-developed countries themselves. However, the United States and other developed countries cannot ignore the need of the less-developed countries to increase their export earnings as an essential part of their development.

In spite of the accomplishments of the Kennedy Round, world trade is still restricted in many cases by tariffs and by a variety of nontariff barriers. Their further reduction or removal, particularly in Europe and Japan, is central to U. S. export prospects.

In some cases the elimination of existing barriers can be achieved by strict enforcement of GATT rules. But, like tariffs, many nontariff barriers —our own as well as those of others—are permitted under those rules and can only be reduced or removed by negotiation. In the shorter term, the United States should negotiate limited agreements concerning particular categories of nontariff barriers or involving both tariff and nontariff barriers in certain industrial sectors that lend themselves to this approach. The reduction or removal of other barriers, however, will have to await another general round of trade negotiations. Planning for this should begin promptly.

The recommendations that follow in this section point to the need for protecting U. S. interest under the GATT and for completing the implementation of the Kennedy Round.

Most tariff and nontariff barriers consist of practices that do not violate existing GATT obligations. In fact, the only important category of a clearly illegal barrier still maintained by developed countries is that of import quotas that were originally adopted because of balance-of-payments difficulties but are no longer justified on those grounds. While most of these quotas have been eliminated on industrial products, there remain important ones, especially in the field of agricultural products and processed foods.

The GATT provides a mechanism for dealing with illegal and other restrictions that nullify or impair the value of a country's benefits under the GATT. In such a case, the country imposing the restriction can be required (under Article XXII) to consult with the injured party or with the Contracting Parties. Alternatively, it can be required (under Article XXIII) to negotiate a satisfactory settlement. If a settlement is not forthcoming, the Contracting Parties may authorize the injured party to withdraw equivalent benefits from the offending party.

It has often been possible to persuade countries voluntarily to bring their practices into conformity with their obligations. But, where this has failed, the United States has invoked these GATT provisions—for example, against countries that maintained quantitative restrictions that could not be justified on balance-of-payments grounds. The use of these GATT provisions to enforce contractual rights should be continued and intensified until our major trading partners are convinced that compliance with the GATT is their most profitable policy.

Where U. S. interests under the GATT are injured significantly by other countries' actions and where a settlement under Article XXII of the GATT does not prove possible, the United States should invoke the remedial provisions of Article XXIII of the GATT.

At the present time, the President's authority to retaliate against illegal foreign restrictions—once approval of the Contracting Parties is obtained under Article XXIII—is not balanced. The sanctions that can be used against imports from countries maintaining illegal restrictions on our agricultural exports are more extensive than those available to defend our industrial exports. Under several provisions of the Trade Expansion Act of 1962, the high rates of duty of the Smoot-Hawley Tariff Act of 1930 could be imposed in retaliation against illegal import restrictions impeding either class of U. S. exports. However, under section 252(a) (3) of the Trade Expansion Act of 1962, the President may impose higher rates of duty— or even quotas—but only in cases where our agricultural exports are being injured through illegal action. In order to put the United States in a position to protect all its export interests as effectively as possible, this arbitrary distinction in the law should be eliminated.

Section 252(a) (3) of the Trade Expansion Act of 1962 should be amended to permit the full range of retaliatory powers to be available, in accordance with the GATT, against illegal foreign import restrictions imposed on either industrial or agricultural exports of the United States.

As the result of reciprocal tariff negotiations conducted over more than three decades, almost all the dutiable items in the U. S. tariff have been bound in the GATT against increases in rates of duty. But occasions can arise when it is necessary to increase a rate of duty: in order to prevent injury to a domestic industry pursuant to an escape-clause action under the Trade Expansion Act of 1962; incidental to the elimination of tariff anomalies; or as the result of a reclassification of a product by the courts. When any GATT country increases a bound rate, it must be prepared to grant compensation to countries that have a contractual right to that rate. If it is not able to offer reasonable compensation, it must face a retaliatory withdrawal of benefits enjoyed by its exports.

Since June 30, 1967, when the tariff negotiating authority in the Trade Expansion Act of 1962 expired, the President has had no authority to reduce tariffs for any purpose. It is essential that the President be given this flexibility. Some of the authority in the Trade Expansion Act remained unused upon its expiration on July 1, 1967. But, even if that authority were now restored, much of it would be unavailable because its use might threaten injury to certain domestic industries, or because the principal beneficiary of a reduction would be a non-GATT country.

In order to provide the needed flexibility over the next several years, the President should be given the authority to reduce any tariff by as much as 20 percent of its post-Kennedy Round rate, subject to the safeguards in the Trade Expansion Act of 1962. Any such reduction should become effective no earlier than one year after the final reduction agreed to in the Kennedy Round becomes effective. The proposed authority should not be sought, however, for the purpose of conducting a new general round of trade negotiations but rather to meet needs, as they arise, for negotiating compensatory tariff reductions on individual products.

The President should be given the authority to reduce any tariff by up to 20 percent of the post-Kennedy Round rate. The legislative record should make it clear that the authority is requested for use in compensatory negotiations and not in a general round of trade negotiations.

During the Kennedy Round the United States negotiated a Supplementary Agreement on Chemicals, subject to enactment of implementing legislation. This agreement traded substantial tariff benefits to the American chemical industry for the elimination by the United States of the American selling price system of customs valuation—a system that gives extraordinary protection to a small segment of domestic chemical production, as well as the production of a few other goods, including rubber-soled footwear. The Congress has not yet taken action to permit implementation of the agreement.

The President should be given the authority to abolish the American selling price system of customs valuation in order to permit, in particular, the implementation of the Supplementary Agreement on Chemicals, negotiated during the Kennedy Round.

Neither the United States nor any other country is likely to be in a position to enter into a general round of tariff and nontariff barrier negotiations until the tariff reductions negotiated in the Kennedy Round have been completely implemented. The final stage of those reductions will become effective on January 1, 1972. In the meantime, there are certain areas—relating to specific nontariff barriers or industrial sectors—in which there is a possibility of reaching agreements benefiting U. S. exports if the President were in a position to negotiate effectively.

However, the prospect of such negotiations in the near future poses a fundamental dilemma. Ever since the first Trade Agreements Act in 1934, tariff reductions have been negotiated and implemented under prior authority delegated to the President. This time-tested method has proven its worth and should form the basis for any future general round of negotiations dealing with tariffs.

But prior delegations of authority are probably not feasible for negotiations concerning particular nontariff barriers or industrial sectors recommended below for the nearer term. Because of the variety and complexity of nontariff barriers, there is no common standard applicable to such barriers that would lend itself to a general and meaningful grant of authority. Furthermore, in the case of an industrial sector, the scope of the tariff and nontariff negotiations involved could probably not be forecast with precision. In these cases, therefore, any necessary Congressional action would, in all likelihood, have to take place after the agreement has been negotiated.

The question of the necessary legal authority breaks down into two subsidiary questions—the authority to negotiate an international agreement and the authority to implement it. So far as the act of negotiation is concerned, Presidents have from the beginning taken the view that they have an inherent constitutional power to negotiate agreements with other countries and do not need any prior Congressional authority or license to do so.

However, as a practical matter, it may no longer suffice to rely on inherent authority alone. The negotiation of three agreements in recent years without advance authorization has led some members of the Senate to oppose this sort of negotiation in principle.

Because of this problem, it would seem advisable for the Executive Branch to seek an expression of the sense of the Congress favoring the negotiation of trade agreements that might require the subsequent enactment of implementing legislation. If such an expression could be obtained, it would facilitate the negotiation of agreements dealing with particular nontariff barriers and individual industrial sectors. But it would not, of course, avoid the need, where relevant, to obtain implementing legislation after an agreement had been concluded.

In order to facilitate the negotiation of agreements for which a prior delegation of authority is not feasible, the Congress should be asked to pass a resolution expressing its general intent that the President negotiate agreements concerning both nontariff barriers and industrial sectors. Any agreement requiring implementing legislation would not enter into force until such legislation were enacted.

In order to make sure that any such agreement is in the U. S. interest, and in order to determine the probable economic effect on U. S. firms and workers of any increased imports that might result, the Executive Branch should conduct public hearings and obtain the advice of the Tariff Commission before entering into negotiations.

Before the negotiation of any trade agreement dealing with particular nontariff barriers or individual industrial sectors, the Executive Branch should conduct public hearings and obtain the advice of the Tariff Commission on the probable domestic economic effect of such agreement.

Nontariff barriers include such disparate devices as quantitative restrictions, arbitrary customs practices, restrictive government procurement policies, and unreasonable application of health and safety standards. They even include such nongovernmental practices as industrial standards and specifications that can make the use of imported products more difficult.

Of the many measures other than tariffs that have the effect of restricting trade and protecting domestic producers, some have been instituted for reasons unrelated to their effect on trade, such as the protection of public health and safety. This adds greatly to the difficulty both of determining their effects on trade and of negotiating their modification or removal.

The nature of nontariff barriers and the wide differences in the practices of different countries are such that an overall nontariff barrier negotiation, conducted independently of a general round of trade negotiations, is probably impracticable. Nevertheless, there is a possibility—and this possibility should be thoroughly explored—of negotiating international agreements, including codes of uniform practices, concerning certain categories of nontariff barriers.

In exploring this possibility, consultations should be held with representatives of industry, labor, and other affected domestic interests. After such consultations and after discussions with other countries, it should be possible to determine those cases in which an international agreement on particular nontariff barriers would be both feasible and in the national interest. The object of such an agreement would be to ensure that U. S. exports receive in foreign markets treatment no less favorable than that accorded to imports into the United States.

When further exploration shows that agreements limiting or eliminating nontariff barriers, including codes of uniform practices regarding particular nontariff barriers, are feasible and in the national interest, the United States should initiate negotiation of such agreements in the GATT.

Another possibility of improving U. S. export prospects before countries are ready for another general round of trade negotiations lies in negotiations within individual industrial sectors. This technique would make it possible to deal both with tariffs and with other matters affecting trade within a sector. This was attempted on a limited basis during the Kennedy Round. For example, an effort was made to reach a special agreement in one sector that would have recognized the multinational nature of the industry concerned. Primarily because of the opposition of a single foreign producer, an agreement was not achieved. The possibilities of similar negotiations in other industrial sectors have not been exhausted, however, especially those in which the industry is organized on multinational lines and where competitive strength is comparable.

A sector negotiation should deal with all impediments to market access, including tariff and nontariff barriers, investment restrictions, and restrictive business practices. After consultations with representatives of industry, labor, and other domestic interests concerned, and after discussions with other countries, it should be possible to identify individual industrial sectors in which negotiations would be both feasible and in the national interest. The object of a sector negotiation should be to establish equality of opportunity for the industry concerned in all major markets.

When further exploration shows that agreements in individual industrial sectors are feasible and in the national interest, the United States should initiate negotiation of such agreements in the GATT.

However successful negotiations in individual sectors or on specific nontariff barriers may prove, substantial impediments to trade will remain. After the Kennedy Round is fully implemented, many tariffs will still be high. Moreover, a preliminary inventory of nontariff barriers recently compiled by the GATT reveals many barriers that are of such limited application or so specialized that they cannot be adequately dealt with in the kinds of negotiations recommended above.

Another general round of trade negotiations is unlikely until the Kennedy Round tariff concessions are fully put into effect. However, the complexity of a future general trade negotiation requires that serious preparatory study begin now.

The form that such negotiations should take will depend upon a variety of circumstances. The discussions now under way in the GATT in relation to specific nontariff barriers and certain agricultural problems will lay the groundwork for, and influence, the final form of a general round of trade negotiations. Domestic considerations within the United States and in the other participating countries will be another important determinant. Before that form is decided and before the nature of the required tariff-reducing authority can be determined, there should be intensive discussion both within the United States and with the other countries concerned, bilaterally and in the GATT.

In preparing for another major round of trade negotiations, much additional work is needed in the collection, automation, and analysis of relevant data. In particular, appropriate weight should be given to the level and characteristics of the post-Kennedy Round tariffs of the prospective participants. Moreover, possible methods of reducing tariffs should be considered in the light of what can be learned of effective, as opposed to nominal, tariffs of the United States and the other participants.

The GATT study now underway concerning nontariff barriers and their protective effects is an essential part of the preparation. This should be complemented by considerably more information than the U. S. Government now has on the impact of foreign nontariff barriers on U. S. exports, both agricultural and industrial.

The experience of previous negotiations should also be taken into account. The item-by-item approach, used in all negotiations before the Kennedy Round, presents serious difficulties, especially in dealing with the EEC. The linear approach used in the Kennedy Round was more successful, but variations would be required, both in order to take account of some of the problems that developed in those negotiations and to ensure that greater emphasis is given to the inclusion of nontariff barriers.

Following further study within the U. S. Government, the United States should initiate an exploration in the GATT to determine the approach in a general trade negotiation that is most likely to accomplish U. S. trade objectives in both industry and agriculture.

C. Questions

1. It has been seen that GATT is based on the principles of nondiscrimination and reciprocity in tariff bargaining; the notion that when protection is allowed in exceptional circumstances, it should be practiced by tariffs and not by nontariff barriers; the provision for compensatory action if the benefits from tariff reduction are subsequently modified; and regular arrangements for consultation among member countries as parties to the agreement.

   a. Do you think the unconditional most-favored-nation principle goes in the direction of increasing or diminishing a country's willingness to reduce its tariffs? Is most-favored-nation treatment the closest international parallel to "equal protection of the laws"? Should most-favored-nation treatment be the universal principle for international trade negotiations?

   b. Do you think that the principle of reciprocity agrees with the free-trader's notion that the "gains from trade" are to be calculated on the side of less costly imports? Or is it actually reflective of a protectionist attitude that other countries should "pay for" the tariff-reducing country's "sacrifice" in having to import more?

   c. It has been argued that the reciprocity principle in multilateral bargaining ensures that the bargaining will be dominated by the more-developed countries, to the neglect of the interests of the less-developed countries. [See H. G. Johnson, *Economic Policies Toward Less Developed Countries* (1967), pp. 14–16.] To what extent did the Kennedy Round recognize this criticism and modify the reciprocity principle for the LDCs ?

   d. If GATT provides for most-favored-nation treatment and nondiscrimination in tariff reductions, how then do you account for the existence of the European Common Market which maintains an external tariff against nonmembers while reducing tariffs among members? (See Articles I and XXIV of GATT.)

   e. Consider the degree of strictness with which GATT treats quantitative restrictions, tariffs, and subsidies to domestic producers. Are all three devices contrary to free trade? Why are the devices treated differently?

   f. What are the enforcement powers of GATT? Can there be freer trade without the provision of more international sanctions?

g. If GATT were now to be rewritten, do you think that many of its Articles would be different from the original 1947 text?

2. a. Do you think the Trade Expansion Act of 1962 was "oversold" as a "new American initiative [that] is needed to meet the challenge and opportunities of a rapidly changing world economy" and as a "new and modern instrument of trade negotiations . . . [that] could well affect the unity of the West, the course of the Cold War and the growth of our nation for a generation or more to come"? (See President Kennedy's statement, pp. 27–28 above.)

b. After the conclusion of the Kennedy Round, how protectionist was United States trade policy? Consider the degree of effective protection (not simply nominal tariff rates), nontariff barriers, and instruments of covert protection.

c. If you were now to propose new trade legislation for the United States, in what ways would you have it differ from the Trade Expansion Act of 1962?

3. It has been said that "The Kennedy Round's neglect of non-tariff trade distortions was as disappointing as its tariff reducing accomplishments were encouraging. . . . It became obvious soon after the start of the Kennedy Round . . . that the prime objective —to achieve a substantial cut in tariffs among the industrial countries would be so difficult to attain that such matters as nontariff barriers and special concessions to the developing countries were unlikely to be seriously negotiated." [See R. E. Baldwin, *Non-Tariff Distortions of International Trade* (1970), p. 2.]

a. Would a round of negotiations on nontariff barriers now be feasible? Or would negotiating on nontariff barriers pose even more difficulties than those of the Kennedy Round?

b. What did the Kennedy Round accomplish for the trade of the less-developed countries? For East-West trade? What might now be done?

4. a. The strategy of trade negotiations might be likened unto those in a "game." Do you think game theory illuminates any of the key decisions in the Kennedy Round? Or might the negotiations be better explained in the old-fashioned terms of "national power" and "personality" of the negotiators and political leaders?

b. Another view would be to liken trade negotiations to a process of dispute settlement. The critical questions then are who shall decide the issues? by what standards? and under what procedures? Consider how these questions were answered in the Kennedy Round negotiations.

c. Were the crucial questions of the Kennedy Round negotiations empirical in the sense that they could be answered by numerical data, or were they political insofar as they involved decisions about competing values?

d. Does the prolonged and complex process of negotiations in the Kennedy Round suggest that a more expeditious method of trade negotiations be instituted? What would you propose? The former Director-General of GATT has suggested that future tariff negotiations could usefully take the form of attempts to reach global free trade in particular industries. But would the elimination of all tariffs in a particular industry generally by itself satisfy the principle of reciprocity? Do you think that members of the world trading community are ready to de-emphasize the principle of reciprocity? If not, do you think it is possible to work out other procedures of tariff negotiations that will allow the principle of reciprocity to be used in the direction of trade liberalization?

5. In closing the Kennedy Round, the former Director-General of GATT characterized the meeting as "eloquent proof" that the "momemtum of world-wide trade liberalization" has never been so marked. [See p. 70 above.]

a. What has happened to this momentum since the end of the Kennedy Round?

b. If you now wanted to regain the momentum of trade liberalization and prevent a further relapse into protectionism, what policy measures would you advocate? Consider this in connection with the next problem on United States import quotas.

Problem II
Neomercantilism:
Textile Import Quotas

A. The Context

1. RISE IN PROTECTIONIST SENTIMENT

Scarcely had the Kennedy Round been concluded when a countercurrent of protectionism gained force. The Trade Expansion Act of 1962 expired in 1967, and threats of trade wars then intensified, with most of the charges and countercharges centering on the use of nontariff trade barriers.[1] Of all the nontariff trade distortions, the most restrictive are import quotas. If objectives of mercantilism are the protection of domestic interests through beggar-my-neighbor policies and the promotion of domestic growth through trade restrictions,[2] then the resort to import quotas certainly symbolizes a resurgence of mercantilist controls.

In 1971, a former White House assistant for international economic affairs was able to observe:

> In 1962, the Trade Expansion Act passed the Congress with the largest majority in the history of the trade agreements pro-

---

1. See H. B. Malmgren, *Trade Wars or Trade Negotiations?* (1970); R. E. Baldwin, *Nontariff Distortions of International Trade* (1970); G. Curzon and V. Curzon, *Hidden Barriers to International Trade* (1970).
2. See n. 4, p. 4, above. Also, Joan Robinson, *The New Mercantilism* (1966).

gram and led to the Kennedy Round of trade negotiations. Since 1962, however, the number of U. S. industrial imports subject to quantitative restrictions, including "voluntary restraint" by foreign suppliers, has risen from seven to sixty-seven —a number which will shortly exceed the total of any other industrialized country, and whose restrictive impact is undoubtedly greater than the liberalizing effect of our tariff cuts in the Kennedy Round. And Chairman Wilbur Mills of the Ways and Means Committee—who helped pilot the 1962 law to its overwhelming passage—commented . . . that the Trade Expansion Act would have been unlikely to attract fifty votes on the House floor in 1970.

The shift has come along an accelerating trend line. In 1964, Congress passed the Meat Import Act—the first legislated import restrictions for a major industry in the postwar period. There were attempts in 1964 and 1965 to negotiate voluntary restraint agreements covering U. S. imports of woolen textiles. The modest trade bill submitted by the Johnson Administration in 1968, whose only significant liberalizing feature was its request for repeal of the American Selling Price system of customs valuation (ASP), was never even reported out of the Ways and Means Committee; and the Administration decided that it had to negotiate voluntary restraint agreements on steel and meat to avoid turning the bill into widespread protectionist legislation. And the Nixon Administration sought to negotiate voluntary restraints on synthetic and woolen textiles throughout 1969 and 1970.[3]

This problem focuses on the policy issues involved in these negotiations, the shift to protectionism in the highly controversial Trade Bill of 1970, and the bilateral textile quota agreements that were ultimately reached in October 1971, between the United States and Japan, Korea, Taiwan, and Hong Kong. There is a fundamental question raised by this problem. What policy measures, if any, should be taken to protect a large domestic industry that faces keen competition from a sharp and substantial increase of imports? Should potential imports be foreclosed through quotas? Or should the economic, social, and political costs of dislocation of local production be endured?

3. C. Fred Bergsten, "Crisis in U. S. Trade Policy," *Foreign Affairs*, July 1971, p. 619.

2. THE DISLOCATION PROBLEM

This type of dilemma for the adherent of freer trade may be termed the dislocation or specific industry problem. In recent Congressional testimony, one authority on American-Japanese relations said:

> "I fear that the most serious difficulties in future U. S.-Japanese economic relations lie in what I term the specific industry problem: the impact of surging competition from other countries for certain large, important, but relatively inefficient industries. Moreover, specific industry problems will plague us regardless of whether the U. S., or Japanese, balance of payments is in global, or even bilateral, surplus or deficit. The general context of the problem is that with economic growth, increasing capital per worker, R and D activities, and evolving comparative advantage, certain large industries in the United States become inefficient relative to other American industries and relative to foreign competition. This same situation is true for Japan as well. Imports of commodities produced by the affected industry are too large and too rapid (due to the enhanced supply capacity of foreign producers) for the normal adjustment process of domestic labor and capital reallocation in that industry to take place rapidly enough without sectoral unemployment and sharply decreased profitability. Adjustment is painful and has high social costs; not surprisingly these also become political costs. Important examples are the textile industry in the United States and the agriculture industry in Japan. Indeed, the analogies in the basic conditions of these respective examples are striking. One main difference however is that since World War II Japanese agriculture has been heavily protected, and now is being slowly liberalized, while American textiles initially operated in a free trade environment, and have gradually become increasingly protected.
>
> The typical response in economically advanced countries is to impose trade restrictions when a large but increasingly inefficient domestic industry is pressured by the foreign competition of evolving comparative advantage. In effect, in an effort to avoid the short-run pain of domestic adjustment, the country is tempted to transform the outside world to fit its own conditions, or to insulate itself from the world. In an increasingly interdependent world economy this is not just inefficient eco-

nomically but highly undesirable in its political and security implications." [4]

The pernicious effects of nontariff trade barriers had been recognized from the start in GATT—especially by the American draftsmen. One of the chief United States negotiators argued the case against quantitative restrictions in no uncertain terms.

> "Quantitative restrictions . . . impose rigid limits on the volume of trade. They insulate domestic prices and production against the changing requirements of the world economy. They freeze trade into established channels. They are likely to be discriminatory in purpose and effect. They give the guidance of trade to public officials; they cannot be divorced from politics. They require public allocation of imports and exports among private traders and necessitate increasing regulation of domestic business. Quantitative restrictions are among the most effective methods that have been devised for the purpose of restricting trade. They make for bilateralism, discrimination, and the regimentation of private enterprise." [5]

A basic tenet of the General Agreement is that if a country is to practice protectionism, it should be through tariffs—not quantitative restrictions (Article XI:1). Only narrow exceptions are allowed for quantitative restrictions, namely, to stop a serious decline in monetary reserves (Articles XII:2, XVIII:9), to meet the balance-of-payments problem of a less-developed country (Article XVIII:9), to support domestic agricultural programs (Article XI:2).

For the specific industry problem, however, tariffs are less effective than quotas. When the differential between domestic and import prices is large and import prices are flexible downwards, then tariff rates would have to be sizable and frequently adjustable. Even so, imports might be sufficiently competitive to seize rapidly a large share of the domestic market. The relative virtue of a tariff for GATT—namely, that the price system may still operate and an exporter can lower his price to get under the tariff—is precisely the disadvantage to the protected industry of a tariff relative to a spe-

---

4. Hugh Patrick, *Testimony on United States Foreign Economic Policy Toward Japan for the Subcommittee on Foreign Economic Policy of the House Committee on Foreign Affairs*, Nov. 4, 1971, pp. 11–12 (mimeographed).
5. Clair Wilcox, *A Charter for World Trade* (1949), pp. 81–82.

cific limitation by quota. What now makes the quota such a dominant problem in international commercial policy is that while it has been imposed because it is more effective than a tariff, it is more difficult to reduce a quota than a tariff. The negotiation procedures of GATT—based on mutually advantageous bargains through compensatory changes in tariffs—are geared to tariff reductions but not to reductions of nontariff barriers. It is more difficult to equate reductions in nontariff barriers in a bargaining situation based on reciprocity.

The dislocation problem became of urgent concern to many countries in the 1950's with the extraordinary growth in Japan's exports, and in the late 1950's with the attention to the significant export quantities of manufactures, particularly cotton textiles, from the less-developed countries. In 1959, the United States asked GATT to study the problem of "market disruption." The contracting parties finally defined "market disruption" as a situation containing these elements in combination:

   (i) a sharp and substantial increase or potential increase of imports of particular products from particular sources;

  (ii) these products are offered at prices which are substantially below those prevailing for similar goods of comparable quality in the market of the importing country;

  (iii) there is serious damage to domestic producers or threat thereof;

  (iv) the price differentials referred to in paragraph (ii) above do not arise from governmental intervention in the fixing or formation of prices or from dumping practices.

    In some situations other elements are also present and the enumeration above is not, therefore, intended as an exhaustive definition of market disruption." [6]

3. COTTON TEXTILE AGREEMENT

Not much more was done by GATT regarding "market disruption" until 1961 when newly elected President Kennedy promised the cotton textile industry some form of relief from the sharp increase of imports from Asian countries. The problem confronting the President was whether to grant the textile industry's demand for quotas. In the end, the GATT accepted a United States request that a meeting of countries interested in cotton textile products be

6. The Contracting Parties Decision of November 19, 1960; *Basic Instruments and Select Documents*, 9th Supp., p. 26.

called, "with a view to reaching agreements on arrangements for the orderly development of the trade in such products, so as to progressively increase the export possibilities of less-developed countries and territories and of Japan, while at the same time avoiding disruptive conditions in import markets." [7]

The resulting scheme—the Long-Term Arrangement Regarding International Trade in Cotton Textiles—was adopted in 1962. The thirty-three signatories to the Arrangement included almost all the main cotton textile importing and exporting countries. The Arrangement has been subsequently extended, the latest three-year pact running through September 30, 1973.

LONG-TERM ARRANGEMENT IN COTTON TEXTILES [8]

Recognizing the need to take co-operative and constructive action with a view to the development of world trade,

Recognizing further that such action should be designed to facilitate economic expansion and promote the development of less-developed countries possessing the necessary resources, such as raw materials and technical skills, by providing larger opportunities for increasing their exchange earnings from the sale in world markets of products which they can efficiently manufacture,

Noting, however, that in some countries situations have arisen which in the view of these countries, cause or threaten to cause "disruption" of the market for cotton textiles,

Desiring to deal with these problems in such a way as to provide growing opportunities for exports of these products, provided that the development of this trade proceeds in a reasonable and orderly manner so as to avoid disruptive effects in individual markets and on individual lines of production in both importing and exporting countries,

Determined, in carrying out these objectives, to have regard to the Declaration on Promotion of the Trade of Less-Developed Countries adopted by Ministers at their meeting during the nineteenth session of the CONTRACTING PARTIES in November 1961,

The PARTICIPATING COUNTRIES have agreed as follows:

Article 1

In order to assist in the solution of the problems referred to in the preamble to this Arrangement, the participating countries are of the opin-

7. GATT Press Release 591, June 30, 1961.

8. *Long-Term Arrangement Regarding International Trade in Cotton Textiles,* GATT, Geneva, 1963. The full text is set out in *Basic Instruments,* 11th Supp. (1963), p. 25.

ion that it may be desirable to apply, during the next few years, special practical measures of international co-operation which will assist in any adjustment that may be required by changes in the pattern of world trade in cotton textiles. They recognize, however, that the measures referred to above do not affect their rights and obligations under the General Agreement on Tariffs and Trade (hereinafter referred to as the GATT). They also recognize that, since these measures are intended to deal with the special problems of cotton textiles, they are not to be considered as lending themselves to application in other fields.

Article 2

The participating countries at present applying import restrictions to cotton textiles imported from other participating countries undertake to expand access to their markets for such cotton textiles so as to reach, by the end of the period of validity of the present Arrangement, for the products remaining subject to restrictions at that date, taken as a whole, a level corresponding to the quotas opened in 1962 for such products, as increased by the percentage mentioned in Annex A.

Where bilateral arrangements exist, annual increases shall be determined within the framework of bilateral negotiations. It would, however, be desirable that each annual increase should correspond as closely as possible to one fifth of the overall increase.

Article 3

If imports from a participating country or countries into another participating country of certain cotton textile products not subject to import restrictions should cause or threaten to cause disruption in the market of the importing country, that country may request the participating country or countries whose exports of such products are, in the judgment of the importing country, causing or threatening to cause market disruption to consult with a view to removing or avoiding such disruption. In its request the importing country will, at its discretion, indicate the specific level at which it considers that exports of such products should be restrained, a level which shall not be lower than the one indicated in Annex B. The request shall be accompanied by a detailed, factual statement of the reasons and justification for the request; the requesting country shall communicate the same information to the Cotton Textiles Committee at the same time.

Article 9

For purposes of this Arrangement the expression "cotton textiles" includes yarns, piece-goods, made-up articles, garments, and other textile manufactured products, in which cotton represents more than 50 per cent (by weight) of the fibre content, with the exception of hand-loom fabrics of the cottage industry.

Article 10

For the purposes of this Arrangement, the term "disruption" refers to situations of the kind described in the Decision of the CONTRACTING PARTIES of 19 November 1960.

Article 11

This Arrangement is open for acceptance, by signature or otherwise, to governments parties to the GATT or having provisionally acceded to that Agreement, provided that if any such government maintains restrictions on the import of cotton textiles from other participating countries, that government shall, prior to its accepting this Arrangement, agree with the Cotton Textiles Committee on the percentage by which it will undertake to increase the quotas other than those maintained under Article XII or Article XVIII of the GATT.

Article 14

This Arrangement shall remain in force for five years.

Article 15

The Annexes to this Arrangement constitute an integral part of this Arrangement.

Annex A

For purposes of Article 2 the percentages referred to in paragraph 3 thereof shall be:

For Austria	95	per cent
For Denmark	15	" "
For European Economic Community	88	" , "
For Norway	15	" "
For Sweden	15	" "

Annex B

1. (a) The level below which imports or exports of cotton textile products causing or threatening to cause market disruption may not be restrained under the provisions of Article 3 shall be the level of actual imports or exports of such products during the twelve-month period terminating three months preceding the month in which the request for consultation is made.

(b) Where a bilateral agreement on the yearly level of restraint exists between participating countries concerned covering the twelve-month period referred to in paragraph (a), the level below which imports of cotton textile products causing or threatening to cause market disruption may not be restrained under the provisions of Article 3 shall be the level provided for in the bilateral agreement in lieu of the level of actual imports or exports during the twelve-month period referred to in paragraph (a).

Where the twelve-month period referred to in paragraph (a) overlaps in part with the period covered by the bilateral agreement, the level shall be:

(i) the level provided for in the bilateral agreement, or the level of actual imports or exports, whichever is higher, for the months where the period covered by the bilateral agreement and the twelve-month period referred to in paragraph (a) overlap; and

(ii) the level of actual imports or exports for the months where no overlap occurs.

2. Should the restraint measures remain in force for another twelve-month period, the level for that period shall not be lower than the level specified for the preceding twelve-month period, increased by 5 per cent. In exceptional cases, where it is extremely difficult to apply the level referred to above, a percentage between 5 and 0 may be applied in the light of market conditions in the importing country and other relevant factors after consultation with the exporting country concerned.

3. Should the restraining measures remain in force for further periods, the level for each subsequent twelve-month period shall not be lower than the level specified for the preceding twelve-month period, increased by 5 per cent.

A comment on the Long-Term Arrangement is of interest.

> In considering [its] provisions . . . one should bear in mind that the Arrangement was proposed and sold by its proponents as a device for increasing international trade in cotton textiles. The premise was that if trade increased gradually and in an "orderly manner" (the adjective "orderly" came to be as important as the noun "disruption" in the vocabulary of the importing countries), the economic and social costs of the displacement of local production by imports from the less-developed countries and Japan could be reduced to the point where the special measures, often illegal under the General Agreement, then being taken by many importing countries could be eliminated. The argument was that slow but steady growth in less-developed country exports to developed country markets would contribute far more to economic development than would sudden increases, often concentrated in a few products, which merely led to governmental measures closing the developed country markets to further increases.[9]

9. Kenneth W. Dam, *The GATT* (1970), pp. 300–301.

The Long-Term Arrangement, however, has been criticized continually by the less-developed exporting countries. A major complaint has been that the criteria of "market disruption"—namely, sharp and substantial increase of quantity, low price, and damage —have been so broadly and vaguely construed that any increase in imports allows the importing country to claim market disruption. This problem of delineating market disruption is crucial if one looks ahead to the possibility of other exports from less-developed countries becoming candidates for such arrangements (not only other textiles, but possibly also transistors, typewriters, toys, cutlery, leather goods, and various electrical appliances).

The developing countries have also emphasized the temporary and transitional nature of the Arrangement, which in their view was to remain confined to the special problem of cotton textiles and not be extended to other sectors of the textile industry. Although some importing countries later concluded bilateral agreements for some increase in the quotas, the increases were considered by the developing countries to be still too small and the agreements burdened with many conditions about categorization of product and complex licensing procedures. As a result, the developing countries have maintained that their exports of cotton textiles have been severely restricted and have remained small compared with the size of the industry and the capacity of certain developing countries to export these products.[10]

As an ad hoc agreement outside the GATT, the Long-Term Arrangement in cotton textiles has been significant in establishing the precedent for quantitative controls on "disruptive" trade. During the Kennedy Round, the importing nations insisted on an extension of the Long-Term Arrangement as a condition to any tariff reductions.[11] Woolen goods were also placed on the United States "exceptions list." Even though cotton textile manufactures still accounted for the largest percentage of total manufactured exports from the less-developed countries (almost 40 per cent in 1965), the exports of cotton textiles had been losing ground relative to other

10. Cf. UNCTAD Secretariat, "Study of the Origins and Operations of International Arrangements Relating to Cotton Textiles," TD/20/Supp. 3.

11. Preeg, *op. cit.*, pp. 106–7, 230–31. The textiles sector did receive average cuts of 18 to 21 per cent.

textiles—especially man-made fibers. From 1960 to 1966, exports of cotton textiles grew only slightly while exports of other textiles grew more than 60 per cent. According to a report of the Tariff Commission, the rise in imports during this period was high "whether measured by quantity, by value or in relation to consumption." Yarn imports increased from 25 million to 121 million pounds, fabric imports rose from 356 million to 1 billion yards, and apparel imports (fiber equivalent) increased from 79 million to 186 million pounds. The report also stated that because of "rapid and profound change" in the industry, with accelerating use of man-made fibers and blends, "many small concerns, lacking adequate resources, found it increasingly difficult to adjust to new conditions of production and marketing." [12]

4. CAMPAIGN PLEDGE OF 1968

During the presidential campaign of 1968, Nixon stated that he believed in freer trade as a matter of principle, but he described textiles as representing "a special case." Recognizing the sensitive role of the textile industry in the South, the presidential candidate offered a pledge to do something about textile imports. The following is a newspaper account of a campaign speech made in Charlotte, North Carolina.

> Nixon, speaking to 7,000 persons in a parking lot at Charlotte's Piedmont Community College, charged that the trade policies of the Johnson administration "have led to a crisis in our economy."
> One particular mistake, Nixon said, was failure to confront the realities of increasing textile imports into the United States.
> "This was part of a whole pattern of failure," Nixon said. He promised "to take the steps necessary to extend the concept of international trade agreements" and knock down barriers to the products of U. S. industry.[13]

As later noted by *The Economist*,

> To Mr. Nixon in the swirl of the Presidential campaign in 1968, textiles were naturally a peripheral matter but one just important enough to elicit a pledge to do something to limit imports. The President wanted southern votes and the textile

12. *New York Times,* Jan. 15, 1969.
13. *Atlanta Constitution,* Sept. 12, 1968.

industry is now concentrated in the South. He gave the pledge mainly for that reason but it was not entirely thoughtless. He was advised, and believed, that Japan, above all, would be reasonable and would go along with a "voluntary" limitation of exports of man-made fibre and wool textiles and clothing, as had been done with cotton textiles in 1962. But, alas, 1969 and 1970 were very different from 1962.[14]

By the time President Nixon took office, the textile problem had actually become a complex of problems. The national unemployment rate was higher than desired, and the usual specific industry arguments for protection were extended in the textile case to emphasize that textiles employed one out of eight workers in manufacturing. National concern was developing also for the plight of disadvantaged minority workers, and it was pointed out that many of the textile workers were minorities who could not readily relocate. The labor movement, in general, had modified its traditional position for more liberalized trade. The AFL–CIO convention in 1969 agreed that the Trade Expansion Act should be modified to bar United States concessions to any country which raises "unfair or unreasonable barriers" to imports from the United States. "Old concepts and labels of 'free trade' and 'protectionism' have become outdated in this world of managed national economies, international technology, the skyrocketing rise of United States foreign investment, and the growth of multinational companies," concluded an AFL–CIO resolution. The call was for measures to prevent "foreign operations . . . that pay workers as little as 15 cents an hour" from making deep inroads into United States markets. And the president of the United Textile Workers warned that "unregulated imports" endanger not only the jobs of "many thousands of workers" in textile and apparel industries but also threaten to shut off "a growing opportunity for employment for blacks, Spanish-Americans, and members of other minority groups." [15]

The textile problem also became part of the United States balance-of-payments problem. Since 1963, American imports had been rising more than American exports, and the large traditional export surplus on current trade account all but vanished in 1968 and 1969.

14. *The Economist*, "Tragedy of Quotas," July 4, 1970.
15. *Christian Science Monitor*, Oct. 17, 1969.

And at the same time, Japan underwent a dramatic change in its balance of payments: from a chronic balance-of-payments deficit to, starting in 1968, a large surplus on current account and rapid accumulation of foreign exchange reserves. The net trade surplus of Japan with the United States grew from less than $300 million in 1967 to more than $1100 million in 1968 and to almost $1400 million in 1969.[16]

Intensifying the criticism of Japan was a belief that Japan maintained a highly restrictive policy against imports from the United States, together with special governmental provisions favoring exports. As expressed by the Assistant Secretary of Commerce for domestic and international business,

> "Our continuing—and growing—trade deficits with Japan are of particular concern to the United States Government and United States business firms, first because they contribute so importantly to our global international payments problem, while Japan maintains import impediments as compared to the relative access afforded by the United States market to Japanese and other world suppliers, and secondly because Japan greatly restricts the opportunity of United States business to participate in her market through investment." [17]

Actually by 1969, Japan had begun to dismantle import quotas at a fairly substantial rate.[18] To an economist, it is by no means clear that Japanese nontariff barriers were harming the United States more than United States nontariff barriers were harming Japan.[19]

16. *IMF / IBRD Directions of Trade*, 1966–70, pp. 106, 145.

17. Quoted in *New York Times*, July 15, 1971.

18. Professor Hugh Patrick's Congressional testimony is informative. "In 1969 Japan still had 'illegal' quotas (RIR—residual import restrictions—by GATT terminology) on 120 of 1096 commodities, plus quota restrictions on 43 items which are regarded as acceptable under GATT regulations, though all cannot really be justified. Today Japan has 'illegal' quota restrictions on 40 items, compared with 39 for West Germany; of these most are on agricultural products, and only 9 are on manufactured goods. In 1971 alone the government eliminated quotas on 50 commodities. The remaining nine items under quota range from important commodities for American trade interests, such as computer hardware, to quantitatively unimportant, such as leather goods." Testimony, *op. cit.*, p. 8.

19. According to Professor Patrick, "More than a year ago the U. S. government learned, after requesting bilateral negotiations with Japan to reduce non-tariff barriers, that the dollar volume impact of all U. S. non-tariff barriers against imports from Japan was larger than the impact of all Japanese restrictions against American exports. This was *before* the recent Japanese reduction in quotas and the latest

Nonetheless, although a careful study had not been undertaken, it was widely concluded that Japanese restrictions were especially severe on imports from the United States and that the restrictions were "unfair." The gist was that, as one problem complicated another, Japan became a highly visible target for defenders of the dollar—and for protectors of American producers and workers.

B. The Issues

5. *PRELIMINARY NEGOTIATIONS*

Contrary to trade policies expressed in his campaign pledge of 1968, President Nixon described the Trade Bill of 1969 which he submitted to Congress as "modest in scope." And indeed it was, containing essentially housekeeping provisions for limited tariff-cutting authority (to allow "compensation" if past tariff concessions were withdrawn), elimination of the American selling price system of customs valuation (in accordance with the Kennedy Round Agreement), a modest easing of the criteria under which the Tariff Commission could invoke the escape clause or extend adjustment assistance, and the extension of a provision of the Trade Expansion Act of 1962 giving the President retaliatory authority in cases of foreign discrimination against any United States export. There was only a brief—almost casual—reference to the textile import problem as being "a special circumstance that requires special measures." The "special measures" were to be the securing of voluntary agreements from the major textile-exporting countries to limit the future growth rate of their man-made fiber and woolen textile exports to the United States.

The task of negotiating these voluntary agreements was given to Secretary of Commerce Stans. His major argument was that if voluntary restraints were not agreed to, then the textile-exporting countries would likely confront the more severe burden of having the Congress unilaterally impose textile quotas. As if to fulfill this prophecy, Representative Mills (Chairman of the House Ways and Means Committee) introduced in May 1969 a mandatory textile

agreement placing quotas on exports of all Japanese man-made and woolen textiles. It has been a case of the pot calling the kettle black; yet the American perception seems to be that Japan maintains high restrictions against U. S. exports while our markets are freely open to Japan." Testimony, *ibid.*, pp. 8–9.

quota bill limiting all textile imports to the average annual amount
of the 1967–68 period, unless agreements were later negotiated to
establish a higher level. But the Administration still sought voluntary agreements. For more than a year, Secretary Stans negotiated
with representatives of Japan's Ministry of Trade and Industry, and
President Nixon conferred with Prime Minister Sato. Their differences could not, however, be reconciled. Secretary Stans appeared
before the Ways and Means Committee and disclosed that a voluntary agreement was unobtainable.

TESTIMONY OF SECRETARY STANS [20]

Mr. Boggs. What are the total imports now of textiles from Japan?

Secretary Stans. As you know, imports of cotton textiles into the United
States are presently restricted under the long-term cotton textile arrangement.

My answer, then, will deal only with manmade fibers and wool, which
are the immediate concerns.

In fiscal 1969, our imports of textiles and apparel made of manmade
fibers were 546 million yards.

Mr. Boggs. I am sorry, I didn't hear you. What was it?

Secretary Stans. 546 million yards in fiscal year 1969.

Mr. Boggs. How does that compare with, let us say, 5 years ago?

Secretary Stans. Let me give you the figures for the 3 years I have here
and we will submit the others. In calendar 1969, imports of textiles and
apparel made from manmade fibers were 585 million yards; in 1968, they
were 448 million yards; in 1967, they were 352 million yards, and in the
preceding 2 years they were considerably less.

Mr. Boggs. That is from Japan?

Secretary Stans. That is from Japan alone.

Mr. Boggs. What about from Korea, Taiwan and Hong Kong?

Secretary Stans. I will give them to you separately for each country.
For 1969, from Korea, 212 million yards; for 1968, 137 million yards; for
1967, 64 million yards.

For Taiwan, in 1969, they were 238 million yards; in 1968, 123 million
yards; in 1967, 59 million yards.

From Hong Kong, in 1969, these imports were 145 million yards; in
1968, they were 99 million yards; in 1967, they were 75 million yards.

Mr. Boggs. Are there any other significant exporting countries?

Secretary Stans. There are no other significant exporting countries at

20. Testimony of Hon. Maurice H. Stans, Secretary of Commerce, *Hearings before
the House Ways and Means Committee on Trade and Tariff Proposals*, 91st Congress, Second Session (1970), pp. 442ff.

this time, although a number of other countries are beginning to export in increasing quantities and have indicated a substantial interest in our market.

I may say also, while you are pursuing this line of questioning, that for the first 4 months of this year, the trend of increases that I indicated in the previous years is continuing and imports are up substantially from all of these countries in the first 4 months of this year.

Mr. Boggs. Does your proposal in any way contravene the GATT provisions that we subscribe to?

Secretary Stans. It does not contravene the GATT provisions. It does involve the right of other countries to ask for compensation or to retaliate on U. S. exports to an equivalent extent if trade expansion should result provided, of course, that the quota limitations in the bill are effective and are not superseded by voluntary agreements.

If there are voluntary agreements, then there is no retaliation provision under GATT that would be applicable.

Mr. Boggs. In your negotiations which I read about in the press, have you discussed with the Japanese representatives what retaliation they might contemplate?

Secretary Stans. I would say that we did not discuss that specifically. We were more interested in trying to see whether it was possible to reach a voluntary agreement at this time that would be of significance in resolving the problem.

Mr. Boggs. Why were you unable to reach an agreement?

Secretary Stans. Well, I suppose they would say that we were asking for too much, and I would say they were offering too little.

Mr. Boggs. Will you be specific about that?

Secretary Stans. Yes. The Japanese offer for textiles was that they would execute an agreement restricting the shipments of textiles to the United States for a period of 1 year provided we would agree that we would not ask for an extension at the end of that year, and that during that year they would be permitted an increase in shipments to the United States in manmade items of 12 to 15 percent, and in wool items of 1 percent.

They also proposed a formula for administration which would permit the shifting within categories on an unlimited basis with the result that they would have the opportunity to add substantially to the labor component of these imports if they set out to do so.

Our proposal was, in contrast, that an agreement would not be of significant help unless it were for approximately 5 years; that we were perfectly willing to allow them during that period of 5 years to share in the growth of the U. S. market, and that the growth formula we proposed would be to allow in each calendar year of the agreement the percentage of increase in the growth of the U. S. market during the preceding year, so their growth in shipments would follow exactly the growth in the U. S. market.

Mr. Boggs. What was it percentagewise in that growth formula?

Secretary Stans. In the last full year it was 5.8 percent, in the fiscal year ended June 30, 1969, and in the fiscal year ending June 30, 1970, we estimate it will be about 4 percent.

With respect to the formula for exercising the controls, we felt that it should, in effect, be comprehensive to prevent shifting of goods from one category to another; that there should be approximately 23 specific categories of goods which had limits on their exports to the United States, subject only to the growth formula, and that with respect to all of the other nonspecific categories there would be a provision whereby if there was a significant increase we could trigger a mechanism that would limit the growth of that category.

These conditions were not acceptable at all to the Japanese, and their proposal was one of general limitations only, as I said earlier, with the right to shift from one category of goods to another.

The divergent positions of the United States and Japan were summarized in the following Aide-Memoire of the government of Japan.

AIDE-MEMOIRE [21]

As has been stated on many occasions, the Government of Japan is unable to accept the proposal by the Government of the United States, dated January 2, 1970, as a basis for discussion. The Government of Japan believes that the Government of the United States has already been fully informed of the views of the Government of Japan with regard to the above-mentioned proposal, but the Government of Japan wishes to reiterate its position, by way of confirmation, as follows.

(1) The above-mentioned proposal differs from the previous United States proposal dated December 19, 1969, in that it does not call for the establishment of aggregate limits and group limits. On the surface, the proposal appears to have done away with comprehensive restrictions. However, in fact, the application of the "trigger" mechanism to all items not covered by specific limits results in the setting up of category by category ceilings and, in this regard, the proposal does not substantially differ from proposals calling for comprehensive restrictions.

This point is greatly to be regretted, inasmuch as the Government of Japan has consistently taken the position that comprehensive restrictions are wholly unacceptable.

(2) The proposal represents some improvement over the December proposal in that specific limits were somewhat increased. Yet, total ex-

21. *Ibid.*, May 20, 1970, pp. 1246–48.

port limits for 1970 under the proposal amount to less than the actual level of exports in 1969. This is contrary to the views expressed by the United States representatives on frequent occasions, including those expressed by Secretary of Commerce Stans on the occasion of his visit to Japan last year, to the effect that the Government of the United States does not seek to roll back the level of past exports.

(3) The proposal calls for an agreement effective for a long and fixed term of 5 years. This is in conflict with the Japanese position that export restraints should be considered as provisional measures undertaken for the sake of expediency until such time as the United States Government is in a position to resort to Article 19 of the GATT.

The basic views of the Government of Japan concerning ways and means for the solution of this issue are as follows.

(1) The Government of Japan can implement export restraints only on a selective basis, solely for those items which are subject to serious injury or threat of serious injury caused by increased imports, and only upon obtaining the understanding of the domestic industries concerned in Japan and following the consent of the major exporting countries.

(2) However, the normal manner to deal with this problem would be resort to Article 19 of the GATT by the United States. As stated in paragraph 2. (3), in case the measures referred to in (1) above should be put into effect, they are to be considered interim measures to be employed until the United States will be in a position to resort to that Article. The Government of Japan reserves its rights under the GATT in case the United States resorts to Article 19.

(3) The Government of Japan can understand the United States position that, under Article 19 of the GATT, judgments as to the existence of injury is made, in the first instance, by the importing country. However, Article 19 provides for the holding of sufficient consultations with exporting countries concerning compensation and other matters. It is also noted that, in the United States, the existence of serious injury or the threat thereof is judged by an authoritative organ, the Tariff Commission, after careful investigation.

(4) However, the present case, where the Government of the United States is requesting that the exporting countries implement export restraints which have substantially the same trade effect as import restrictions, differs completely from normal Article 19 procedure. In this case, it is felt that it is only reasonable to ask for full consultations with the exporting countries, who are to implement the restraints, for obtaining their understanding concerning injury or the threat thereof.

As the Government of Japan has explained during the preliminary discussions in Geneva and on other occasions, the existence of serious injury or the threat thereof due to increased imports with respect to individual items on a selective basis, should be determined on the basis of economic factors normally taken into account, such as production, imports, prices, employment and etc. On the basis of the incomplete data and explanations thus far presented by the Government of the United States, the Government of Japan cannot but conclude that it can find no items causing or threatening to cause injury.

While the Government of Japan is of the view that such matters as the duration of the restraints and the growth rate of the specific limits should be discussed in depth only after agreement is reached as to whether or not restrictions are necessary, and, if so, what items are to be subject to export restraint, its views with respect to the major elements of the United States proposal of January are set forth below.

(1) The restraints should be in effect for as short a period as possible inasmuch as export restraints are considered to be interim measures to enable the Government of the United States to resort to Article 19 of the GATT, as stated in paragraph 3. (2) above. The restraints should cease to be effective one year after the coming into effect of the new United States Trade Act or by the end of 1971, whichever comes earlier.

(2) Since restrictions are to be in effect only for a short period, the Government of Japan does not consider it appropriate to establish in advance a uniform growth-rate of the specific limits. In any case, the United States proposal to adjust the limits in accordance with the fluctuations of the United States domestic market is wholly unacceptable, because such a scheme freezes the share of imports in the years to come.

(3) The level of specific limits and growth-rates for the limits should not be determined uniformly in advance, but should be determined individually, depending on the nature of the injury caused or threatened to be caused. For this reason also, inquiry into the existence of injury or the threat thereof for individual items should be the initial task; discussion on reasonable growth rates can be held on the basis of the judgment of injury or the threat thereof.

As reported in the following extracts, the Nixon administration finally endorsed mandatory quotas on textiles.

THE ADMINISTRATION'S "RELUCTANT" SUPPORT [22]

WASHINGTON, June 25—The Nixon Administration threw its "reluctant" support today behind legislation to impose import quotas on textiles. In so doing, it may have opened the way to much broader import restrictions.

The position of the Administration was conveyed to the House Ways and Means Committee by Secretary of Commerce Maurice H. Stans only a day after a final effort to negotiate a voluntary agreement on textile trade with Japan had failed.

The questioning of committee members indicated a strong undercurrent of sentiment that it was not fair to solve the import problems of

22. *New York Times*, June 26, 1970.

only the textile industry. During a month of testimony producers of about 70 product categories have asked for relief.

Mr. Stans said today: "The need for a solution to the textile import problem is clearly apparent. In the absence of agreements with Japan and with other key exporting countries, it is our reluctant judgment that the only means presently available for solving this problem is the textile legislation now before this committee."

However, Mr. Stans made these additional points:

The legislation "allows negotiated agreements to supersede the quotas," which under the bill would roll back imports below their level of 1969.

The legislation should be amended to permit the President to exempt from quotas products and exporting countries where imports are not "disruptive."

The Administration continues to oppose the provision in the legislation imposing import quotas on shoes.

There is great statistical dispute about the impact of the imports on the industry, its profits and its employment. But only one member of the committee today, Representative Sam M. Gibbons, Democrat of Florida, raised doubts about whether the industry really needed protection. And his comments came late in the day after both the audience and nearly all the committee members had left.

Much of today's questioning centered not on textiles but on the general trade situation of the nation, with emphasis on allegations that other nations—particularly Japan—were using various devices to help their exports and impede their imports.

Mr. Stans conceded that during the whole postwar period, as tariff barriers were gradually being reduced but some nontariff trade barriers were erected, "in many respects we have been Uncle Sucker to the rest of the world. It is time to say, 'Let's play fair'."

But Mr. Stans emphasized that the Administration "in principle is not in favor of quota legislation." He was cautious about suggestions from committee members for a formula that would "trigger" quotas for any product where import penetration reached a certain level.

He was also cautious about suggestions that the United States set a deadline of three or four years, after which it would retaliate against imports from any country that refused to negotiate the removal of nontariff barriers. These barriers range from border taxes to government procurement regulations, from health standards to import licensing.

TRAGEDY OF QUOTAS [23]

There is blame enough to go round in the sad story that last week finally forced the essentially free-trade-minded Nixon Administration into supporting restrictive quotas imposed by law on imports of textiles. The

23. "American Survey," *The Economist*, July 4, 1970.

current cliché, inevitably, is Pandora's box and it is apt. No man can say what evils will fly out of a Congress given this simple opening of presidential backing for a major restriction on trade, even if it is only one quota. But a more apt analogy is Greek tragedy itself—the inexorable following of one thing from another, with very little in the way of bad intentions.

Mr. Miyazawa, the suave minister of trade and industry, arrived in Washington early last week with a "new" offer of restraint on textile exports, amid great fanfare; when the offer turned out to be as limited and unacceptable as before, it was really the final insult. Mr. Edwin Reischauer, the former American ambassador to Japan and an admirer of the country, said, after the negotiations collapsed, that Japan was "basically to blame."

Mr. Nixon has made a thing of living up to pledges, whether or not the Japanese (or many Americans) believe it. Mr. Stans, the Secretary of Commerce, heard Mr. Miyazawa's offer on the first day and gave him two more chances to improve it. When on the Wednesday it was clear that no agreement was possible Mr. Stans, who had gone through this agony for 14 months, decided to end it. He announced that the negotiations had failed and within 12 hours the President had decided that enough was enough and that a pledge had to be kept.

On Thursday morning Mr. Stans announced to the Ways and Means Committee of the House of Representatives the Administration's "reluctant" support of legislation to impose quotas on imports of woollen and man-made fibre textiles. He stressed, however, that one reason for the support was that the level of imports permitted by the formula in the bill—which would be a substantial rollback from current levels—could be increased if there were a voluntary agreement later. Although the domestic textile industry was on the whole jubilant, a thoughtful spokesman for it pointed out that, in backing the legislation, the industry was relying wholly on the President in power not to negotiate agreements that would permit even more imports than at present.

When Mr. Stans announced his decision, nearly all the 25 members of the Ways and Means Committee were in their seats. And immediately after his statement, the troubled sentiments of the committee became clear. The members asked why should textiles, and only textiles, obtain relief? True, the bill to limit imports of textiles had the support of some 230 members already, more than a majority of the House. But, asked Mr. Byrnes of Wisconsin, the senior Republican on the committee, why should "political clout"—in this case based on the size of the industry and its geographical spread—determine who should get relief from imports?

Mr. Mills, the chairman, explored all of Japan's violations of the General Agreement on Tariffs and Trade, the country's tax and other benefits for exports, and wondered whether the United States "can survive as an industrial power" as "the only really open market in the world." Mr.

Stans, who insisted—genuinely—that he still believed in freer trade, said that he had come to think that the United States had played "Uncle Sucker" in its negotiations in the postwar period. In an almost humorous choral note to the Greek tragedy, the small rubber footwear industry— far more hurt by imports than is the textile industry—sent a telegram to Mr. Stans after his testimony asking to be included in import quotas; earlier it had insisted only on a high tariff. This made it the 71st industry to claim relief.

PRESIDENTIAL NEWS CONFERENCE [24]

Q. Mr. President, how do you view the trade bill that seems to be developing in the House Ways and Means Committee, and if it contains the provisions that apparently will be voted on, would you veto it, sir?

A. I would certainly veto it, if it contains the provisions which I did not recommend. Speaking in general terms, first, quota legislation, mandatory quota legislation, is not in the interest of the United States. We are an exporting nation rather than an importing nation. It would mean in the end, while it would save some jobs, it would cost us more jobs in the exports that would be denied us, the export markets that would be denied us; and, second, even more important, it is highly inflationary, as anybody who has studied tariffs and quotas through the years is well aware.

Consequently, I have always opposed quota legislation as a general proposition.

In the case of textiles, for 16 months we have been attempting to negotiate a voluntary quota agreement with Japan without success and also with other nations. In view of that lack of success, and in view of the enormous importance of the textile industry to this country, the fact that one out of eight workers in manufacturing is in textiles, we feel that for the Congress to pass a limited bill dealing with textiles only and providing that mandatory quotas will come into effect and will remain in effect only if voluntary quotas are not negotiated, we believe that that approach is acceptable.

But if the bill goes beyond that, if it, for example, includes other items, I would not be able to sign the bill because that would set off a trade war.

6. TRADE BILL OF 1970

The cliché Pandora's box may be apt in describing the situation created when the Nixon administration was forced into "supporting

24. *New York Times,* July 21, 1970.

restrictive quotas imposed by law on imports of textiles" as *The Economist* observed, for it did not take the House Ways and Means Committee long to report out the most quota-ridden piece of trade legislation since the early 1930's. Proceeding beyond the President's desire for "a limited bill dealing with textiles only," the Committee's bill opened the way for introducing any number of quotas and imposed other trade restrictions.

HOUSE UNIT BACKS BROAD TRADE BILL [25]

WASHINGTON, July 14—The House Ways and Means Committee approved today a many-sided trade bill that would substantially alter the nation's 35-year-old policy of gradual reduction of tariff and other trade barriers.

The bill would impose mandatory import quotas on textiles and shoes. It also contains a new formula that could set off import quotas on other products when imports are shown to damage a domestic industry.

Even before the committee took its final action, Nixon Administration officials knowing which way the committee was heading, expressed dismay and alarm. The President had "reluctantly" supported import quotas on textiles but not the other provisions.

There is some dispute about how much import quotas would raise prices. Most authorities believe they would have at least some impact in that direction. In addition, some cheap foreign imported goods, such as apparel and footwear, might not be available at all.

The committee also approved a change in the tax laws designed to spur United States exports. It would authorize a new entity called a Domestic International Sales Corporation, or DISC, through which exporting companies could defer taxes on their profits from export business.

The bill also contains provisions aimed at the tougher administration of three laws already on the books that can be used to curb imports:

Antidumping: This permits special duties where a foreign seller is found to be "dumping"—that is, selling in the United States market at prices lower than in the seller's home market.

Countervailing duties: This long-dormant statute requires extra duties to be imposed when foreign countries are found to be subsidizing exports through tax or other measures.

The escape clause: This permits higher duties, or even quotas, when an industry can prove to the Tariff Commission that it has been injured by imports. The tests imposed by the present law have proved very difficult to meet and the bill would ease them substantially.

Under the committee's procedures, a formal vote must still be taken on each provision of the bill after legal language is drafted. While it is

25. *Ibid.*, July 15, 1970.

unlikely that any of the decisions disclosed today will be reversed, such reversals have occasionally happened in the past.

Yesterday the drift of the committee's sentiment was disclosed when it rejected the request of the Administration for repeal of the 50-year-old "American Selling Price" system of customs valuation applied mainly to imports of certain chemicals.

Under the provisions of the bill, the volume of imports allowed by the formula—which is lower than the present rate of imports—could be increased if the President negotiated voluntary agreements with supplying countries. This is the route that is expected to be taken. The effective date of the quotas has not yet been decided upon.

The same general provisions will apply to imports of shoes.

The sponsor of the more general mechanism to set off other quotas was Representative John W. Byrnes, Republican of Wisconsin, the senior minority member. He persistently argued during the hearings that it was not fair to provide protection only for industries—textiles and shoes—that had "political clout" because of their size and geographical dispersion.

The formula for the general quota is complex, involving percentage penetration of the United States market, rate of increase of imports and proof of injury to a domestic producer. But it was clearly designed to force the President to impose quotas when the specified conditions were met, though he could decline to do so on a finding that the national interest would be damaged.

TRADE WAR BREWS [26]

Talk of a world trade war has suddenly grown louder and more ominous.

Through recent months, strains in the United States trade relations with the European Economic Community and Japan had made such a conflict a possibility, although there was hope that it would be avoided.

But last week, the danger of a free-swinging trade war was sharply heightened. In completing its consideration of new trade legislation, the House Ways and Means Committee voted to include a provision that could lead to import quotas on any product considered "disruptive" to domestic production.

Apart from questions of whether the bill will be enacted without change, or whether it will be vetoed by President Nixon, the moves to restrict trade have brought alarmed protest by advocates of liberal policies.

Import quotas, they warn, will surely set off a trade war that will mean sharp losses in American exports at a time when a larger export surplus is essential for checking the new rise in the nation's balance-of-

26. *Ibid.*, July 19, 1970.

payments deficit. They view these effects as more damaging to domestic production and jobs than import competition.

Speaking as a member of the Emergency Committee for American Trade, David Rockefeller, chairman of the Chase Manhattan Bank, said he was sympathetic to problems of the textile industry, particularly its increased unemployment.

But he noted that it was "very difficult to start a quota system for one industry without having it spread to others.

"If we start on this tack," he added, "it will hurt more people than it will help. It is very dangerous and against our over-all interests to adopt protectionist policies that could unleash repercussions that would damage us over many years. The Common Market countries and others are certainly in a position to take very strong retaliation."

Mr. Rockefeller said that he believed that President Nixon very definitely favored liberal trade policies and would take an increasingly firm stand against protectionist legislation. The Emergency Committee consists of more than 50 top executives of major corporations with large-scale domestic and international operations.

In a comment pointing up election-year interests that appear to be a factor in the trade legislation, Donald M. Kendall, president and chief executive officer of PepsiCo, Inc., who is chairman of the Emergency Committee, asserted:

"A recent count showed that 22 member companies of E.C.A.T. have operations in the Congressional districts of the members of the House Ways and Means Committee.

"I don't know how many of these operations would suffer from foreign retaliation against legislated import quotas, but it is obvious that there will be money lost and men and women out of work if these quotas go into effect."

Prospects of broad import-quota legislation are not pleasing to the textile industry, which all along has feared that too many restrictive measures would lessen its chances for obtaining some restraint on textile imports.

Robert C. Jackson, executive vice president of the American Textile Manufacturers Institute, commented:

"The Textile industry supports the import-control legislation in its entirety as introduced by Chairman Mills and 253 other members of the House."

He added that "we strongly oppose any amendment that would undermine the basic purpose of the Mills bill, which is to provide the framework within which textile imports can be brought under reasonable regulation by means of comprehensive voluntary agreements or statutory limitation."

Senator Jacob K. Javits, Republican of New York, commented that "the United States would be making a great mistake in imposing quotas that would risk triggering a trade war."

"Quota schemes," he added, "attract a majority of Congress, but we should recognize that we all have a tremendous stake in export markets."

Rather than write broad import restrictions, the Senator commented that he felt it would be better for the Congress to give the President authority to take action in any cases "where we have been put upon because of our trade liberalization."

Much of the support that has grown in the Congress for import restrictions reflects a conviction that the United States has not received equally fair treatment by other countries as a result of its own trade liberality. Representative Mills expressed this view last week in the comment that "the United States is becoming the only open market in the world," while other countries are resorting to various devices to restrict imports and subsidize exports.

Joining in the expression of alarm were any number of economists —in fact, 5000 economists endorsed "An Appeal for Freer World Trade." [27]

> The United States is faced once again with a momentous decision in its foreign trade policy. Should our trade policy promote genuinely and consistently freer international trade in the total national interest, or government-controlled trade reflecting perversion of the national interest by the shortsighted pressures of special interests? . . . Forty years ago, in the midst of a growing economic crisis at home and abroad, Congress enacted and the President signed the highest tariff law in the nation's history. . . . We now seem on the threshold of another massive mistake, which would seriously damage the trade agreements system that since 1934 has replaced the anarchy of the 1920's and early thirties.
>
> Our country's response to the adjustment problems of U. S. producers and to the need for truly reciprocal liberalization of trade barriers throughout the industrialized areas of the Free World should show clear determination to solve problems at home and foster close cooperation abroad. At present, however, it seems little more than rudderless drift. The Administration's own efforts to restrict textile imports, without a coherent, constructive textiles policy that documents the need for such controls in the context of balanced government attention to the industry's needs, seems ill-advised. Congressional legislation imposing unilateral import quotas—even on textiles alone, con-

27. Circulated by the Committee for a National Trade Policy. The full text is reproduced in a pamphlet published by the Committee, *Time to Raise Our Sights in Trade Policy* (Spring, 1971).

sidering the wider implications of such a move—would be as perilous to the nation's interest today as was the Tariff Act of 1930 four decades ago.

We therefore urge Congress to reject import controls—direct or indirect, explicit or implicit. The bill reported out by the House Ways and Means Committee in August 1970 provides for and encourages such controls. If such a bill is passed by Congress, we urge the President to veto it. We urge instead a realistic foreign and domestic policy aimed at getting all countries to cooperate in furthering the expansion instead of the contraction of international trade, and at finding durable answers to the adjustment problems of U. S. industries, workers and communities.

Also noteworthy was the statement by ten former Presidents of the American Economic Association.[28] The text of their statement said, in part:

The policy of progressive liberalization of international trade pursued by both Democratic and Republican Administrations during the postwar period has made an important contribution to the growth and prosperity of both the American and world economies.

But we stand at the brink of a serious reversal of this trend, a reversal which could lead us back to the heavy protectionism of the nineteen-thirties and the great Depression.

Protectionist trade policies will benefit a few but they will harm many. Quotas are particularly damaging to the efficient functioning of the economy. They place an absolute maximum on the level of imports and hence largely remove international competition as a factor influencing domestic pricing policies.

Such quotas would intensify inflationary pressure, raising costs to domestic producers and consumers. Likewise, much more even than in the case of tariffs, quotas would limit the spur to technological improvements presently provided to domestic producers by the forces of international competition.

The imposition of quotas would represent a serious breach of our international commitments under the General Agreement on Tariffs and Trade. They would invite legal retaliation against our exports even if they failed to generate a genuine trade war.

Neither facts nor theory support the contentions that we should turn our back on the principle of liberal trade which has served us so well.

28. The signers begin by saying that "this statement is made by us as individuals and not in the name of the Association." Statement is quoted in *New York Times*, July 20, 1970.

As could be expected, "Letters to the Editor" were many.

TEXTILE-APPAREL QUOTAS [29]

To the Editor:

The five members of Columbia University's Department of Economics who wrote July 10 in opposition to textile-apparel quotas must have gotten their knowledge of foreign trade from very old textbooks. Times have changed and so have the facts of international trade. Repeating the bromides of the past isn't very productive when facing a serious problem today.

Their warning about a possible trade war doesn't make much sense in light of the network of non-tariff barriers already established by such exporting nations as Japan and the European Economic Community. These nations already curb imports of competing products and have very little ammunition left with which to conduct a trade war.

The five economists also suggest that it would be economically disastrous to underdeveloped nations if we were to regulate imports—in the face of the fact that the largest exporter of textiles and apparel is Japan, which cannot by any definition be called underdeveloped. And so far as textiles and apparel are concerned, many of the manufacturing facilities in Taiwan and South Korea, two other large exporters, are owned by Japanese manufacturers.

As a matter of fact, the most helpful step for underdeveloped nations would be if Japan and the E.E.C. would open their doors to trade. It does not make sense economically for the United States to remain the only industrial nation with an open-door policy.

Finally, the economists raise the question of fighting inflation at home through low-cost imports. The trouble is that in our own field of apparel, imports are not much of an inflation deterrent. They are usually sold at the same price as domestic products, with the retailers capturing the difference in higher mark-ups.

The greater damage to our economy, incidentally, would come not from inflation but from rising unemployment caused by the unregulated flood of imports.

Our members, many of them belonging to minority groups who would have a hard time relocating, are not going to watch their jobs slip away to the economic melodies of the 1930's. It's time the economists updated their tunes and learned about the facts of international trade today.

Howard D. Samuel
Vice President, Amalgamated
Clothing Workers of America
New York, July 13, 1970.

29. *New York Times*, July 22, 1970.

PROTECTED TEXTILES [30]

To the Editor:

The public should know that the textile industry in the United States is highly protected. An approximation of prevailing United States duties (in percentages) follows:

Synthetic fabrics, 40; cotton goods, 13–15; synthetic yarns, 12; cotton yarns, 13–15.

Therefore, exporters to the United States must overcome this duty charge, plus high shipping, packing and insurance costs.

The industry has for years enjoyed the benefit of quota limitations negotiated by the Commerce Department. In addition, voluntary agreements between the United States and Japanese industry have been in force for many years.

Then, during the Johnson Administration, a 6½-cents-a pound cotton subsidy payment was legislated which equalized that being paid on cotton exports. The industry lobbied for this relief, claiming gross disadvantage because foreign competitors enjoyed this 6½-cents-a-pound advantage. Subsequent to this, prices of cotton textiles, both domestic and export, rose uninterruptedly. Moreover, textile exports did not increase.

The United States textile industry enjoys the largest per capita consuming market in the world. The highest percentage of its production is concentrated on mass production staple fabrics in which the unit of labor content is the lowest in the world. [Editorial July 5]

A mature industry such as textiles which demands ever-greater protection, even at the expense of United States international trade policy, does a disservice.

Perhaps Howard D. Samuel, Vice President of the Amalgamated Clothing Workers of America [letter July 22], may have overlooked some of these considerations. The economists he criticized did not.

Harry Goodwin
Vice President
Textures International, Inc.
New York, July 23, 1970

While the domestic consequences were aired, there was little concern with the broader context of the GATT. A notable exception is the next letter.

30. *Ibid.*, July 28, 1970.

TRADE BILL AND GATT: COLLISION COURSE [31]

To the Editor:

"Retaliation" is the term often used for consequences predicted to follow if the United States enacts the trade bill currently before the Senate. Some efforts have been made to minimize the significance of such retaliation, but seldom is it mentioned that such retaliation would not be simply the spiteful action of foreign pique, but a deliberate and legally authorized sanction under GATT (The General Agreement on Tariffs and Trade) for the breach of an obligation of GATT.

GATT Article XI prohibits the United States (and all members of GATT) from using quotas as a means of restricting imports. This is one of the most important rules contained in the GATT Agreement. At the 1947 negotiations the United States was the strongest advocate of the rule against quotas (because of bitter memories of the effects of quotas on trade in the 1930's).

Over the two decades of GATT history the United States often used arguments which relied on GATT obligations to urge removal of European quota systems. This effort was largely successful with one important exception—agricultural goods. Not so coincidentally, it was on agricultural goods that the United States had, inconsistently with GATT, imposed quotas itself.

GATT specifically provides a remedy or "sanction" for certain actions of members which breach its obligations. Article XXIII of GATT, for instance, allows a majority of GATT members to determine that reciprocal measures may be taken against the trade of a breaching member. Thus, if the new United States quotas reduce imports from its trading partners, those trading partners may be allowed to prohibit certain United States exports from their markets.

Serious consequences of a United States breach of GATT obligations are not limited to sanctions under GATT or retaliation from our trading partners, however. There are several other consequences of such a breach which could be very damaging. First, there will be the difficulty, if not impossibility, of renewing efforts to prevent the spread of quotas in the world, or indeed of other protectionist measures (including various nontariff barriers).

Just as United States diplomats were often neutralized in their efforts of the 1960's to liberalize world agricultural trade by the fact the United States had introduced and maintained a quota system on agricultural goods, so will future United States diplomatic efforts to obtain trade outlets for United States goods be severely hampered by United States disregard for its GATT obligations.

Second, and perhaps more significant, a breach by the United States

31. *Ibid.*, Dec. 20, 1970.

of the solemnly sought GATT prohibition on quotas will put in question the integrity of all United States international economic commitments. Can any foreign nation feel confident of developing rational international regulation for the turbulent international economic problems of today, when the largest trading nation of the world demonstrates its disregard for legal norms concerning trade matters?

John H. Jackson
Ann Arbor, Mich., Dec. 9, 1970
The writer, Professor of Law at the University of Michigan, is author of "World Trade and the Law of GATT."

6.1. *Quota Provisions.* Although the provisions in the Trade Bill of 1970 raised a number of policy issues—all worthy of detailed appraisal, our central concern in this policy problem is with the provision for textile quotas. The Bill provided for the establishment of annual quotas.

QUOTA PROVISIONS IN TRADE BILL OF 1970 [32]

Title II provides temporary measures to restrict imports and avoid the threat of serious injury to the textile and footwear industries and further deterioration in the domestic market for textiles and apparel and nonrubber footwear.

This is to be accomplished by—

(a) The establishment of annual quotas, based on imports during 1967–69, by category and by foreign country of production for all categories of textile articles and footwear articles which may be imported during each calendar year beginning after December 31, 1970;

(b) Authorizing exemptions from such quotas when the President determines that exemption will not disrupt the domestic market or that exemption is in the national interest; and

(c) Authorizing negotiation of agreements with foreign countries which would result in the regulation of imports into the United States of textile articles or footwear articles or both and would supersede the statutory quotas for the articles covered by the agreements.

Within this general framework, title II authorizes increased imports where the supply of articles subject to limitation is inadequate to meet domestic demand at reasonable prices; provides for certain exclusions with respect to noncommercial entries and to articles already subject to international agreement; and establishes the applicability of the rulemaking provisions of the Administrative Procedure Act to various actions under title II of the bill. Title II terminates at the close of July 1, 1976, un-

32. H. R. Rep. 1435, 91st Congress, Second Session (1970), pp. 35–40.

less extended in whole or in part by the President following his determination that such extension is in the national interest.

These provisions are designed to provide a mechanism for establishing a reasonable and effective limitation on United States imports of textile products and of non-rubber footwear products for the broad purpose of remedying market disruption in those cases in which it now exists, and of preventing the spread of market disruption to other categories of articles. It is intended that, insofar as may be possible, the limitation of these imports will be accomplished through the negotiation of voluntary agreements provided for under section 202 and that the quota provisions of section 201 will assist in the negotiation of such agreements as well as to provide protection for the domestic market and workers in cases where such agreements are not concluded.

The quota, exemption, and agreement provisions of title II are intended to assure that all textile articles and all footwear articles, as defined, come within the scope of such provisions and may, at any point in time, be subject to quota or agreement if they are not at such time exempted.

A. Annual Quotas

Annual quotas are established by statute on the total quantity of each category of textile articles (defined in subsec. 206(1)), and of footwear articles (defined in subsec. 206(2)), produced in any foreign country which may be imported during 1971 and in each subsequent year. The limit for 1971 for each category of articles produced in each country is the average annual quantity of such articles from such country which was imported during the years 1967, 1968 and 1969.

Textiles.——The average of imports from all countries of the principal textile articles not at present subject to import limitation (or to voluntary export restraint to the United States), i.e., principally wool and man-made fiber textile articles, amounted to an annual average of 1,390 million square yards equivalent in the 1967–1969 base period for man-mades, and 184.5 million square yards for wool textile products. (These figures include tops, yarns, fabrics, apparel, and made-up and miscellaneous textile products.) In 1969, imports were 1,782.6 million square yards equivalent for man-mades and 191.1 million for wool textiles. As of June 1970 imports are running at an annual and all time record rate of 2.4 billion square yards for man-made fiber textiles. However wool textile imports are expected to total 150 million square yards.

At the same time, cotton textile imports, which are subject to the terms of the Long Term Arrangement Regarding International Trade in Cotton Textiles, are continuing at a high rate. They are expected to again reach more than 1.6 billion square yards in 1970.

Apparel, the most labor intensive sector of the textile-apparel industry is experiencing a continuing sharp increase in imports. At present rates, 1970 apparel imports will rise to 1.6 billion square yards equivalent, of which more than 1 billion yards will be manufactured from man-made fibers, 500 million will be cotton apparel and 50 million will be wool apparel.

The committee heard substantial testimony from industry and government witnesses about the damage these excessive imports are causing to American firms and workers and the disruption that already has been caused in the domestic market for these goods. These imports pose a threat to the future of a strong textile-apparel "industry" in the United States unless import growth is more closely brought into balance with growth in the domestic market and in domestic production.

6.2. Variety of Views. Many different views on the Trade Bill were presented at the hearings before the House Ways and Means Committee. The following excerpts from testimony indicate a number of arguments pro and con, as submitted by interested parties.

STATEMENT OF DONALD F. McCULLOUGH [33]

Mr. Chairman and members of the committee:

I am Donald F. McCullough of New York City, president of Collins & Aikman Corp. I appear before you today in my capacity as president of the American Textile Manufacturers Institute, the major trade association of the U.S. textile manufacturing industry.

The ATMI represents some 85 percent of the spinning, weaving, and finishing capacity in the cotton, silk, and manmade fiber sectors of the industry, with member companies located from Maine through Texas.

In response to the chairman's request in the announcement of these hearings, this testimony begins a joint presentation on a consolidated basis by key textile trade organizations. In addition to ATMI, these include the American Yarn Spinners Association, the Cordage Institute, the National Association of Wool Manufacturers, the National Knitwear Manufacturers Association and the Northern Textile Association; also the Alabama, Georgia, North Carolina and South Carolina Textile Manufacturers Associations. . . .

We submit, Mr. Chairman, that the American textile-apparel industry, with its 2.4 million employees along with the additional hundreds of thousands of people engaged in the allied activity of cotton, wool, and manmade fiber production, is far too valuable a national asset to be traded off to foreign producers.

We appreciate as well as anyone that questions of international trade policy must be weighed carefully in the light of overall foreign and domestic economic and diplomatic policy. We do not want to see a so-

33. *Hearings before the House Ways and Means Committee on Tariff and Trade Proposals, op. cit.,* May 20, 1970, pp. 1217–22.

called "trade war" any more than anyone else does, and there is no reason in the world why one should occur.

But the textile import problem has been unresolved for so long, and the accelerating impact of virtually unlimited volumes of low-wage textile imports is so great, that the future course of one of this Nation's most basic and essential industries is being shaped not here, but in Tokyo, Hong Kong, Taipei and other overseas areas.

This is a problem that transcends any narrow geographic boundaries, partisan political considerations, or any particular product category. The basic issue, in simplest terms, is the very future of this industry and whether it will continue to function as one of the country's major sources for employment of men and women at all skill levels, as a customer for great amounts of supplies and services that sustain jobs in many other industries, and as a major consumer of important agricultural products.

That is why the administration has spent the past 15 months in a concerted effort to negotiate voluntary agreements with other textile nations on sharing the domestic market in a way that will sustain and expand the American industry's growth.

That is why you, Mr. Chairman, have taken such a continuing interest and now, with some 200 of your colleagues, have moved ahead with this legislation as the only reasonable solution to this long-festering problem.

That is why all segments of the textile industry, including manufacturers, organized labor and all who comprise the fiber-textile-apparel complex are wholeheartedly behind your efforts to legislate a meaningful, long-range solution.

But time is running out. No industry, no labor force, no nation can long endure the type and trend of low-wage import penetration which is assaulting the textile industry. And no nation that wants to preserve such a vital asset as this industrial-agricultural complex represents, should be expected to permit the import situation to get so out of hand.

In less than 10 years we have seen a tripling of textile imports, creating a mammoth textile trade deficit now running well over $1 billion.

The raw cotton industry is being battered by a volume of cotton textile imports which are equivalent to more than 1 million bales of cotton annually.

Man-made fiber textile imports have leaped geometrically, from 221 million square yards in 1963 to double that amount in 1965, then double again to 934 million in 1967, and double again to 1.8 billion yards in 1969.

Wool imports have also increased relentlessly. Today, one out of every 4 yards of wool products sold in the United States is of foreign origin.

What does all this mean in lost production, and in lost potential? For one thing, obviously, it has meant lost job opportunities for thousands upon thousands of American men and women. The import volume in 1969 alone represented the displacement of well over a quarter of a million American textile and apparel jobs.

This is not a regional problem, but a national one that strikes at the heart of our entire economy.

My own company is headquartered in New York City. In our town, some 270,000 people are employed in the textile and apparel industry. The textile-apparel payroll of $1.7 billion in New York City is about equal to the city's annual welfare bill, as it was last year. More and more textile-apparel workers will be showing up on those welfare rolls unless the process of large-scale job transfers via imports is halted.

The several rather unique characteristics of the textile industry—its size, dispersion, its many competitive centers of initiative—have important social and economic significance for this country's future. It has been referred to as a "gateway industry," for example, because it offers opportunities for people of diverse skills and talents to hold down good jobs—ranging from those who can be trained in just a few weeks to scientists, engineers, data processors and other highly specialized technicians.

The industry employs an unusually large number of black Americans, considerably more than the national manufacturing average. Minority employment is increasing at a faster rate in textile mills than the average for all types of manufacturing.

We offer broad opportunities to women, likewise. Many women in textile and apparel occupations gain supplemental income for families that simply could not make it otherwise. The Labor Department reports that 80 percent of the apparel workers and 43 percent of the textile workers are women. This is a fact not generally appreciated. Where would these thousands of women turn if it were not for their textile and apparel jobs?

This is why we are so distressed when the labor force drops by 59,000 jobs in a little over a year—as it has done—and our industry is forced to cut back substantially on operations and on investment in the new plants and equipment necessary to create the jobs of the future.

Large-employment industries such as textiles, apparel and footwear, that have a high increment of labor in the cost of their finished products, cannot avoid being particularly hard hit by concentrations of imports in unchecked amounts. Let me mention just two or three examples of the kinds of situations happening at this very moment throughout the textile industry.

One is plant closings. No doubt you of the committee are aware that these have been reported extensively in the press and they continue to occur.

Secondly, many companies are being forced to reduce their workweek. Much of the basic textile-manufacturing structure is geared to operate three shifts 6 days a week—this has been the historical pattern for many years. Countless employees depend on that sixth day, at overtime pay, for extra money to make their payments on homes, cars, TV sets, refrigerators or what other necessities and luxuries they want. Cutting off this sixth day hurts them individually and, of course, slashes into the total economy of their communities.

Third, outlays of funds for plant and equipment are being either curtailed or postponed. These reductions have been substantial over the past 3 years. Yet, modernization is essential for any company that hopes to stay competitive and keep its employees on the job.

With markets and manufacturing operations constantly being washed away by imports and nobody able to foresee where it all will end, the textile-apparel industry faces an uncertain future. Yet, any business seeking to move forward in America's dynamic, competitive environment needs to set clear future goals.

Managements must make crucial long-range decisions. Money decisions: what they can afford to spend and whether they can earn it back.

Sound judgments are impossible to reach for textile executives who do not know when and where to expect the next attack from abroad. I can tell you from personal experience, Mr. Chairman, that this cloud of doubt, of wondering what may happen next in imports, hangs over almost every meeting of textile company directors when forward plans are discussed.

If the items entering this country in such volumes were better designed or more attractive, more durable or more efficiently produced, we would have little reason to object. But the vast majority of imports sell here primarily because they are cheaper; and they are cheaper for one reason only—they are made at wages and under working conditions that would be illegal and intolerable in this country.

Only until and unless the textile industry gains some measure of assurance that imports will not indefinitely go on gaining a larger share of the American market, can our industry look to the future with confidence. This whole Nation stands to gain—in terms of broadening job opportunities, the buttressing of industries allied to textile activity, and the generation of economic activity in hundreds of cities and towns—if the import problem can be alleviated.

It is our opinion that H.R. 16920 provides the framework for an eminently fair and reasonable solution, by assuring both domestic and foreign producers opportunities for sharing in the growth of the American textile market.

U. S. textile import policies under H.R. 16920 would remain so generous relative to those of other members of the General Agreement on Tariffs and Trade that there should be absolutely no reason for any nation to retaliate against us or claim compensation from us.

We are well aware that certain textile exporting nations—Japan, in particular—might threaten to reduce their buying of our raw cotton, soybeans, wheat or other commodities if their textile shipments to the United States were brought under orderly control. Contentions that this might happen do not hold up, however, in light of the realities of international trade as it actually is practiced today.

You can look at the trade in commodity after commodity and see that there is little, if any, relationship between what a major exporting country like Japan buys from us in relation to its textile shipments to us. The record shows quite clearly that Japan buys her raw materials wherever and whenever she can get the best deal, with no evident regard for her exports to a given country.

Take cotton, for example. We have seen our exports of raw cotton to Japan decline steadily during the past 10 years—the very time that we have experienced such a phenomenal rise in textile imports. On the other hand, Mexico, which permits virtually no textile imports from Japan, sold Japan more cotton last season than the United States did.

I am not aware of any trade war between Mexico and Japan.

Another contention is that import restraints will bring an automatic increase in the price of textiles to consumers. This is either a misrepresentation of the bill's objectives or a misunderstanding of economic reality. First, there is nothing in the legislation that necessarily would alter substantially existing relationships between foreign and domestically produced textiles in the U. S. market.

Moreover, import growth is permitted and anticipated. So how can it be valid that prices automatically will increase?

But there is an overriding consideration. It is that the U. S. textile industry historically has been and remains one of this country's most competitive big industries. Unlike some other major industries where a few companies dominate production and distribution, textiles is composed of hundreds of efficiently operated competitive companies constantly vying with one another for the business at hand.

Maintaining a highly competitive, expanding domestic textile-apparel industry is the consumer's best assurance that he or she will receive quality textiles at reasonable prices. It is this competition to attract consumer's interest and to cater to their needs and wishes that has created in America the world's greatest textile market.

However, when any segment or large part of that market falls under foreign domination, the competitive influence on prices can be lost. Let us look at one area where this has happened. Prices of silk products have leaped 69 percent since 1957–59. The U. S. market for raw silk and silk textiles is dominated by foreign suppliers. Once any foreign interest gains this kind of domination, provisions of U. S. law for protection of consumers and employees alike—antitrust regulations, prohibitions against conspiracy to fix prices, wage and hour laws and so on—no longer prevail.

And in looking out for the consumer's interest, we must never forget that in order for a person to be a consumer, he must first be an income earner.

It is high time, Mr. Chairman, to end the present insanity of exposing the American home market to indefinite, no-end-in-sight increases in textile and apparel imports from countries that have no obligation whatsoever to feel any legal or moral responsibility toward American employees, consumers, or communities.

This your bill can do. Thank you for this opportunity to present our views.

STATEMENT OF WILLIAM POLLOCK [34]

Mr. Pollock. Mr. Chairman, I have filed with this committee a copy of a statement by my organization, the Textile Workers Union of America.

I would like to say, at this point, that the United Textile Workers of America is joining with us in support of this statement.

It goes into some detail regarding the problems our industry faces as a result of the growing volume of textile imports.

It also expresses our complete support for import quotas on synthetic fibers and all textile products, as provided for in H.R. 16920.

I will not burden the members of this committee by going over all of the ground covered by our statement. Instead, I would like to confine my testimony to some special reasons for action to regulate textile imports. They go beyond the interests of the industry. They involve the interests of the entire country.

I am aware, of course, that to the people in each industry, nothing is more important than that particular industry. But what happens in the textile industry does have an impact upon the rest of the Nation.

And I believe it is possible to demonstrate that the national interest is indeed involved to a significant extent.

This is true because of the geography and the vital statistics, if you please, of the textile-apparel industry.

Let me start by saying that we are talking here about 2½ million Americans whose livelihood is directly linked to this industry.

The outstanding fact is that a large majority of the plants are located in small towns and rural areas. . . .

Therefore, textile workers who lose their jobs as a result of mill curtailment or liquidation have nowhere else in the area to turn to for employment.

This means that many displaced textile workers are forced to gravitate to the larger cities. Without the experience to cope with big-city life, without the skills necessary for big-city employment, they tend to fall by the wayside.

As a result, they contribute to the social and economic problems that plague all of our big cities.

If they remain in the rural areas in which they live, they are without jobs. And the rural counties lose tax revenue. These counties can ill-afford the increased cost of public assistance needed to care for the poverty-stricken unemployed.

34. *Ibid.*, May 20, 1970, pp. 1277–87.

This means a decline in the quality of rural life and, with it, substandard schools, roads, and community facilities. It also brings on a further tilting of the national scale in the direction of rural-urban imbalance.

What I have said is particularly true with respect to the black population. It is now engaged in a great effort to reach parity with the rest of our population. And all of us should share in that effort.

In the last few years, particularly, the textile industry has provided employment opportunities for the Negroes who have been driven off the farm. It represents an important road which enables them to enter our industrial society.

If that road is now shut off as a result of mill closings or curtailments caused by the flood of imported textiles, we will be piling yet another frustration on top of a pile that already has grown too high.

The impact of imports has been particularly severe in those situations where plants have been forced to close down.

Last year, 32 textile mills were liquidated, wiping out more than 8,000 jobs. In the first 4 months of this year, nine additional plants have been closed, wiping out more than 1,500 jobs.

Earlier this month, the West Point-Pepperell Co. announced plans to close its sheeting divisions at Biddeford, Maine, destroying 900 jobs in a small town which is dependent upon this plant for its economic mainstay.

Mr. Chairman, the committee has all of the facts and figures it needs —perhaps even more than it needs. They add up to a clear, economic justification for import quotas on textiles, textile products, and synthetic fibers.

But I would like to emphasize this aspect of the situation.

The Textile Workers Union of America is not an isolationist organization. We are willing to see a reasonable level of textile imports enter the domestic market. We would have liked to have seen agreements negotiated between the various trading countries on a voluntary basis.

As you know, the U. S. Government vigorously attempted, for more than a year, to reach such agreements. But these efforts have been rejected by Japan and other exporting countries.

Now there is no choice but legislation to establish quotas on such imports.

Even so, Japan and the other exporting countries do have a choice under the proposed terms of this legislation.

The bill before this committee provides that quotas will not be imposed on any category which is covered by a voluntary agreement.

So there is an alternative. The exporting countries can either accept the quotas fixed under this bill, or work out voluntary arrangements.

Finally, I would also like to emphasize this factor:

In this instance, there are far-reaching questions of social policy and national concern that involve the well-being of each of us—no matter how far removed we may be from a textile mill or a synthetic fibers plant.

This is not simply a matter of tariff policy—or tariff mechanisms—or a narrow construction of particular laws or regulations. Nor is it a matter of narrow sectional interest.

I predict that what this committee does with respect to import quotas on synthetic fibers and textile mill products will have as much impact upon the welfare of millions of Americans as any other legislation now pending in the Congress.

It is in that context that I urge your favorable consideration of H.R. 16920.

STATEMENT OF RICHARD L. ROWAN [35]

Mr. Rowan. I am Richard L. Rowan. I am an associate professor of industry and associate director, industrial research unit, Wharton School of Finance and Commerce, University of Pennsylvania. . . .

We are not here to plead the special interest of an industry. Rather, we wish to indicate some of the social and economic problems that are likely to ensue if imports of textile products are permitted to cause unemployment among southern textile employees.

Our analysis is based on studies of Negro employment in American industry. . . .

Mr. Rowan. I have the facts about the number of jobs held by Negroes in this industry, which until recent years employed only a few blacks, and I will point up the fact that if jobs are lost, the only recourse left for the displaced will be migration to the cities and further aggravation of our welfare problems.

The decade of the 1960's witnessed the beginning of major changes in the employment of Negroes in the southern textile industry. At this time, a combination of factors, including a tight labor market and Government pressure, began to open job opportunities to both male and female blacks. The record of Negro employment in textiles in the late 1960's and early 1970's is impressive, particularly if it is compared to the whole period of 1890 to 1960, when blacks were systematically excluded from the industry, except in the most menial jobs. . . .

As long as employers were able to staff their operations with whites, Negroes were denied employment opportunities. While some change began to occur in the 1950's, the dramatic increases in Negro employment did not take place until the mid-1960's. New industry of all types moved into the South in the late 1950's and early 1960's, and this created alternative employment opportunities for both blacks and whites. Whites, in particular, began to shift into jobs that were more attractive than those in textiles leaving vacancies to be filled by blacks. This labor market phenomenon coincided with strong equal employment measures of the Federal Government. . . .

Several important facts emerge from the statistical summary: (1) In re-

35. *Ibid.*, May 21, 1970, pp. 1561–68.

gard to total employment, the number of employees increased by 6,430 (2.4 percent), but Negro employment increased by 11,348 (45.3 percent), which indicates that all of the net addition in employment in the plants studied resulted from Negroes entering the industry. On the basis of sex, total males increased by 185 (0.1 percent), while Negro males increased by 5,910 (28.3 percent); total females increased by 6,245 (6.0 percent) while Negro females increased by 5,438 (129.9 percent).

The statistics are necessary to place the employment situation for blacks in perspective, but what are their real significance for those involved? Blacks included in the numbers represent people who for years were denied opportunities to enter the mainstream of economic life of the region. This is changing, rapidly. Today, the Negro, who enters the textile mill, may be a person who has never worked before in an industrial setting. It is the beginning of a new way of life. The Negro female, for example, who has served heretofore only as a domestic is able to find a productive employment experience.

Our major concern before this committee is simply one of what happens to those Negroes who are now receiving, for the first time in their lives, an opportunity to enter a useful, productive life in the event any internal or external activity should eliminate their jobs. Most likely they would not find employment anywhere else; they would not appear in the frictional unemployment statistics as those shifting job location. They probably would appear in the category of the hidden unemployed among those who have dropped out of the labor market because no work was available to them. Any addition to the discouraged worker group should be avoided. Black people without jobs in the southern textile areas are likely to become part of the welfare rolls in the big cities or they may return to some unproductive agricultural pursuit.

The social, political, and economic environment in which people live in the South can benefit from the positive racial employment changes that are now occurring in the textile industry. People who work together have an opportunity to learn and understand each other. A mill owner in Alabama reported to the author: "One of the major byproducts of the Civil Rights Act, which forces us to integrate our plants, is that we have begun to understand people as human beings."

The prospects for the future are encouraging, but the final outcome will depend on the quality of the employer's effort and the continued availability of jobs. . . .

Mr. Watts. Thank you very much for your statement.

Are there any questions?

Mr. Conable.

Mr. Conable. Is this trend likely to continue irrespective of any overall effects on the textile industry?

Is there likely to be a continuing shift?

Mr. Rowan. In my judgment, yes.

Mr. Conable. It is still not majority employment in the industry, is it?

Mr. Rowan. It is not.

Mr. Conable. But you feel that the shift that has so accelerated during the later part of the sixties will continue for a foreseeable period of time?

Mr. Rowan. Yes.

Mr. Conable. Of course, many of these same people have been released from other jobs by the agricultural revolution, have they not?

Mr. Rowan. Some of them have come from agriculture and are now entering the industrial mainstream by the textile industry, yes.

Mr. Conable. Many of them you would conclude, were not employed at all unless they were employed on a comparatively low level agricultural basis?

Mr. Rowan. I would say for the most part that is correct, in particular, the Negro female who has either worked in some kind of an agricultural pursuit or perhaps has worked as a domestic. She is making up a very important part of the employment picture in the textile and apparel industry in the South today.

Mr. Conable. What about the future? What about the quality of life of people in this type of employment? Is this likely to be upgraded? Are they highly represented by unions, for instance?

Mr. Rowan. No, they are not highly represented by unions.

Mr. Conable. Has there been a consistent pattern of wage growth over the years both as a result of Government action and as a result of collective bargaining?

Mr. Rowan. There has been some wage growth in the industry, but it is still a low-wage paying industry, textiles and apparel.

Mr. Watts. Mr. Betts.

Mr. Betts. Professor, relating what you have said to the question before the committee of imports, I assume you take the position, then, that this favorable trend toward increasing employment of Negroes would depend to a large extent on protecting domestic industry from imports, is that correct?

Mr. Rowan. It depends in large measure, Mr. Betts, on some expansion of employment in the industry.

I would assume that any activity that would cause employment to decline, or even to remain relatively stable, would influence the number of blacks who go into the industry.

Mr. Betts. And assuming that what our friends in the industry tell us, that industry is in danger from imports, you would naturally, then, favor some means which would protect the industry from these imports, to continue the trend of Negro employment, is that correct?

Mr. Rowan. That is correct.

Mr. Watts. Mr. Conable.

Mr. Conable. Professor, I would like to ask you this question: The source of your information has been entirely industry sources, has it not, or have you also corroborated the evidence they have given you with outside sources?

Mr. Rowan. We have had some assistance where it has been possible to get it on a confidential basis from the Equal Employment Opportunity Commission and the Office of Federal Contract Compliance.

Mr. Conable. Was your study subsidized by the textile industry?

Mr. Rowan. No; it was subsidized by the Ford Foundation.

Mr. Conable. And you acquired the subject in the usual way, through your own initiatives?

Mr. Rowan. Yes.

Mr. Watts. I would assume, in answer to a question that was put to you, that if this is the first industry in which they have been able to work, that the experience gained in that industry is going to go a long way toward qualifying them for different types of industry, would it not?

Mr. Rowan. Absolutely, Mr. Watts.

Mr. Watts. In other words, when you first step into any industry, you gain a knowledge of how to work with groups of people, how to operate machines, and so forth, that will lead you to better qualify yourselves for other types of industrial employment.

Mr. Rowan. Yes.

Mr. Watts. That is all. Thank you.

STATEMENT OF RALPH H. CUTLER, JR. [36]

Mr. Cutler. Mr. Chairman, members of the Ways and Means Committee, I am Ralph H. Cutler, Jr., vice president of C. Tennant, Sons & Co. of New York, and chairman of the trade policy committee of the American Importers Association. With me today is Mr. Gerald O'Brien, executive vice president of the American Importers Association.

Mr. Burke. We welcome both of you to the committee.

Mr. Cutler. My company was founded in 1825, and today has annual sales of over $300 million in industrial raw materials. I appear today on behalf of the American Importers Association, which was organized in 1921 and is the only trade association representing importers on a national basis. Since 1934, we have supported the trade agreements initiated by successive administrations since 1934.

We are deeply concerned that legislation to establish quotas and other types of restrictions on imports will be harmful to the consumer, the American economy, and the import business. Bear in mind that there are millions of Americans whose jobs are dependent on international trade. Based on Bureau of Labor statistics for 1969, we estimate that over 5 million persons today are partially or wholly dependent for their livelihood on foreign trade activities, including over 3.3 million engaged in the production and transportation of merchandise for export. Comparable figures for imports do not exist for 1966, but using 1962 data, we estimate about

36. *Ibid.*, May 18, 1970, pp. 933–37.

2.2 million people are employed in the transportation and distribution of imported items or the processing of imported materials.

Experience has shown that a limitation of imports tends to raise prices in the domestic market. The most recent example is the "voluntary" agreements on steel. Since these have been effected, American steel producers have steadily increased prices because of shortages both in the United States and abroad.

Quotas of whatever nature are bound not only to limit the consumers' freedom of choice, but also to restrict this choice in the market place to more expensive goods. Any limitation on imports will very soon affect American export sales. This will come at a most unfortunate time both as regards our balance of payments and the American economy as a whole. If the United States imposes unilateral quotas, we can expect retaliation against American exports, or the need to compensate the countries affected.

For many years, we have emphasized that trade is a two-way street. We feel that a liberal import policy is the only way to increase U. S. exports. We also believe that if world trade is to increase in the future as it has in the past 20 years, it will be necessary that our trading partners substantially relax their restrictions against American imports. We strongly urge the administration to maintain its efforts to secure such relaxation.

The American Importers Association opposes restraints on trade by any country. We deplore those of other countries, but at the same time we must point out that the United States is far from blameless. At the present time, more than 15 percent of total imports in 1969 are subject to mandatory or "voluntary" quotas, covering cotton textiles, steel, oil, dairy products, brooms, wheat flour, peanuts, and others.

We recognize that world conditions and domestic inflation have reduced the substantial trade balance our country enjoyed until recently. We submit that a modest trade balance is a more normal situation. In our view, protectionist legislation should not be enacted in a misguided attempt to create a large trade surplus. On the contrary, if enacted, we could surely expect a chain reaction of trade restrictions throughout the free world.

The American Importers Association is strongly opposed to H. R. 16920 and all others like it. . . .

Now, I wish to explain our reasons for opposing H. R. 16920. . . . The establishment of restrictions on the imports of all textile products and nonrubber footwear is unwarranted and dangerous. It has not been established by the Tariff Commission or by any independent investigating committee that increased imports of these items have injured the domestic American industry. There is a provision in the Tariff Act by which the domestic industries involved can present their case to the Tariff Commission, if they feel they are injured. We believe that these industries have avoided this road to relief because they cannot prove injury. We believe that using political means to gain their ends will undermine the safeguards established by the Congress over many years. Furthermore, we feel sure that other countries would retaliate, and the United States would have no chance to soften the blow through compensatory negotiations. . . .

H.R. 16920 seeks to change the criteria of increased imports for escape clause relief from "major cause" to "substantial cause." This is weaker than the criteria proposed in the Administration bill, and a lower standard than is appropriate to make the escape clause an effective and workable mechanism. It would eliminate those provisions of the present Trade Act which limit the duration of an escape clause action to 4 years, and require an industry to justify an extension beyond that time. It would seriously change the definition of "domestic industry," and permit unlimited segmentation of an industry and an arbitrary carving out of a single company or even part of a company which might be injured by imports.

The Textile and Apparel Group and Footwear Group of our Association will present much more detailed arguments against this legislation when they appear before you later in these hearings.

In conclusion, our opposition to quota legislation is based on our conviction that of all trade barriers, quotas are the most onerous and the most self-defeating. They tend to carve sections of the market into exclusive preserves both for domestic industry and for some importers.

The importing business is a bastion of strength in the free enterprise system. Thousands of independent American businessmen are scouring the world for products which the American consumer wants at a price that he is willing and able to pay. This is free competition at its very best, and it should be the policy of our Government to give it the maximum encouragement.

Many thousands of people, including importers, shipping companies, customs brokers, and lawyers, in almost all the 50 States are rendering this service to their community.

We think that H.R. 16920 will be self-defeating, and will inevitably bring retaliation.

STATEMENT OF NELSON A. STITT [37]

Mr. Stitt. Mr. Chairman and members of the Ways and Means Committee, I am Nelson A. Stitt, Director of the United States-Japan Trade Council, an association of approximately 800 firms doing business in the United States and interested in promoting a growing healthy trade between the two countries. We appear here in support of proposed legislation which would advance this purpose and in opposition to proposed legislation which would inhibit the mutual exchange of goods. . . .

[Our statement follows.]

37. *Ibid.*, May 19, 1970, pp. 1066–1129.

Summary

Introduction

1. Japan has moved from a state of dependence on the United States, to a state of full independence and consciousness of national pride. Consequently, the United States demand that Japan impose limitations on its textile shipments to the United States, as well as the manner in which the demand has been made, is regarded in Japan as offensive to its self-respect.

2. Japanese goods are sold in the United States because Americans want and need them. The problems caused by imports involve a balancing of domestic interests, chiefly consumers versus groups requesting protection. Imports should not be discussed as if they were solely an issue between the supplying nation and the United States.

3. Japan is steadily removing its own restrictions on imports. The controls still remaining in Japan have little significant effect on the volume of United States transactions with Japan.

4. Contrary to some of the comments made during these hearings, Japan is cooperating loyally with the United States on both economic and political issues. There is no valid basis for invidious comments about Japanese business and government officials—because of the current United States trade balance deficit with Japan—when the United States runs similar trade deficits with Canada and Germany, about whom such comments are not made. . . .

The Mills Bill

We strongly oppose the provision of the Mills bill, H.R. 16920, which would place additional barriers upon United States imports, reduce the discretion of the Tariff Commission, unduly enlarge the reach of the escape clause, and hold to a minimum the President's authority to reduce tariffs. . . .

Textile Quotas

We are strongly opposed to legislatively-imposed quotas on textiles and apparel for the following reasons:

1. The United States textile and apparel industries have shown a healthy growth over the past decade in production, sales and profits and new investment.

2. Employment in these industries, in the face of growing automation, has risen about 300,000 between 1961 and 1969.

3. Textile imports in 1969 represented only 8.5% of total United States consumption.

4. Restrictions on textile imports would result in inflationary price rises to American consumers, especially in the low income brackets.

5. Mandatory import quotas on textiles would have a serious adverse

effect on United States exports of manufactured products and agricultural commodities.

6. Textile quotas would have a severely damaging impact on the economies of many underdeveloped countries in Asia and Latin America.

We urge that the textile issue be examined on a sector-by-sector basis, rather than seeking comprehensive across-the-board limitations.

United States–Japan Reciprocity

1. *Japan's Residual Import Restrictions.*—The Japanese Government has escalated its tempo of import liberalization in the past six months. It has decided to advance the final stage of Kennedy-round tariff cuts from January 1, 1972 to either January 1 or April 1, 1971, a move which will increase Japan's imports $400–$500 million next year. In spite of continued criticism in this country of Japan's import restrictions, United States exports to Japan during the past ten years have nearly tripled, and have increased more during that period than U.S. exports to any other country.

2. *Japan's Trade Surplus.*—It is well known that Japan had a $1.4 billion trade surplus with the United States and a $3.8 billion surplus with the world in 1969, but not generally realized that Japan had a record deficit in invisible trade which amounted to $1.3 billion in the same year. Japan's dependence on raw materials imports is so great that the government must maintain substantial foreign exchange reserves for protection against market fluctuations abroad.

3. *Voluntary Export Restraints and European Discrimination.*—Japan currently restricts "voluntarily" a wide range of exports to the United States. In addition, Western European countries maintain numerous discriminatory restrictions aimed solely at Japanese exports. European discrimination is gradually being reduced, but the Japanese are concerned about current United States moves in the direction of greater restrictions.

4. *Capital Liberalization.*—Japan is steadily liberalizing in the field of capital investment. Even under present restrictions, there are already in Japan more than 700 foreign subsidiaries, branch offices and joint ventures with foreign share ownership of 20% or more. The fourth round of liberalization, now expected in October, 1971, will complete liberalization in the sense of 50% foreign share ownership. . . .

The Chairman. We appreciate very much, Mr. Stitt, your bringing to us a very fine paper.

I want to thank you and tell the members of the committee about how you worked so hard with some of us a year or so ago to accomplish what I thought was an important elimination of an irritant that was arising through the arrangement of voluntary controls of steel imports from both the West, Japan, and the European Common Market.

Mr. Stitt. Can I inject a point there? I did work with the Japanese but, with the problems of antitrust that might be involved, I didn't work with Europe.

The Chairman. No, you didn't work with Europe.

Mr. Stitt. No, I worked with the Japanese.

The Chairman. You worked with the manufacturers of steel in Japan.

Mr. Stitt. Yes, sir.

The Chairman. None of us worked with the Japanese Government.

Mr. Stitt. That is right.

The Chairman. Our Government didn't do that.

Mr. Stitt. The Japanese Government didn't entirely agree with the arrangement.

The Chairman. I know. That arrangement was for 3 years.

Mr. Stitt. Yes, sir.

The Chairman. Will it just be a 3-year arrangement or do you think it will be extended?

Mr. Stitt. This, Mr. Mills, has to be a personal opinion.

The Chairman. I know it. I want your personal opinion.

Mr. Stitt. My personal opinion is that it will be extended for some period.

The Chairman. I am glad to hear that, because had you said no—

Mr. Stitt. Remember, this is a personal opinion.

The Chairman. Yes, I understand. But had you said no, there would have been another flock of people down here wanting a quota. You know that.

Mr. Stitt. Yes, sir.

The Chairman. You realize, of course, as an attorney more than most people around, because you have been here a long time, and you have dealt with the Congress, how the Congress itself reacts, too, to the pressures that are constantly on the Congress for some course of action. I have been telling some of our friends about these developments for some time.

I agree with you that it isn't good to write quota legislation. I don't like it. I don't like voluntary quotas. But I don't like to see one of our own industries, whatever that industry is, lose its position in the United States and not be able to grow as increased consumption grows in the United States. I must admit that the importation of textiles is not as great, percentagewise, as many of the other items that I can describe. There is some unemployment in the textile industry, so the Department of Commerce tells us, between April of this year and April of last year.

I believe they said there were 53,000 fewer jobs. What do you do about a thing like that when it happens? We all have these people as constituents. They vote for me if I do them right and they vote against me if I do them wrong. It is the same with all of us.

What do you do about a situation like that?

Mr. Stitt. I have two answers, sir. First, speaking as an economist rather than as a political person, I think that the textile industry is one of the low-paid industries in the country.

The Chairman. Yes.

Mr. Stitt. I think our unemployment level has not yet reached alarming proportions, and I think, as an economist, that the shift from low income industry to high income industry is to be encouraged.

The Chairman. I know it is fine to talk like that as an economist, but it is very hard for people involved to have to hear it.

Mr. Stitt. Now speaking as a pragmatic politician—

The Chairman. And I can understand you better.

Mr. Stitt (continuing). I have prepared a statement on the textile issue, sir, outside my regular statement because I thought this question might arise.

Much has been said about the textile issue during these hearings. First, let me define some terms. The entire question as it has been put to the Japanese by the U. S. negotiators seems to be a political question rather than an economic question.

The U. S. administration has tried to make an end run around the normal statutory procedures for injury determinations and has insisted that foreign governments agree to limit their shipments on an across-the-board, comprehensive basis.

Japan, after suggesting use of the GATT escape clause, article XIX, and declining to discuss the question in other terms, has since come a long way toward accepting a negotiated solution. But in my opinion the United States has not compromised significantly since the talks began. Therefore, the current impasse exists. Japan's major objections to the U. S. proposals are that they have been comprehensive and do not contain any proof-of-injury feature. In view of the official U. S. Government statistics indicating prosperity in the U. S. textile industry as a whole— and I have the figures if you would like to have them, sir—the Japanese Government cannot justify to its textile industry and its own people the need for comprehensive across-the-board export controls or even for semicomprehensive controls subject to a trigger formula on the products excluded from the semicomprehensive control.

There is such a thing as politics in Japan, too, sir. Their textile industry is just about as tough as ours.

Thus, a more selective approach, with a clause for proof of injury, would be a better basis for negotiation.

My own opinion is that if the United States were to propose a selective plan with a proof-of-injury factor, a textile agreement could quickly be negotiated.

The domestic textile industry has exerted tremendous pressure, as you know better, perhaps, than anyone else. The result has been a U. S. position of all or nothing in negotiations. It sometimes seems that the entire approach is calculated to invite the Congress to legislate quotas. If there is no negotiation, and the pressure for quotas becomes difficult to control, I hope you and the other members will realize that the situation has been occasioned by the rigidity of the U. S. negotiating position rather than by a reluctance on the part of Japan to negotiate on fair and reasonable terms.

I would suggest that before you take a step as drastic as legislating quotas—the Mills bill—and if at the time you mark up this bill a voluntary agreement is not reached, you follow two actions: One, direct the U. S. Tariff Commission or some other objective body to make an investigation of sectors of the industry that claim injury. I, myself, would be inclined to agree with you, sir, that men's shirts is one of the sectors of the industry that may well have an excellent claim, either before the Tariff Commission or anybody else, for some temporary remedy against the increasing imports.

Or, two, direct the U. S. negotiators to propose selective controls following some viable proof of injury to industry segments.

I think that an agreement would soon be forthcoming if such a proposal were made.

I want to make two comments about quota legislation of the type proposed in H.R. 16920.

First, the major loser would be American consumers, especially those in the lower income brackets, because, with the competitive effect of imports removed, their prices will rise and in the process the entire inflationary spiral will be stimulated.

Second, if provisions of H.R. 16920 were enacted, there is no assurance that there would be any greater incentive for Japan or any other nation to enter into voluntary agreements. The reason for this is that foreign nations might choose to have the United States establish a unilateral quota under which circumstances the foreign nation would be eligible for compensation under the GATT, and such compensation could only do harm to our higher income, highly productive, export industries.

The Chairman. The low-income consumer is going to be the loser if we enact the bill, and there are those who tell us that if we don't enact the bill the low-income people are going to be the losers, too. You must bear in mind that it is the high-labor-content industries in the United States that are having the problems.

The shoe industry doesn't have a very good record of wage payments to its employees in the United States. They are low-paid employees. Most of the textile industry, compared to other industries in the United States, is low-paid industry.

Most of these operations are in what we call the Appalachian areas of the United States, where there is underemployment to begin with, or unemployment to begin with. Most of the shoe plants in the country operate 300 to 500 employees and they are scattered around in practically every little county seat and town in my district and everywhere else. Textiles are in every little valley you come to throughout North Carolina, South Carolina, my State, and other States. You can't go over one hill and cross another hill without passing a textile plant in North Carolina, for instance. All of them are in the areas where poverty is prevalent.

So we actually may be on the horns of a dilemma. If we do one thing, we hurt; if we don't do one thing, we may be hurting the same people.

Mr. Stitt. I would say in the long run, Mr. Mills, that the answer for the poor people in Appalachia, in Arkansas, and some of these other areas, perhaps in some areas of Massachusetts, the best answer the U. S. Government can give to them, is adjustment assistance rather than affecting our foreign policy by erecting tariff walls or quotas.

The Chairman. If we can once get this family assistance program into operation and get our trade relations properly equated, we are going to eliminate poverty in the United States at least by 1975. We can't go along any longer than that with it.

Mr. Stitt. Adjustment assistance, sir, I believe—

The Chairman. That won't do it by itself.

Mr. Stitt. For these poor people in Appalachia and elsewhere, imports are only part of their problem. There are technological changes, changes in the market, changes in productivity. There are many, many things operating here. Imports do contribute. But I would be inclined to say that in many of these depressed areas, imports are not the greatest factor, not the greatest reason why these people are living on the poverty line.

The Chairman. Mr. Stitt, what would your response be if I tell you that I can envision this committee, with the capacity it has, developing a program that will apply across the board to provide for more orderly reception of imports into the United States without cutting anybody back, that would not in any way be in violation of GATT?

Of course, anything we do, they are going to say it is, but they can't prove it. Nobody is going to be injured as a result of our action here or abroad. We are just not going to let them have all of our market.

Mr. Stitt. I would deplore such action on the part of this committee.

The Chairman. I know you would. But I am asking you, if I told you that, would you think we could do it?

Mr. Stitt. I think it would be bad.

The Chairman. I am not talking about whether it would be good or bad. I know your opinion is that it would be bad.

Mr. Stitt. But don't you want the reason for my opinion? My reason is we live in a world which is shrinking very rapidly. To the extent we would erect barriers on the border to protect the domestic market, we would be losing ground to the rest of the nations of the world.

The Chairman. No; we would just be doing what the rest of the nations of the world have been doing since World War II and agreeing to undo with a great deal of reluctance.

Mr. Stitt. That is the general tenor about a great deal of conversation we have heard here. I do know about Japan and they are lowering barriers, not raising them.

The Chairman. If we enacted the bill that I had in mind, Japan's export of textiles to us would be reduced by four percent.

Mr. Stitt. That is right. No, of textiles across the board. In synthetic fibers, it would be reduced by about 40 percent.

The Chairman. I am talking about textiles across the board. For Taiwan, it would be about 50 or 55 percent.

Mr. Stitt. And we want to do that to Taiwan. Do we want to do that to South Korea, to Indonesia, to Singapore? No.

The Chairman. You have had tears in my eyes all the way through your testimony but you haven't changed my mind. You have affected my eyes but not my mind.

I have said repeatedly that I didn't get to be chairman of the Ways and Means Committee to preside over the destruction of any segment of our American industry, and I mean it.

STATEMENT OF GARDNER ACKLEY [38]

Dr. Ackley. Thank you, Mr. Chairman.

My name is Gardner Ackley. I have recently returned to the University of Michigan after having served, as you mentioned, as U. S. Ambassador to Italy and before that as a member and later chairman of the U. S. Council of Economic Advisers.

With me this morning is Mr. Eugene Keeney, president of the American Retail Federation, on whose behalf I am appearing here today. This organization, as you know, is a federation of 28 national retail associations and 50 statewide associations of retailers. It is the only organization which speaks for retailing as a whole, an industry which employs 8½ million persons.

I very much welcomed the invitation of the American Retail Federation to appear on its behalf before this distinguished committee, because my views on the legislation you are considering appear to be identical in all major respects with those of the federation. That this is so is not surprising: as the businessman closest to the consumer, the retailer tends to identify his interests with those of consumers. As social scientists concerned with the economic welfare of the Nation, economists tend also to identify with the consumer interest. The economist, however, sees no contradiction between a producer interest and a consumer interest. For all producers are also consumers. Their economic welfare is maximized when they direct their productive activities in the way which will earn them the highest possible real incomes—that is, when they produce that set of goods and services with the largest total real value to themselves as consumers.

It is a basic postulate of economic analysis that the economic welfare of the producer-consumer is maximized by the freest possible trade, both domestic and international. There are, of course, certain well-recognized, although limited, exceptions to this general presumption. But apart from these trade permits each producer to maximize his real earnings by producing those goods and services in which his efficiency is greatest, measured in terms of their value to consumers. Indeed, not only does trade permit each producer so to allocate his effort, it encourages him to do so, because, if he allocates it otherwise, competition forces him to earn less than is available to him elsewhere. This is no less true of international specialization and trade—through which the citizens of all participating nations benefit—than it is of the domestic specialization and trade which maximizes real income domestically.

Members of this committee have proved that they are well aware of these benefits of trade, through the constructive leadership they have given to the evolution of U. S. trade policy from that crucial turning point in 1934 through the Trade Expansion Act of 1962. Under the legislation you have guided through the Congress over these years, the United States has been able to take the leadership in the steady and accelerating progress of mutual trade liberalization which culminated in the Kennedy round of 1967. In significant part as a result of this mutual liberalization, there has been an extraordinary expansion of world trade, which has quadrupled since 1950. In turn, as a result of this amazing expansion of trade—and of other factors—the rate of world economic growth—as well as the rate of growth in almost every major trading nation—has been faster since 1950 than in any earlier period for which we have reliable data. . . .

I turn now to title I of H.R. 16920, which would impose highly restrictive import quotas on textiles, apparel, and footwear.

The American Retail Federation strongly opposes this proposal, for a number of reasons. The most basic reason is because it would interfere drastically and, in our view, unnecessarily, with an international trade in textiles, apparel, and footwear which benefits the overwhelming majority of Americans in their role as consumers. The reverse of the coin is less obvious but equally significant: the bill would provide an artificial incentive for too many productive resources to be directed toward industries in which U. S. productive efficiency—and therefore our ability to earn incomes—is relatively low. It would do this by restricting export markets for those American goods in which our productivity—and therefore the ability of U. S. nationals to earn incomes—is relatively high. We would lose both as consumers and producers.

Put this way, as the economist prefers to put it, it all seems very abstract. It can easily be made more concrete. The bill would directly raise prices for shoes and for textiles, both domestic and imported, in four different ways.

First, it would reduce the supplies of imported items which are relatively lower in price than their domestic counterparts, forcing consumers to purchase instead more of the latter. Exhibit A, attached to this statement, compares the prices of selected imported and domestic items of apparel, of essentially identical quality. These comparisons were supplied to the American Retail Federation by buyers for a number of retail establishments, and represent their best judgments of prevailing market conditions. The difference, especially when expressed as percentages, are striking.

Second, it would cut off some imports—especially of "low-end" goods —which have no domestic counterparts. They are not and would not be produced domestically even if there were no imports. For instance, about half of all footwear imports retail at prices less than $3 a pair. Imports of such low-end goods would not merely be reduced in the same proportion as all imports; with limited quotas, there would be strong incentive to export to the United States merchandise with maximum unit value. This form of price increase would, of course, bear most heavily on those Americans least able to pay higher prices. These include Americans with whose circumstances this committee has been concerned very recently —the recipients of public welfare and social security.

Third, it would raise the prices of the goods that continued to be imported. Price competition among foreign producers for entry into our markets would be materially lessened once they were unable to expand their sales by lower export prices.

Fourth, it would raise the prices of domestically produced goods. No longer needing to fear that higher prices would lose them markets beyond the quotas, American producers could and would raise prices directly. Moreover, with a lessened spur of foreign competition, the pressure on them to become more efficient would be reduced, so that their costs, and then their prices, would tend to drift up even more.

It is clear that these consequences fly directly in the face of the enlarged interest in consumer protection recently evidenced both by the administration and by the Congress.

The direct cost of quotas would thus be paid by consumers. But, it is argued, this may be a cost worth paying because:

(*a*) It will create, or at least protect, American jobs; and

(*b*) It will improve, or at least avoid a further deterioration of, the U. S. balance of payments.

I believe that neither of these advantages will ensue, and for the same reason: any reduction of U. S. imports as a result of quotas will be fully offset by a reduction of U. S. exports.

Reduced imports of textiles, apparel, and footwear would reduce the number of dollars flowing to foreigners. To some extent, this would directly reduce our exports, as well. But the main reason is that other nations whose exports would be hurt by our quotas would—as they have every right to do—impose equivalent barriers on U. S. exports. As a result, our balance of payments would not be improved and we would export as many jobs as we protected, and, on the whole they would be higher-paying jobs. Many of these jobs would almost surely be in agriculture.

If a nation suffers from a chronic general shortage of jobs—that is, from chronically excessive unemployment—it cannot ordinarily expect to find the remedy in exporting its unemployment; the intended recipients will simply reexport it—if possible, back where it came from. The remedy for excessive unemployment, we know, lies in another direction completely—in monetary and fiscal policy.

If a nation suffers from a serious and persistent balance-of-payments deficit that threatens to exhaust its international reserves, the remedy again must be found elsewhere—in basic structural changes in its economy; or, failing these, in uniform and temporary emergency surcharges on all imports or a uniform export subsidy; or, failing all else, in a realignment of exchange rates.

In the case of the U. S. deficit, the most important structural change we need to accomplish is to halt domestic inflation. We will not help to halt inflation by unnecessarily and substantially raising the prices of goods that make a significant contribution to the cost of living. We would thereby tend, as well, to enlarge wage increases, and thus give an extra lift to the prices of everything we produce, including, of course, our exports and our goods that compete with imports.

So far, however, I have not come directly to grips with the most immediate reason advanced for quotas: that they are the only remaining remedy available to redress or to prevent serious injury to two important American industries. Now, I have no doubt that there are segments of both industries which could demonstrate serious injury or the threat thereof. This is not demonstrated, however, merely by reciting phenomenal percentage increases in the imports of certain categories or classes of goods of which imports had previously been exceedingly small.

Serious injury is not demonstrated by showing that profits or wages or both in these industries are lower than in other industries or have recently declined. They have been chronically lower, long before any recent events which have created or threatened to create an alleged crisis. Nor should we expect profits or wages to move always in the same percentage in all industries. During most of the 1960's, for example, textile profits increased substantially faster than manufacturing profits generally, and I believe that textile wages also increased faster than all manufacturing wages.

Nor do we demonstrate serious injury merely by showing that employment has declined—as it has, slowly, in shoes, but not in textiles until 1969—or that sales or production have risen less or fallen more than in industry on the average. There are always many industries in which employment or sales or production have declined or risen less than the average.

If serious injury can be shown, relief should be granted—either through the liberalized escape clause or adjustment assistance, or, possibly, by some kind of voluntary limitation on exports to the United States. But, fundamental to any solution should be the proof of injury. The figures I have seen for the textile, apparel, and footwear industries do not demonstrate that injury has occurred to any of those industries, overall.

I was much impressed by the emphasis in Ambassador Gilbert's testimony before your committee last Monday on the concept that a nation can take measures of the sort here being considered only when injury occurs or is threatened—a concept which he called the keystone of the GATT international trading system.

With this concept, he said, "there could be no rule of law in trade, no reasonable expectation of certainty so necessary for economic activity, no means of policing or enforcing binding obligations. . . . It would not be difficult to envision the results if we were to cease to respect this concept or to embark on a unilateral course affecting the vital interests of others."

It is very easy to argue that the world trading system is already far from perfect, and that we here propose to do only what others are already doing even more than ourselves.

It is surely true that some important exporters to the United States of textiles, apparel, and footwear—Japan, in particular—have trading arrangements less liberal than ours. In the case of Japan, there can be no valid excuse for the slow progress it is making in removing its quotas and other restrictions. U. S. policy has been and must continue to be directed aggressively toward persuading Japan to liberalize more rapidly. Yet, we can hardly take a completely "holier-than-thou" attitude toward Japan's restrictions. The data in table 1 show that some $6.2 billion of U. S. imports in 1969—17 percent of our total imports—were of products on which the United States maintains import quotas.

Moreover, Japanese import barriers have not prevented a 3-percent increase in our nonagricultural exports to Japan over the 11 years 1958 to 1969, a 335-percent increase in our nonagricultural exports. They have not prevented an increase of our exports at an average annual rate of 18.8 percent a year over the years 1965 to 1969. This must be the highest of our export increases to any major trading nation.

I suggest that our only chance to persuade Japan—or other nations—to move more rapidly down the road toward more liberal trade would be destroyed were we to enact H.R. 16920. Some may take a certain gruesome satisfaction in pulling the house down on our heads because we find it is so imperfect. I do not. I would rather try to improve it.

In my view, the most dangerous of all consequences of the passage of H. R. 16920 is the danger that such action could set off a new chain reaction of protectionism and economic nationalism. During the great depression, nearly 40 years ago, we learned something of the disastrous effects —not only economic, but political, and ultimately perhaps military—of that kind of economic warfare. I hope you are aware that there is tinder lying around that would not be difficult to ignite. Protectionism and economic nationalism are sentiments found in every country. I should not want the United States to be the nation that lit the match.

Consequently, the American Retail Federation urges that this committee vote down H.R. 16920. Even in the event that the administration is unable to negotiate some appropriate voluntary restriction of textile imports, and even if the administration's promised proposals on footwear should fail to meet any legitimate problems of serious injury in that industry, the action proposed in H.R. 16920, in our view, is worse than no solution at all.

Thank you, Mr. Chairman.

7. *JAPAN'S VOLUNTARY RESTRAINT*

Despite the expressions of alarm and negative testimony, the House of Representatives passed the Ways and Means Committee's trade bill without change on November 19, 1970, by a vote of 215 to 165. The time of the 91st Congress ran out, however, before the Senate could approve an even more protectionist version of the House bill that had been reported out by the Senate Finance Committee.

The 92nd Congress could start the legislative process again—but both Representative Mills and President Nixon wanted to avoid another round of highly protectionist import legislation. Representative Mills even went so far as to undertake negotiations himself with the Japanese Textile Federation, saying, "If an agreement is worked out, it would diminish the chance that quotas would be included in this year's trade legislation." [39] The Japan Textile Federation announced its own plan of export restraint (March 8, 1971).

MILLS AND THE JAPAN TEXTILE FEDERATION [40]

TOKYO, March 8—The Japan Textile Federation, which represents all major groups in the textile field, declared today that it would voluntarily restrict exports of textiles to the United States for a three-year period beginning July 1.

The declaration, announced at a crowded news conference here by Toyosaburo Taniguchi, the federation's president, was immediately relayed to Representative Wilbur D. Mills, chairman of the House Ways and Means Committee, in Washington. The federation hopes the declaration, which was hedged with several important reservations, will prove sufficient to kill trade-quota legislation in Congress.

In today's declaration, the Federation proposed to restrict cotton textiles, wool textiles and man-made-fiber textile exports, excluding yarn and raw materials, to the United States for three years, after a three-month preparatory period—in other words, beginning July 1.

During the first year of the restrictions, textile exports would be 5 per cent higher than during the previous year. The second year would see a

39. *Wall Street Journal*, Feb. 26, 1971.
40. *New York Times*, March 9, 1971.

6 per cent increase beyond the first year's total and the third year another 6 per cent increase. These quotas would be imposed on a physical —that is, quantitative—basis rather than a value basis.

The most important reservation in this declaration concerned actions by other textile-exporting countries. These countries were not specified, but Mr. Taniguchi made clear in his news conference that the federation was thinking of South Korea, Taiwan and Hong Kong, not of European countries.

If these "other countries" do not enforce similar restrictions, Japan will not do so either. Japan's restrictions will begin from the first calendar month after restrictions imposed by these "other countries." The three-month preparatory period is for the purpose of getting the United States to persuade these "other countries" to go along with Japan, Mr. Taniguchi explained.

In a preamble to the declaration, the federation said it was restricting exports not because it admitted that such exports had caused "serious injury or market disruption" but in order to prevent the rise of "trade protectionism in the United States," which it said would "pose a serious threat to free trade throughout the world."

Officials of the federation are said to respect Representative Mills as an influential opponent of protectionism, despite his sponsorship last year of a trade-quota bill that was passed by the House but died in the Senate. They say that today's declaration does not differ in any important respect from proposals they say were relayed to them last month from Representative Mills via Michael Daniels, their lobbyist in Washington. They hope their declaration will provide Mr. Mills and other free-trade advocates in Congress with the ammunition needed to head off any new protectionist legislation this year.

The officials also expect their declaration to make unnecessary further negotiations over textile restraints, which the Japanese and United States Governments have been carrying on intermittently for nearly two years.

Without actually saying so in their declaration, federation officials believe that the main reason for textile restraints is political, not economic. They believe Premier Eisaku Sato made a political promise to President Nixon to restrain textile exports in gratitude for the President's decision to return Okinawa to Japan.

The imposition of over-all quotas instead of detailed categorization as demanded in earlier negotiations by the United States Department of Commerce allows the industry some possibility of shifts between manmade fiber textile exports, which have been growing rapidly, and cotton and woolen textiles, which have been declining.

Whereas the United States prefers restrictions by value, the Japanese have insisted on restrictions on a quantitative basis, saying that this is the only way they can encourage producers to shift from low-cost, low-profit items to sophisticated high-profit items especially in the manmade-fiber field.

Today's declaration was accepted by all 23 major textile groups represented at the federation's executive council meeting this afternoon and evening, Mr. Taniguchi said. At the same time, considering the plight of small- and medium-sized enterprises, especially in the apparel field, the federation appealed to the Government for tax relief, loans and other measures to compensate members of the textile industry for any losses suffered because of these restrictions.

The Federation's declaration was immediately denounced by American textile producers and unions. Howard W. Swank, chairman of the Man-Made Fiber Producers Association, said the Japanese plan "does not solve the problem brought about by the flood of imports." And leaders of the four major American textile unions called the Japanese move "inadequate and totally unsatisfactory" and said it would lead to "utter chaos in the American market." [41]

Within three days, President Nixon joined in rejecting the announced plan as inadequate, and once again he threw his "strong support" behind legislation that would restrict textile imports by mandatory quotas. But he also left open the possibility of resuming negotiations on voluntary textile quotas with the Japanese government, provided they were "meaningful."

STATEMENTS BY NIXON AND MILLS [42]

Statement by the President

For two years, this Administration has attempted to negotiate a voluntary agreement with the Government of Japan curtailing the excessive wool and man-made fiber textile imports from Japan. The United States has sought to be as flexible as possible concerning the details of an agreement while consistently adhering to certain basic principles, which we consider essential to any agreement designed to curb these excessive imports. These principles are reflected in the following terms which have been presented to the Japanese Ambassador by the United States negotiator in meetings through January of this year:

A limited number of categories of particularly sensitive products, covering about one-half of those imports, would be assigned specific import ceilings. The ceilings would be based upon imports from Japan in 1969, plus a reasonable growth factor. Shifting of imports among these categories would be permitted so as to reflect changing conditions in the

41. *Ibid.*, March 10, 1971.
42. *Ibid.*, March 12, 1971.

United States market, subject to limitations to avoid excessive concentration in any of these sensitive categories.

If imports from Japan of any other category exceeded the 1970 import level, plus a more liberal growth factor, the United States could request consultation with Japan, and impose specific limitations if a mutually satisfactory solution was not reached.

On Monday, following discussions between its Washington representative and the Chairman of the House Ways and Means Committee, the Japan Textile Federation announced that the Japanese textile industry is undertaking a unilateral program to limit future exports of textile products to the United States. At the same time, the Government of Japan issued a public statement endorsing this unorthodox action by a private Japanese group and terminating its negotiations with the United States Government. On its face, this unilateral program falls short of the terms essential to the United States in the following significant respects:

Only one over-all ceiling for all cotton, wool and man-made fiber fabric and apparel textiles is provided, with only a general understanding by the Japanese industry "to prevent undue distortions of the present pattern of trade." This allows concentration on specific categories, which could result in these categories growing many times faster than the over-all limits.

The over-all ceiling would be based on imports from Japan in the year ending March 31, 1971, plus a growth factor. During the two years that we have been negotiating with the Government of Japan, imports of man-made fiber textile products have greatly increased, and in January, 1971, they entered this country at a record-breaking level. Moreover, the program magnifies the potential growth of the sensitive categories by including in the base exports of cotton products which are already limited by agreement and which have been declining.

The deficiencies in the Japanese industry program make it clear that it will not result in an acceptable solution. It is well known that I would prefer a negotiated agreement to solve this problem. The answer of the Japanese industry, now apparently ratified by the Government of Japan, has effectively precluded further meaningful Government-to-Government negotiations, the resumption of which this country would welcome.

Consequently, I will strongly support the textile quota provisions of the legislation now pending before the Congress, H.R. 20, a bill passed by the House of Representatives last year and reintroduced this year by Chairman Mills and Congressman Byrnes of the Ways and Means Committee.

At the same time, I am directing the Secretary of Commerce to monitor imports of wool and man-made fiber textile products from Japan on a monthly basis. I am instructing that this monitoring begin immediately, with the results, including an analysis of any differences from what would have been the results under the terms we presented, to be made available to the entire Congress.

Under the circumstances and in order to provide the relief necessary for United States textile workers and businesses this government must now give the fullest consideration to other alternative solutions to the textile problem.

Statement by Mills

I understand that the President and his advisors, after considering the recent initiative of the Japanese Textile Federation toward a solution of the problem of textile imports, have decided to reject the Japanese proposal. Having responded on many occasions to requests from Administration officials during the past two years to assist in furthering a negotiated settlement of this problem, I am both surprised and disappointed at this decision.

This rejection of the Japanese initiative not only involves honest differences of opinion as to the extent and the nature of restraints on textile exports to the United States, it involves the very core of our trade relations with the textile exporting countries and indeed with our ability to deal on a realistic basis with the problems all our industries face in competing in our own markets and abroad.

While I can perhaps understand the position taken by the leaders in the textile industry in opposing the proposal, and I assume that they have given it serious study, it is difficult to understand an out-of-hand rejection of the proposal after two years of unsuccessful attempts to negotiate a settlement. My support of the industry's efforts and my support of the Administration's efforts to obtain a solution to this problem are a matter of public record. I regret that at this time the decision has been made to reject this avenue toward a meaningful accommodation of the international textile trade problem.

The President apparently knows of another way to obtain the protection which the textile industry is seeking, and, at the same time, prevent other protectionist developments from accompanying that relief, but I do not.

As I have pointed out before in several different ways, the stakes involved in an early settlement of the textile controversy are very great. Obviously, our trade problems go far beyond just the question of textiles, and I cannot understand how under any circumstances a statutory program for the protection of a single industry can be developed which is exclusive of consideration of statutory programs for other affected industries. As I have already said, I await with considerable interest the presentation of such a program by the Administration.

At this point, as one commentator concluded, the situation seemed to be in a state of impasse: Japan said negotiations were over; the President backed legislated quotas; Mr. Mills, whose role was crucial, opposed quotas.[43]

A bleak picture continued to confront the textile industry. And industry executives and union representatives were becoming ever-more anxious for the conclusion of government-to-government agreements.

TEXTILE WOE [44]

The $21-billion a year American textile industry, which understandably doesn't like bad news, is pointing to some recent negative announcements as confirmation of its oft-expressed fears over the flood of imports.

Domestic industry sales have been mostly stagnant since 1968, textile-company heads point out, while total textile and apparel imports from Jan. 1 through April 30 have risen 42 per cent over 1970's level. But developments in the last few weeks underscore the industry's problems, one of which is imports.

Those developments are a reduction in its quarterly dividend by J. P. Stevens & Co., the industry's second-largest company, the closing of three worsted plants by Burlington Industries, Inc., the largest producer, and lowered stock values for textile concerns. . . .

Industry earnings in the year's first quarter have declined about 14 per cent to $93-million from $109-million in the like 1970 quarter, according to the American Textile Manufacturers Institute, a trade group.

Last week, Donald F. McCullough, chairman of the Collins & Aikman Corporation, a leading textile company, said that the recent developments "prove at least to some degree what we in the industry have been saying for the last 3 or 4 years on the imports problem."

Some media and some opponents of legislated import quotas have criticized domestic textile producers for their insistence on new restrictions, he said. "They have called us greedy, conniving and downright wrong," observed Mr. McCullough, "but the fact remains that the latest figures on man-made fiber imports are simply staggering. The erosion of our industry is continuing and getting worse."

On the total man-made fiber imports, an A.T.M.I. spokesman in Charlotte reported that the levels in both March and April had reached record proportions. . . .

In 1971's first quarter, man-made fiber imports rose 81 per cent to 1,380,000,000 square yards from 764,000,000 square yards.

However, in the midst of this rather bleak picture, there are some hints of a likely pickup in industry sales for the year, mainly because of

43. Edwin L. Dale, Jr., *ibid.*, March 12, 1971.
44. *Ibid.*, July 4, 1971.

an improved environment in the economy, which should help the textile industry, according to A.T.M.I.'s spokesman. . . .

Industry sales were $21.5-billion in 1968, $21.3-billion in 1969 and $21.2-billion in 1970, and should be between $21.5-billion and $21.6-billion in 1971, he said.

But, as far as industry earnings this year, the trade group spokesman believes that the first-quarter decline indicates an annual rate below the $413-million of 1970. That year's industry net compares with $621-million in 1969 and $654-million in 1968.

A GLOOMY PICTURE [45]

[I]ndustry claims that imports have cost the U. S. 150,000 jobs in the textile and apparel industry since the start of 1970 and that imports have soared by 33% so far this year to an annual rate equal to about 15% of U. S. consumption in a stagnant market. As a result, the industry asserts, the nation's trade deficit on textile products now is running at an annual rate of nearly $2 billion.

Executives of the U. S. industry, which has annual sales of $22 billion, express more uncertainty over the industry's near-term prospects than do some financial analysts, who cite some strengthening of production, price, and employment statistics at mid-year. The analysts also are bullish on the outlook for carpets and other textile home-furnishings on the basis of this year's increased housing starts and completions.

But so far, and with few exceptions, textile profits are gloomy. Industrywide earnings per dollar of sales are down to 1.7 cents this year from 3.8 cents in 1965. That far exceeds the retreat in profits for all nondurable manufactures, to 4.4 from 5.5 cents.

Red ink now smears the ledgers of such historically profitable textile producers as J. P. Stevens, Dan River and Bibb Manufacturing. Three-year-long earnings declines aren't uncommon, with even Burlington expected to join that list when it reports for the fiscal year ended Oct. 2. And West Point-Pepperell just confirmed its profits retreated in the year ended Aug. 28 for the fifth consecutive year.

The industry has responded to these setbacks by slashing dividends, curtailing employment and closing mills. And by intensifying its campaign to reduce import competition.

Dan River halted dividend payments in mid-1970 and this spring laid off 600, or over 15%, of its salaried employees. Last November, West Point-Pepperell closed a 900-employee plant in Maine, and Bibb Manufacturing will by year's end padlock four Georgia mills in which 1,100 workers now toil. (Bibb, blaming its troubles on past tariff cuts,

45. *Wall Street Journal*, Oct. 18, 1971. Reprinted by permission of the *Wall Street Journal*.

recently appealed to the Tariff Commission for adjustment aid to forestall further retrenchment; a decision is due Nov. 1.)

All told, says the American Textile Manufacturers Institute, 92 textile mills that employed at least 19,911 workers in 17 states (but mostly in the Carolinas and Georgia) have been closed since October 1968. The trade association's tally includes the toll since last October of 30 mills with 9,718 workers in nine states.

Some textile men privately blame much of this attrition on President Nixon's failure until now to grapple with either the import avalanche or the domestic economic stagnation.

Textile workers' wages now average $2.56 an hour, or about $1 below the average for all manufacturing workers, and for the first time in 10 years they aren't going up—and not just because of the wage-price freeze. They wouldn't be increased, anyway, most industry leaders agree, because profits are too depressed.

8. GOVERNMENT-TO-GOVERNMENT TALKS

Despite President Nixon's strong rejection of voluntary Japanese export controls, the Japan Textile Federation maintained that it would proceed with its own unilaterally declared three-year export control plan beginning July 1, 1971. Throughout the summer months of 1971 American officials were attempting to reach some agreement with South Korea, Hong Kong, and Taiwan. But their positions remained far apart on the amount of exports of noncotton goods to be allowed, in what specific categories, and for what time period. After the announcement of the Nixon Administration's New Economic Policy on August 15, 1971, there was less patience with continued attempts at negotiation. The Administration let it be known—or rather, issued an ultimatum—that it would impose mandatory quotas by an October 15, 1971, deadline unless the Asian governments reached agreement with the United States.

If Presidential advisers were insisting to the Japanese government that the United States now had no intention of compromising on the textile trade dispute, Japan's textile industry was equally determined to resist moves toward a pact between the Japanese and American governments. The Japan Textile Federation issued a statement that the Tokyo Government was about to conclude a "humiliating" agreement with the United States, "under strong American pressure and based on harsh terms that would deal a crushing blow to the industry for a long time." The textile industry, with almost 2 million workers, stated it would unite to combat any Government surrender to the American demands.[46]

Notwithstanding the strong opposition from its own textile industry—but recognizing the continued pressures from the United States and the progress by the United States toward agreements with the other Asian textile-exporting countries—the Japanese Cabinet decided to resume government-level negotiations. Japan's government now recognized that negotiated quotas might be a lesser evil than mandatory import quotas, and they also saw the possibility of the removal of the 10 per cent surcharge on noncotton textiles in exchange for a government-guaranteed textile agreement.

8.1. Formal Agreements Reached. On the deadline date for concluding agreements, it was announced that the negotiators for Japan and the United States had initialed an agreement limiting the flow of Japanese exports to the American markets and that the United States agreed to remove its import surcharge. Central to the agreement were these provisions:

A base level of 900 million square yards for all man-made fiber textiles and a base level of 50 million square yards for wool textiles. These were to be distributed in categories according to Japanese exports to the United States during the year ending on March 31, 1971.

An overall growth rate in exports of 5 per cent a year for man-made fibers and 1 per cent a year for wool products.

Six groups of man-made and wool textiles accounting for 450 million square yards subdivided into eighteen categories for which specific growth rates would range from 2½ to 10 per cent.

The formal agreement was signed on January 3, 1972.

UNITED STATES-JAPAN TEXTILE AGREEMENT [47]

Preamble: The purpose of this Arrangement is to prevent an abrupt increase and to provide for orderly development of export trade in wool and man-made fiber textiles from Japan to the United States consistent with the healthy development of the textile economies of both countries.

For this purpose and in accordance with the provisions of this Arrangement, Japan will conduct her exports to the United States of wool and

46. *New York Times*, Oct. 9, 1971.
47. The full text is in Department of State Press Release, No. 1, Jan. 4, 1972.

man-made fiber textile products to see to it that an aggregate annual increase in the exports of such products will not be in excess of the levels provided for in the Arrangement, and the United States will give consideration in implementing this Arrangement to assuring the full utilization of such levels by Japan.

1. (a) The provisions of this Arrangement will be implemented by the two Governments in accordance with the laws and regulations applicable in their respective countries.

(b) The Government of Japan will apply the restraints provided for in this Arrangement to exports of wool and man-made fiber textiles to the United States for three years beginning October 1, 1971.

2. The two Governments recognize that their rights and obligations under the General Agreement on Tariffs and Trade are not affected by this Arrangement.

3. (a) The annual overall limits for wool and man-made fiber textiles for the three years of this Arrangement are as follows:

Square Yards Equivalent

October 1, 1971 — September 30, 1972	997,500,000
October 1, 1972 — September 30, 1973	1,047,400,000
October 1, 1973 — September 30, 1974	1,099,800,000

(b) Within the annual overall limits provided for in subparagraph (a) above, the annual overall limits for wool textiles will be 42,833,000 square yards equivalent for the first arrangement year, 43,261,000 square yards equivalent for the second arrangement year and 43,694,000 square yards equivalent for the third arrangement year.

(c) Within the annual overall limits provided for in subparagraph (a) above, the annual overall limits for man-made fiber textiles will be 954,667,000 square yards equivalent for the first arrangement year, 1,004,139,000 square yards equivalent for the second arrangement year and 1,056,106,000 square yards equivalent for the third arrangement year.

4. Within the applicable annual overall limits for wool and man-made fiber textiles set forth in paragraph 3, the annual limits for certain groups of categories, subgroups of categories and specific categories are as set forth in, or determined in accordance with, Annex A. . . .

6. (a) (i) If, during any arrangement year, the Government of the United States of America considers that imports from Japan in any category not set out in Annex A or in any particular product within any category set out in Annex A are increasing so as to cause or threaten to cause disruption in the United States market, the Government of the United States of America will request consultations with the Government of Japan.

(ii) Pending a mutually satisfactory solution between the two

Governments, the Government of Japan will limit exports for that arrangement year in the category or product, as to which such consultations have been requested, to 105 percent for man-made fiber textile categories or products and 103 percent for wool textile categories or products of the level of imports into the United States from Japan of such category or product during the most recent twelve month period preceding the month in which the request for consultations was made for which relevant data are available to the two Governments.

(b) With respect to categories not set forth in Annex A, consultations referred to in subparagraph (a) above will be requested whenever imports from Japan in a twelve month period in such category increase to the level of the imports from Japan of such category for the twelve month period ending March 31, 1971, compounded for each arrangement year by 10 percent for each man-made fiber textile category and 3 percent for each wool category.

Consultations will not be requested for any category under this subparagraph when imports from Japan in such category are not more than 500,000 square yards equivalent for each man-made fiber textile category other than apparel, 350,000 square yards equivalent for each man-made fiber apparel category, and 100,000 square yards equivalent for each wool category. . . .

In the event such consultations are requested at the levels indicated in this subparagraph and pending a mutually satisfactory solution between the two Governments, the Government of Japan will limit the exports in the category in question in the arrangement year in question to the level of imports in such category to the United States from Japan which formed the basis for the consultation request.

(c) Any consultations provided for in this paragraph will be held and concluded promptly. The Government of the United States of America will provide a detailed factual statement of reasons and justification for its request for consultations, including relevant data on imports from third countries. The Government of the United States of America will make similar consultation requests to the Governments of other countries whose exports to the United States of wool and man-made fiber textiles are subject to restraint in cases where imports from such countries in the same category or product are increasing. . . .

12. The validity of this Arrangement is for the period of three years beginning October 1, 1971. During the third year of this Arrangement, the two Governments will consider extending the Arrangement for a further period of time.

13. Each Government may at any time propose modification of this Arrangement. The other Government will give sympathetic consideration to such a proposal.

Annex A. Textile Quotas

Group and Category	Category distribution within group (per cent)	Group limits First year	(Square yards equivalent) Second year	Third year
Group I (7.5 per cent)	100.0000	156,837,000	164,965,000	173,502,000
206 Woven fabrics, cellulosic, wholly of continuous man-made fiber	23.8945			
210(a) Woven fabrics, other, of man-made fibers except glass fibers	12.5392			
211 Knit fabrics	63.5663			
Group II (5 per cent)	100.0000	152,409,000	160,307,000	168,603,000
208 Woven fabrics, other, wholly of continuous man-made fiber	77.5503			
209 Woven fabrics, other, wholly of noncontinuous fibers	22.4497			
Group III				
Subgroup A (10 per cent)	100.0000	35,411,000	37,246,000	39,173,000
216 Dresses, knit	17.4836			
222 Trousers, slacks and shorts, knit, women's, girls' and infants'	42.3622			
236 Skirts, not knit	9.1853			
238 Trousers, slacks and shorts, not knit	30.9689			

Annex A. Textile Quotas cont.

Group and Category	Category distribution within group (per cent)	Group limits First year	(Square yards equivalent) Second year	Third year
Subgroup B (2.5 per cent)	100.0000	92,596,000	97,394,000	102,435,000
219 Shirts, other (including blouses), knit	26.1617			
221 Sweaters and cardigans, knit	42.6556			
229 Coats, not knit	31.1827			
Group IV (5 percent)	100.0000	35,298,000	37,127,000	39,048,000
228 Blouses, not knit	29.7074			
234 Dress shirts, not knit	38.0051			
235 Shirts, other, not knit	32.2875			
Group V (2.5 per cent)	100.0000	27,343,000	27,616,000	27,893,000
104 Woven fabrics of wool, including blankets (carriage robes, lap robes, steamer rugs, etc.) over 3 yards in length	100.0000			
Group VI (5 per cent)	100.0000	3,945,000	3,985,000	4,025,000
120 Men's and Boys' suits	35.5068			
124 Trousers, slacks and shorts	64.4932			

NOTE: Exports in any category within a group or subgroup may not exceed 103 percent of the group or subgroup limit for that category (as adjusted by the percentage shown) multiplied by the percentage which the category accounted for of the total of U. S. imports from Japan of the categories in that group (subgroup in Group III) during the twelve-month period ending March 31, 1971.

Taiwan, South Korea, and Hong Kong agreed to similar textile export limitations—but for five years, with an allowable export growth rate of 7½ per cent a year for man-made textiles and 1 per cent a year for wool textile products. In signing the Agreements for the United States, Ambassador-at-Large David M. Kennedy stated in each case that the Agreement will significantly contribute toward improving the friendly climate between the two countries and specifically provide the framework for helping their textile economies. He further expressed the view that the Agreement will allow reasonable growth of each exporting country's textile industry while preventing sudden and inordinate penetration into the United States market causing harm to the United States textile industry.

8.2. *Reactions.* President Nixon hailed the Japanese agreement as "a hopeful sign for the continuation of good relations with Japan" and as having prevented the "erection of permanent protective walls around the United States." [48] But other reactions were distinctly different. A *New York Times* editorial stated:

TEXTILE AGREEMENT [49]

The agreement bludgeoned out of the Japanese and other Asian synthetic textile exporters yesterday represents a victory on the part of President Nixon and the Southern textile industry, but at a cost to American long-range international political and economic interests that has yet to be fully calculated.

By threatening the Japanese, South Koreans, Taiwanese, etc., with an economic atom bomb in the form of mandatory import quotas, the Administration has indeed forced all these close allies of the United States to capitulate on an economic "Missouri." Whatever rationalizations or justifications can be advanced for specific terms of the agreement, the manner in which this policy is being carried out bodes ill for the future of America's economic relations with the rest of the world.

It cannot be denied that the Japanese have a highly protectionist record themselves and proved generally recalcitrant and uncooperative in the long negotiations aimed at loosening their autarkic economic policy. To this extent, they invited American retaliation. But, no matter how great the provocation, the sea waves emanating from this turn in American trade policy can have disastrously self-defeating consequences in the context of proclaimed American political goals and the relationships with this country's closest allies in Asia and Europe as well.

The agreement severely limits the growth of noncotton textile imports

48. *New York Times*, Oct. 16, 1971.
49. *Ibid.*, Oct. 16, 1971.

from the Asian countries for a three-to-five-year period, and in return the United States is lifting the 10 percent import surcharge that had been imposed in August. However, the surcharge has not been applied to items covered by quota arrangements, so this concession was in line with already existing policy. While there is no question that the meteoric rise of Asian textiles, particularly synthetics, has been a source of great and legitimate concern to certain segments of the American industry, there is also little doubt that the newly imposed limitations will ultimately increase the costs of these products to the American consumer— even though Japanese textiles last year accounted for only 1.2 percent of the dollar value of the American textile market.

The agreement certainly represents a victory for President Nixon and the textile lobby; but it will turn out to be a pyrrhic victory if it sets the pace for increasingly restrictive policies in the field of world trade.

As could be expected, Tokyo officials did not share the satisfaction of the American administration.

WITH TEXTILE PACT, ILLWILL [50]

TOKYO, Oct. 15—The Japanese have a proverb, "Nama byoho wa okizu no moto," which means "Crude tactics cause great injuries."

By using diplomatic tactics that American officials here readily concede were rough and unorthodox, representatives of the Nixon Administration succeeded tonight in getting the Japanese Government to limit textile exports to the United States. The American officials justified their tactics by contending that the Japanese would not believe the United States would take action. They said that no agreement would have been reached without resorting to a tough line.

That agreement has resolved a prolonged trade dispute. But it has left the Japanese angry, resentful and determined to retaliate sooner or later. They are unhappy with the terms of the understanding—but they are outraged by the way they believe it was forced on them.

A senior Japanese official, asked what he thought the repercussions would be, said: "It's going to be bad, very bad. People here just won't forget how this was done."

The official, who deeply believes that Japan's best interests are served by a close alliance with the United States, said he feared the illwill generated by the manner in which the negotiations were handled would only add bitterness to Japan's already deteriorating relations with the United States.

American officials acknowledged that they expected more resistance from the Japanese Government on other economic issues, such as the reduction of trade barriers, elimination of restrictions on American invest-

50. *Ibid.*, Oct. 16, 1971.

ment in Japan, and revaluation of the yen—all objectives of President Nixon's economic policies.

But they argue that it had been necessary to take a tough stand on the textile issue to win the respect of the Japanese.

Some American businessmen said they have long felt that the United States Government was not exerting itself enough on their behalf. But they contended that the Nixon Administration had chosen the wrong issue on which to take a stand and had gone about it the wrong way.

Several argue that the Administration has used up bargaining chips on a relatively insignificant issue. American officials said tonight that Japanese exports of the items at issue would take only about 3 percent of the American market.

Japanese sources reported that Kakuei Tanaka, the Minister of International Trade and Industry, who negotiated for Japan, was furious over the American approach. Mr. Tanaka is the most powerful member of Parliament here and a potential Premier.

POLITICS AND TEXTILES [51]

TOKYO, Oct. 14—"The Japanese, Taiwanese, South Koreans and the people of Hong Kong are together going to contribute to the campaign funds which President Nixon hopes will get him re-elected next November."

This statement, by Derek Davies, editor of the Far Eastern Economic Review, sums up the attitude of embittered Government officials and industry leaders in the four countries over the United States position and tactics in the textile dispute.

Faced with an ultimatum threatening stiff import quotas, which officials contend would cripple their industries, Japan, Hong Kong, Taiwan and South Korea agreed to negotiate Government-enforced restrictions on their exports of non-cotton and wool textiles to the United States. They believe politics in America forced them to do it.

Three years and two months ago, Richard M. Nixon, Republican Presidential candidate, made a campaign pledge, aimed at attracting Southern votes, to curb these textile imports, just as President Kennedy had done with cotton eight years before.

Now, President Nixon appears on the verge of keeping part of his promise, but many Asian leaders question whether the prize was worth the cost. The cost, they contend, includes the following:

The price of clothing in the United States will eventually go up, contributing to the inflation the President is battling to curb.

Already strained United States-Japan relations have been worsened by Washington's ultimatum and basically uncompromising position, and the already wobbly Government of Prime Minister Eisaku Sato faces the wrath of a powerful Japanese textile industry.

Hundreds of small factories are expected to close, putting hundreds of

51. *Ibid.*, Oct. 15, 1971.

thousands of workers out of jobs in Taiwan and South Korea, after the United States has spent millions of dollars in foreign-aid funds to help develop the industry.

In Japan, according to a spokesman for the Japan Synthetic Fibers Association, an estimated total of 300,000 workers would lose their jobs because of a decline in production specifically due to conclusion of a Government agreement with the United States. But industry spokesmen probably tend to exaggerate, much as American industry did earlier when the Japanese challenged them to prove losses caused by Japanese imports.

In 1969 and 1970, a total of 830 small and medium-sized textile manufacturing companies in Japan went bankrupt. The cause was a sharp decline in orders, due not only to the general recession but also to the anticipation by traders of the voluntary export restrictions that went into effect.

The number of workers put out of jobs by these bankruptcies was not known, the Synthetic Fibers Association spokesman said.

But it is the feeling that politics is at the bottom of the dispute that especially disturbs the Asians. As Mr. Davies wrote:

"The most objectionable aspect to the American ultimatum is not simply that it probably violates the rules of the General Agreement on Tariffs and Trade or that it is of doubtful legality even under American law. The unforgivable fact is that it has no economic justification whatsoever."

While American officials argue that it is justified as one way of reducing the United States trade deficit, Asian officials argue that this case is less than convincing. Of the total United States non-cotton and wool imports, they note, these four countries contribute only 28 percent. And this amounts to less than 6 percent of what the United States consumes each year. Most of what the United States consumes it produces itself.

Special concern was expressed over the adverse impact of quotas on the less-developed textile-exporting countries. Korea, for instance, had been heralded (not least by the United States Agency for International Development) as a "success story" of development: it was a model of structural transformation and export-led growth, with a marked rise during the 1960's in manufactured exports, of which textile products had come to comprise more than 41 per cent in 1971. And it had been a major recipient of American foreign aid, with close political relations. The third Five-Year Plan (1972–76) envisaged an average annual increase of 8.6 per cent in real GNP, with textile exports expected to grow from $421 million in 1971 to

$1237 million in 1976, for a total increase in GNP between 1972 and 1976 of $4628 million. Textile quotas were now unhappily expected to force a retreat from these targets.

KOREANS BITTER [52]

SEOUL, Korea—Two months after an agreement with the United States that limited Korean textile exports to the American market, South Korea officials have assessed the consequences of the pact and do not like what they see.

Similarly, four months after President Nixon imposed the 10 per cent import surcharge and floated the dollar, those economic officials are unhappy with the results although they have been unable to assess them as well as the textile impact.

Both actions have left the South Koreans a bit bitter. They contend that the two policies do not make sense after the United States has poured so much economic aid into Korea over the last 20 years to get it onto its feet—and then set the nation back with restrictive trade barriers.

Moreover, South Korean officials express chagrin because they believe that both policies were intended to hit the Japanese but the blows glanced off and hurt Korea, a much weaker nation economically.

The Korean officials said the textile agreement, which limits exports of synthetic fibers, would not have much over-all impact on this year's export figures since they were running ahead of projections before the pact went into effect on Oct. 1.

But they project a $1-billion shortfall of targets over the next five years as a result of the agreement. That is a lot of money in an economy with a gross national product of $6.9-billion in 1970 and one that officials plan to raise to $13.3-billion in a third five-year plan ending in 1976.

The Korean textile industry currently provides about 20 per cent of industrial production, one-third of all exports, one-third of Korean exports to the United States, and 400,000 jobs in an industrial labor force of 1.3 million people.

Korean economic officials say that they hope to offset some of the anticipated foreign-exchange losses by switching the textile industry to higher-quality, higher-priced goods. But that will not help the production figures, where a 1.5 per cent decline is expected next year.

More important, the switch will not help employment because fewer people will be needed to make the same amount of products even though they cost more money. The officials predict that textile employment will fall 1 per cent next year.

52. *Ibid.*, Dec. 11, 1971.

The following report by the Korea Exchange Bank offers greater perspective on the development of the textile industry and some possible consequences of the restraints on textile exports.

ROUGH ROAD AHEAD FOR TEXTILES [53]

As delegates from Korea and the United States initialed an agreement on the voluntary control of the export of Korean synthetic and woolen textiles to the U. S., the long-contentious subject of the limitation of shipments of textiles, which the U. S. had attempted since 1969 to impose on Korea, was finally settled along American lines. . . .

From 1964 to 1970, Korea's textile exports have increased at an annual rate of 48.8 per cent, and the U. S. market has absorbed the largest portion. In particular, the increased rate of U. S. imports of Korean textiles, especially of knitwear, sweaters and clothing of woven fabrics, has been surprisingly high. As a result, the textile pact put the future of the Korean textile industry in jeopardy, simply because the nation's fastest growing foreign market confronted stringent restrictions.

Moreover, with gloomy prospects for notable increases in the export of textiles, which have constituted over two-fifths of the nation's recent total overseas sales, it now seems certain that the export target for 1971 will not be reached, that many textile production facilities will have to cease operation, and that numerous workers will become unemployed.

The textile industry was one of the first modern industries to come to Korea. The first cotton textile mill was established in 1917 and by 1930 the production of cotton textiles practically sufficed the domestic demand. By the end of World War II, and of Japanese colonial role in Korea, the country had 13 cotton textile mills with a total of 9,075 looms and 316,000 spindles.

The Korean War (1950–53) resulted in the destruction of some 70 per cent of the nation's textile production facilities with the result that hundreds of millions of dollars, including $2.8 million from the United Nation's Korea Rehabilitation Agency, had to be invested in the reconstruction of the industry. By 1956, the production of cotton fabrics and yarn had exceeded its pre-war level, and this was enhanced by development of wool and silk production facilities.

However, it was not until the early 1960s that textiles emerged as an important part of the nation's export potential. During the period of the First and Second Five-Year Economic Development Plans (1962–71), substantial amounts of foreign capital were invested in the textile industry, particularly in the production of synthetic fibers (between 1959 and 1970 investment in the textile sector totaled over $250 million or 9.2 per cent of all foreign funds poured into the country during the period).

53. Korea Exchange Bank, *Monthly Review*, Nov. 1971, pp. 1–10.

The proportion of textiles to the total value added by the manufacturing sector during 1970, 26.7 per cent, was the largest of any sub-group in the manufacturing sector, and the annual growth rate of textile production averaged 19.5 per cent between 1962 and 1970. Total production of the manufacturing sector as a whole rose at an average annual rate of 18.6 per cent during the same period. Thus, the textile industry has contributed most to the development of the nation's manufacturing sector.

The labor-intensive textile industry did much to alleviate unemployment problems by giving work to 210,000 persons (as of the end of 1969) or 25.9 per cent of total employment in the manufacturing sector.

The following study of the production and export of textiles in recent years is designed to limelight the internal and external problems facing Korea's textile industry.

As of the end of 1970, Korea's cotton textile industry consisted of 951,800 spindles (up 50 per cent over 1965) and 10,973 looms (a slight decline when compared to 1965). The increase in the production facilities of woolen textiles has been remarkable. Some 369,600 spindles, more than three times as many as in 1965, were in operation in 1970, while the number of looms doubled during the same period. In addition, the number of silk reeling machines and looms, which can also be used to produce synthetic fiber fabrics, also rose sharply, while knitwear equipment saw a substantial buildup by virtue of a soaring export demand.

Changes in the composition of textile yarns produced in the late 1960s are noteworthy. Until 1965, cotton yarn constituted 90 per cent of all tex-

Table I. Position of Textile Industry

	1962	1964	1966	1968	1970	Average increase rate per cent (1962–1970)
Total exports (thousands of dollars)	56,702	120,851	255,751	500,408	1,003,808	42.3
Exports of textiles (thousands of dollars)	8,390	34,005	78,124	208,061	384,391	49.8
Ratio (per cent)	15.7	28.1	30.5	41.6	38.3	
Value added in manufacturing (millions of won)	95.14	116.78	165.76	263.01	379.27	18.6
Value added in textiles (millions of won)	24.87	29.96	44.98	68.18	106.57	19.5
Ratio (per cent)	26.1	25.7	26.8	25.9	26.7	

NOTE: Increase rates for exports are averaged from 1964 to 1970 due to unusual growth from 1962 to 1964.

SOURCES: Ministry of Commerce & Industry and The Bank of Korea.

tile yarns produced in Korea, but the increase in the demand for synthetic fibers in the succeeding years lowered the relative importance of cotton, as well as woolen, yarn. Many woolen yarn spinners therefore began to use more and more synthetic fibers. Meanwhile, the production of silk during 1970 was up four times over that for 1965 as a result of official policy to encourage the cultivation of cocoons and to increase production capacity with imported automatic reeling equipment.

It was not until the Korean War that synthetic fibers started to flood the country. Lack of necessary techniques and sufficient investment capital hindered the establishment of related plants until domestic production became an absolute necessity. Nylon and vinylon plants were built early in the 1960s while since 1968 the domestic production of polypropylene and polyester fibers has almost met the demands of the home market. In addition, plants for the production of viscose rayon and acetate rayon went into operation in 1966 and 1969 to raise the production of man-made fibers in 1970 to 53,000 tons.

The production of woven fabrics has seen similar trends. In 1970, 291.6 million square yards of cotton cloth, 103.6 million square yards of synthetic fiber fabrics and 95.9 million square yards of rayon fabrics were produced, while the output of woolen fabrics and silk fabrics recorded 21.4 million and 12.6 million square yards, respectively.

The production of cotton cloth and rayon fabrics has seen steady growth during recent years, while that of synthetic fiber fabrics and silk fabrics more than tripled in five years owing to a notable rise in both export and domestic market demand. But, as in the case of woolen yarn, woolen fabrics have seen little increase in recent years.

The remarkable increase in the output of knitwear was mainly due to a brisk export demand, with sweaters leading the field. In 1970, over 89.7 million synthetic-fiber sweaters were produced, as compared to a mere 3.7 million in 1965. Furthermore, the proportion of synthetic fiber yarns used in the production of knitwear has grown at the expense of cotton and woolen yarns. During 1970, 113.9 million square yards of tricot knitted cloth were produced, compared to 9.9 million square yards in 1965, while raschel knitted cloth set a production figure of 16.2 million square yards in 1970.

Production statistics for knitwear are available from export enterprises only, but the unrecorded output is considered to be substantial. Likewise, there are numerous small manufacturers of nonknitted cloth, but it is impossible to obtain their production records.

Most of the raw materials for Korea's textile industry have been imported. In particular, the country has no production of raw cotton and wool, while despite a growing capacity to produce synthetic fibers, large quantities of synthetic fiber tops continue to be supplied from foreign sources, especially Japan. Also, the nation is importing considerable yardage of fabrics, especially synthetic materials, to support the growing export demand for clothing.

Imports of textiles during 1970 were valued at over $247.6 million, a figure equivalent to 67 per cent of total textile exports. It was not until 1967 that textile exports forged ahead of imports. Synthetic fiber tops and yarns, which constitute basic materials for Korea's textile export business, lead imports, while lack of techniques has resulted in a sharp increase in imports of fabrics.

Shipments of textiles during 1970 were valued at $384.4 million or 38.3 per cent of Korea's gross export earnings of $1,003.8 million. In 1966, textile exports grossed $78.1 million, thus to record an annual increase rate of 49.8 per cent. One important factor in the expansion of textile exports from underdeveloped nations is low costs resulting from cheap labor. Southeast Asian countries, including Japan and Hong Kong, commenced exporting textiles much earlier than did Korea.

In considering export data, it is convenient to classify textiles into two groups, woven fabrics and clothing. Among woven fabrics, raw silk, cotton cloth and Japanese sash (shibori) were major export commodities, recording $49.6 million, $39.7 million and $34.6 million, respectively, in 1970. Japan was the largest market for raw silk and sash, while cotton cloth was shipped to Hong Kong, Japan, the United States and Italy. Synthetic fiber fabrics, embroidered cloth and tricot knitted fabrics were mainly exported to the United States.

Exports of clothing increased so rapidly as to recently exceed those of woven fabrics. During 1970, exports of shirts of woven fabrics, sweaters and knitwear other than sweaters grossed $51.1 million, $72.4 million and $34.0 million, respectively. More recently, shipments of trousers of woven fabrics, knitted underwear and socks have increased remarkably. In 1970, as much as 75 per cent of the clothing from Korea was sold to the United States, while the major markets in 1966 were Sweden, Hong Kong and the United States, in that order. Exports of clothing to the United States have soared since 1966.

Of Korea's total textile exports in 1970, the United States took 45 per cent, while Japan and Hong Kong bought 28 per cent and six per cent, respectively, and were followed by West Germany, Canada, Sweden, Singapore, the Netherlands and South Vietnam. Korean textiles were sold even to the Republic of South Africa and Nigeria but most textiles exported are to a few countries.

Of the major textile products exported, 85 per cent of the woolen fabrics, 74 per cent of the sweaters, 87 per cent of the woven shirts, 79 per cent of other woven clothing items and 55 per cent of knitwear other than sweaters were shipped to the United States, while 80 per cent of the raw silk shipped out as well as all the Japanese sash, went to Japan.

The recent expansion of Korea's textile industry was based on the rapid increase in exports. Thus, any notable fluctuations in exports could have dire results for the nation's textile industry. The recent restrictions on imports of synthetic and woolen textiles instituted by the United States will have a serious effect on the export of Korean textiles and, thus, on the production of textiles, since synthetic and woolen fabrics and products have been among Korea's leading export commodities to the United States.

The direct impact of the restriction will be the failure of the textile sector to attain its export target. Textile exports to the United States over five years from 1972 have been set at $1,893 million, but the quota for Korea for the five years totals a mere $995 million, or only slightly over half the amount planned.

Thus, the textile and textile good manufacturers will undoubtedly suffer much from the pact, particularly in view of the recent additions to production facilities to meet rising export demands. Particularly hard hit will be producers of knitwear and synthetic fiber goods. It has also been estimated that the pact will put 20,000 looms out of commission, and that 10,000 knitting machines will stop production and 40,000 workers will be laid off.

9. ADJUSTMENT ASSISTANCE

Beyond the immediate question of the particular merits of quotas, this problem more generally seeks answers to how there might be new, more efficient, and more equitable means of containing the dislocation problem. Traditionally, countries have relied on escape clause negotiations under GATT and safeguard clauses in their own trade legislation. The General Agreement (Article XIX) does provide the possibility of escape from previously made tariff concessions that as "a result of unforeseen developments" are causing or threatening "serious injury to domestic producers of like or competitive products." Action under this escape clause is intended to be of an emergency character: a tariff concession may be suspended, withdrawn, or modified only "to the extent and for such time as may be necessary to prevent or remedy" the injury resulting from the concession.[54]

American trade legislation has long provided some form of escape clause procedure, but relief has not been easy to obtain. For escape clause relief, the Trade Expansion Act of 1962 required proof that (a) imports were increasing at an absolute rate, (b) the increase had resulted in "major part" from concessions granted under trade agreements, (c) serious injury had occurred or was imminent, and (d) the increased imports had been the "major factor" in causing that condition. If the Tariff Commission found that relief was justi-

54. For a more detailed analysis, see Dam, *op. cit.*, pp. 99–107.

fied, the President could give tariff assistance or certify the eligibility of firms or workers in the injured industry for adjustment assistance. The certification for adjustment assistance was a new form of policy response that—without resorting to tariff or quota restrictions—was intended to alleviate the dislocating effects of increased imports. The assistance to firms could take the forms of technical assistance, including engineering, marketing, and management advice; financial assistance such as loans or guarantee of loans; and tax assistance through a special carry-back of operating losses. Assistance to workers could be provided in the forms of cash payments as compensation for a period of adversely affected employment; retraining for other types of employment; and relocation allowances.

The eligibility criteria of the 1962 Act have proved extremely rigorous, and provisions to ease the standards have been submitted to Congress in subsequent trade bills.[55] Some liberalized provisions were advocated in the Report to President Johnson by his Special Representative for Trade Negotiations, William M. Roth.

NEW APPROACHES TO DOMESTIC ADJUSTMENT [56]

Although most American workers—as consumers of imported products and as producers of exported products—have undoubtedly gained from the growth of world trade and from price restraints resulting from import competition, some workers have been hurt. Imports can cause dislocation and hardship by displacing American products. Even in years of full employment, imports can create short-run problems for workers—problems of seeking another job, moving to another location, or learning a new skill. In doing so, they may risk the loss of seniority or other employment rights. The problems of adjustment to import competition become social problems when trade adversely affects jobs.

Thus, the challenge of imports to a high-wage, high-living-standard country is not only to find satisfactory means of adjustment, but also to

55. Adjustment assistance provisions for a three-year transitional period were incorporated in the 1965 United States–Canadian Automotive Trade Products Agreement, which provided duty-free trade to manufacturers of automobiles and automotive parts. The policy was notable in assisting and encouraging, rather than restricting, factor reallocation in production. See J. E. Jonish, "Adjustment Assistance Experience Under the U. S.–Canadian Automotive Agreement," *Industrial and Labor Relations Review*, July 1970, pp. 553–60.

56. *Future United States Foreign Trade Policy*, Report to the President submitted by the Special Representative for Trade Negotiations, Jan. 14, 1969, pp. 41–47.

provide new opportunities for the increased productivity of its citizens. The U. S. Government can help ensure that the benefits of trade are not gained at the cost of unemployment for some, and that workers are trained in skills that are in demand. . . .

The criteria in the Trade Expansion Act of 1962 for adjustment assistance to workers should be amended to eliminate the requirement that increased imports be causally linked to past tariff concessions.

The criteria for adjustment assistance to workers—as well as to firms —should instead be based solely upon the relationship between increased imports and the economic injury in question. The need under the present law to establish that increased imports are the major cause—that is, the cause greater than all other causes combined—of economic injury presents formidable problems of evidence as well as of analysis. In particular, it is very difficult to isolate one cause from all other causes.

Instead, it should be sufficient to require that increased imports are *a substantial cause* of economic injury. This would require that a petition by workers demonstrate that increased imports have an actual and considerable bearing upon the unemployment or underemployment that is alleged. The petition would not need to show, however, that increased imports are greater than all other causes of the injury combined, nor even greater than any other single significant cause. . . .

The criteria in the Trade Expansion Act of 1962 for escape-clause relief for industries should be amended to eliminate the requirement that increased imports be causally linked to past tariff concessions.

Further, as already noted, there is a serious question whether it is possible to determine the single cause of serious injury—whether it be increased imports or any other single factor—that is greater than all other causes combined. However, because of the economic consequences of escape-clause relief in the form of higher tariffs or quotas, a fairly rigorous test should be substituted requiring that increased imports should be *the primary cause* of serious injury.

This test should prove workable. It does not demand that increased imports be the major cause of serious injury, that is, the cause greater than all other causes combined. It does require, however, that increased imports be greater than any other single significant cause. This test for escape-clause relief is more demanding than the recommended test for adjustment assistance.

The present escape-clause criteria should be amended to require only that increased imports be the primary cause of serious injury to an industry.

While there is an established need to change the criteria for escape-clause relief, no case has been made for altering the concepts of "serious injury" and "industry" now embodied in the Trade Expansion Act of 1962 and its legislative history. In the first place, serious injury, and not simply injury, must be found, as indicated by such factors as idling of productive facilities, inability to operate at a level of reasonable profit, and unemployment or underemployment. In the second place, serious injury must be widespread throughout the establishments in the industry in which the product is made. Finally, because of the expertise that the Tariff Commission has developed over a number of years in investigating the economic condition of particular industries, it should continue to apply the criteria for escape-clause relief.

The concepts in the present escape-clause criteria concerning "serious injury" and "industry" should be retained, and the role of the Tariff Commission with respect to escape-clause petitions should remain the same.

If the U. S. Government has a responsibility for granting temporary import relief to an industry seriously injured by imports, the firms in that industry should also bear the responsibility for taking prompt and effective action to improve their ability to meet competition at home and from abroad. Present policy provides them with an opportunity to adjust, but places no responsibility upon them to do so. . . .

The Tariff Commission should be required to seek annual reports from the firms in an industry granted escape-clause relief on the specific efforts they are making to adjust to import competition, and the Tariff Commission should take these efforts into account in its annual report to the President on the escape-clause action. In addition, midway in the period for which the relief is granted, the Tariff Commission should be required to report to the President on the probable economic effect of reducing or terminating such relief, and to include in that report its judgment of the progress being made by the firms in adjusting to import competition. . . .

In some cases a program of assistance to groups of workers, industries, firms, or establishments may not be enough. A community-wide problem can arise, for example, when firms or industries adjust by relocating or by consolidating plant operations. This problem can be particularly critical in a community heavily dependent upon a single plant.

It is government policy to assist community and regional development in areas suffering from economic distress. Such assistance is particularly appropriate when imports resulting from government trade policy are the cause of this distress.

There is a need, therefore, when dislocation occurs in a community because of imports, to find better means of coordinating the many already existing community programs, to stimulate further community-wide development efforts, and to provide constructive new solutions. The existing programs of community assistance cover many possible approaches— such as rural renewal loans, technical assistance in the development of local economic plans, loans to development companies and private firms, vocational education, relocation financing, and management counseling.

Some similar proposals were submitted to President Nixon in a report by the Commission on International Trade and Investment Policy. The Commission concluded that major reforms of the existing program are necessary to strengthen materially the scope, content, and administration of adjustment assistance and thereby achieve its purposes.

A MORE EFFECTIVE PROGRAM OF ADJUSTMENT ASSISTANCE [57]

The government can ease adaptation to import competition in two ways. First, programs of adjustment assistance can enhance the mobility and upgrade the quality of both our manpower and our capital. Second, methods of temporary protection—"orderly marketing agreements," or import restrictions (tariffs or quotas) under the escape clause—can provide time for industries to achieve a viable competitive position in the same or different lines of activity.

These policies designed to ease adjustment to import competition can operate more effectively within the context of a coordinated industrial and manpower policy—an approach which the United States has thus far pursued in piecemeal fashion.

Adjustment assistance and import restriction differ sharply. While the former is focused on the particular firms or workers injured by increased imports, the impact of the latter cannot be confined to those firms actually suffering injury. Moreover, successful programs of adjustment assistance should help to develop a more competitive economy, including in particular a more highly skilled work force, and thereby offset at least part of their cost.

Use of adjustment assistance also avoids the adverse effects on costs of U. S.-produced goods in both domestic and foreign markets, the restrictions on access for those goods to markets abroad, and the strains on U. S. foreign relations that are associated with increased protection against imports. Hence the Commission feels that in general the government should encourage adjustment rather than impose restrictions—except in those circumstances where orderly marketing agreements or escape-clause restrictions may be more appropriate. . . .

With respect to eligibility, workers or firms applying for adjustment assistance should be required to show that an increase in imports contributes substantially to causing or threatening serious injury, but they should not be required to show a connection between increased imports and a previous reduction of duties which resulted from a trade-agreements concession.

The program for workers should be improved by instituting a series of administrative or legislative changes addressed to the principal shortcomings of the present programs, including action to:

---

57. *United States International Economic Policy in an Interdependent World,* Report to the President submitted by the Commission on International Trade and Investment Policy, July 1971, pp. 66–69.

—speed access to, approval for, and delivery of adjustment assistance;

—provide greater incentives, including wider benefits, to accept training or relocation assistance;

—make allowances available for the full period of retraining;

—give qualified workers the opportunity to pursue technical, professional, or academic as well as vocational training;

—relax the requirement concerning previous work and earnings;

—provide family health benefits for workers; and

—provide subsidies to allow older workers to enter the Social Security program without reduction of benefits.

In addition, a way must be found to protect the pension rights and health and welfare benefits of workers who have to change jobs.

In the Commission's view, adjustment assistance to firms should normally be available only to small businesses. To increase the effectiveness of adjustment assistance to firms, we recommend that:

—operating responsibility be centralized to expedite the delivery of benefits;

—more attractive terms of financial assistance and tax benefits be provided; and that

—interim financing between approval and delivery of assistance be made available.

In some instances the problem of adjustment might best be dealt with if weaker firms were merged into stronger units or were acquired by more successful firms, whether or not in the same industry. U. S. antitrust legislation should be altered or so administered as to permit mergers if the firm in question is encountering serious difficulty because of import competition. In such cases, the fact that imports are entering in significant quantities will normally ensure that competition in the industry will not be substantially lessened by domestic mergers.

To ensure effective administration of these expanded programs, an Office of Trade Adjustment Assistance should be created. The Office should have an independent budget to carry out the adjustment assistance program, including ongoing analysis of current and likely future adjustment problems.

Adjustment assistance can function best within an expanding domestic economy which provides alternative job and investment opportunities for workers and firms unable to compete in particular product lines. For this reason, the success or failure of the adjustment assistance program is in part determined by overall monetary and fiscal policies pursued by the U. S. Government.

At a different level, the Executive Branch should establish an industrial and manpower policy which would coordinate and augment programs for anticipating and assisting adjustments to economic change arising from international trade and investment. Elements of these policies would include: provision of data on likely trends in American and foreign production and employment patterns; identification and governmental encouragement of promising new areas of productive economic activity; greater coordination of existing, as well as new, governmental programs of regional, community, business, and manpower development; and liaison with voluntary private groups involved in the promotion of economic adjustment.

President Nixon's assistant for international economic affairs also called for a new focus in adjustment assistance.

THE ADJUSTMENT PROCESS [58]

As regards adjustments due to import competition, while it may be true that they may be but a fraction of those which occur for domestic reasons, it is nevertheless a fact that the burden may be a heavy one for a particular industry to bear. Furthermore, a program to build on America's strengths by enhancing its international competitiveness cannot be indifferent to the fate of those industries, and especially those groups of workers, which are not meeting the demands of a truly competitive world economy. It is unreasonable to say that a liberal trade policy is in the interest of the entire country and then allow particular industries, workers, and communities to pay the whole price. This is particularly unacceptable at a time when unemployment levels are high and there is widespread concern over jobs. To correct the defects of the present program, several avenues are already being explored by a task force of the Council on International Economic Policy. The most important of these are summarized below.

The broad national policy purpose of adjustment assistance should be to strengthen the U. S. economy by helping facilitate the processes of economic and social change brought about by foreign competition. The objective of an adjustment assistance program should be to make U. S. industry as a whole, including existing industries, more productive and competitive and thereby provide better paying jobs for American workers. When necessary, the program should be oriented toward encouraging the movement of workers and capital resources from activities no longer economically viable to those that are. In fact one index of the competitive strength of an economy is the proportion of its resources that are employed in activities in which the country excels.

Adjustment assistance should be given a new focus. Early action mechanisms (including strengthened governmental information systems) should be developed to spot trade import problems and begin dealing with them at the earliest possible moment. This would entail not only

58. Peter G. Peterson, *A Foreign Economic Perspective*, Report to the President, Dec. 27, 1971 (U. S. Government Printing Office), pp. 39–41.

identifying actual and potential import-impact areas, but also pinpointing foreign trade distorting or disruptive practices on a world-wide basis, which are likely to give rise to significant U. S. adjustment problems. As part of this effort, we need to speed up the process of making anti-dumping determinations and the decision-making process related to escape clause and unfair practices legislation.

The program should be strengthened by building means for analysis of trade problems on an industry-wide basis, and providing a variety of assistance to encourage maximum self-assistance and market-oriented responses on the part of industry. Delivery of workers' benefits should be greatly accelerated. Finally, we need to determine whether and if the program could be broadened to include assistance to communities severely affected by foreign competition.

Clearly, the whole adjustment assistance effort is of great concern to organized labor. Developing a program which can be accepted by the unions, and communicated positively by union leaders to their membership will not be easy, but union support is critical to the program's success. Unions standing to lose membership through the retraining of their members for new crafts will have to be convinced that their workers will enjoy real benefits as a result.

Even when accelerated by a program of assistance, the adjustment process takes time—and in recent years some economic changes associated with increased imports have occurred very fast. When increasing imports have the potential to bring change faster than the adjustment system can cope with it—and thus to bring hardship—some have suggested that temporary orderly marketing mechanisms should be available. We are now exploring this possibility to develop criteria for invoking such mechanisms, and to see how these criteria can be internationalized so that such *temporary* protection could be available in all countries on an equitable basis.

However, if temporary mechanisms are used to restrict the volume of trade, it would seem to me to be desirable to consider the requirements of a concurrent, orderly adjustment program for the domestic industry which is gaining protection. By introducing a domestic adjustment program as well, we would ensure that the period of special protection is actually used to assist an orderly adjustment, and not used as a permanent crutch, at the expense of consumers at home and efficient producers in other countries.

The main thrust of the foregoing proposals is to change the substantive and procedural standards employed in the determination of eligibility for adjustment assistance, so as to make relief from the dislocation of imports more easily obtainable. But why should this be done? Some would support these proposals simply to forestall the more protectionist policies of trade restrictions. Others believe that the government has an obligation for the costs of dislocation and should subsidize the injured firms and workers. If, however, it is to make economic sense, the adjustment assistance must ensure adjustment: it cannot merely perpetuate the retention of inefficient resources in the depressed industry. It must either promote measures to increase productivity or stimulate an exodus of factors from the industry. No matter what their particular form, adjustment measures must avoid trade-distorting effects: an inefficient adjustment-assistance measure has no more merit than does an inefficient tariff or quota.

Not only should assistance facilitate the conversion of resources to higher productivity uses, but it could also be argued that it should do so as early as possible. The United States approach to adjustment assistance has been an ex post facto approach, becoming operative only after it has been established that injury to an industry has already occurred because of increased imports. This tends to keep the program as narrow in scope as possible. And in delaying action, it allows protectionist forces to gain momentum, and it makes the adjustment problem all the more difficult. It may, therefore, be more sensible to shift to an "early warning" approach that makes it possible both to anticipate probable difficulties and to deal with these at an earlier stage. In essence, the problem is to devise an anticipatory, comprehensive approach that will be harmonious with the changing character of the international division of labor and facilitate the movement of resources in the direction of more efficient international resource allocation. Already revealed in the case of textile quotas, this problem of dislocation will become more acute—and the time for adjustment much shorter—as technology is diffused more rapidly to newly developing countries, multinational enterprises expand, the developing countries accelerate their industrialization process, and these countries acquire a wider comparative advantage in the well-standardized, labor-intensive manufacturing industries that will become increasingly competitive with the older labor-intensive, import-sensitive industries of the United States.

10. CAMPAIGN PLEDGE OF 1972?

With the final selection below, we reach no neat solution—but are brought back once again to the start of this policy problem!

"SITUATION REPORT" ON AN IMPORT BILL [59]

WASHINGTON—There is now a good chance that at least one serious candidate for the presidency this year, Hubert Humphrey, will endorse in principle the strongly anti-import, anti-international-investment bill in Congress backed by organized labor. . . .

There is also a good chance that President Nixon—philosophically more a free-trader than his performance in office suggests—will propose a trade bill to Congress this year limited to remedies for damage to companies and workers suffered because of imports—mainly better "adjustment assistance" but also import limitation in some cases. Such a decision would necessarily put off until later a request for bold new negotiating authority aimed at moving the world away from trade barriers.

The "situation report" here is chiefly a description of how seriously must be taken—and is being taken—the pressure of organized labor, backed by parts of industry, for a major change in this nation's basic foreign economic policy.

The vehicle, now familiar, is called the Hartke-Burke bill, after Senator Vance Hartke of Indiana and Representative James Burke of Massachusetts, both Democrats. No one expects its early enactment. But the citizen signature campaign and other pressure behind it cannot be sneered at. The bill is unique among seriously considered items of international economic legislation in modern United States history in two respects.

First and most important, it essentially declares the multinational company adverse to United States interests. It is an investment bill just as much as it is a trade bill. The bill would hamper the international companies in any number of ways, from taxation to licensing.

It is safe to say that the underlying instinct in this town, whether among "liberals" or "conservatives," is to oppose this kind of restriction. But the feeling is not unanimous, and troubled minds abound. Anyone who wonders about the evolution of American foreign policy—where it has led us—must question instinctive support for the "free flow of capital" and the "optimum allocation of resources" just because these are the conventional wisdom of economists, bankers and many businessmen.

The attack of United States corporate investment abroad by the American Federation of Labor and Congress of Industrial Organizations —chiefly on the ground that it costs jobs at home—can be and is being refuted, though the figures inevitably remain somewhat fuzzy. But there is much quiet puzzlement here about a world in which United States foreign commitments diminish and the role of the dollar in the world diminishes—both now widely desired—while the role of United States companies continues to expand at a breath-taking pace.

The second aspect of the bill is not so new, but it would be striking if

59. Edwin L. Dale, Jr., "Washington Report," *New York Times*, Jan. 23, 1972.

enacted. It is a straightforward declaration that, because of all sorts of changes in the world, the only way damaging import competition can be limited is by quantitative restriction—quotas.

It might seem remarkable how little the steam behind the bill has been diminished by the recent sizable effective devaluation of the dollar, and the resulting relative price changes in imports vis-à-vis domestic products. But then it really isn't remarkable at all.

The attitude that relative price changes will not help is entirely consistent with the view that higher tariffs would not help—a view that has been gradually but persistently developed, for example, by Oscar Strackhein. Mr. Strackhein has made a sincere effort to describe what he regards as a profound change in the world and U. S. competitiveness in it; even if the great majority of economists do not agree, other people have listened.

The conclusion is that only quotas will save us. Note that the new quotas on textiles came along just as the dollar was being devalued.

Members of the House Ways and Means Committee now regard it as a serious possibility that trade legislation—the customary name had better be changed to trade-investment legislation—will be considered this year. If it is, it will be in the middle of presidential politics.

That does not argue for enactment of any restrictive legislation this year. But it raises the serious possibility of a set of statements and commitments by presidential candidates and others that they will not be easily shaken off. For anyone who thinks politicians never live up to commitments, let there be offered the reminder of Richard Nixon, the importation of textiles and three years of United States relations with Japan.

C. Questions

1. Consider the various policy options open to President Nixon.

a. Why did the President not try to achieve his goal of protecting the textile industry by using the escape clause and imposing tariffs?

b. Why did he insist on government-to-government agreements instead of the mandatory quotas of the Trade Bill of 1970?

c. Why did he not support the Mills agreement with the Japan Textile Federation?

d. Why did he not settle for adjustment assistance to the domestic firms and workers?

e. Why did he emphasize bilateral agreements instead of proposing a GATT conference on textiles with the objective of arriving at multinational rules?

2. President Nixon's assistant for international economic affairs (Peter G. Peterson) stated that the Nixon agreements negotiated with the Asian countries were superior to the Mills agreement with the Japan Textile Federation in three respects. "First, it's between governments and thus provides more assurance of performance. Second, it also covers Korea, Taiwan and Hong Kong, which now export more man-made fibers to the U. S. than Japan does. Third, there is significantly more coverage of categories." (*Wall Street Journal*, Oct. 18, 1971.)

a. Do you agree with Peterson's reasoning?

b. Would there be any case for restricting imports from Japan but not Korea, Taiwan, and Hong Kong?

3. Why was it easier for President Kennedy to negotiate restraints on cotton textiles in 1961 than it was for President Nixon to negotiate additional textile quotas?

4. Appraise some of the arguments advanced in favor of protection for the textile industry.

a. Does the fact that Japan imposes nontariff barriers on imports from the United States justify United States retaliation?

b. In 1970–71, was the bilateral balance of trade between the United States and Japan really at issue in the problem of removing the American balance-of-payments deficit?

c. Does the employment of minority disadvantaged workers strengthen the case for protection?

d. Can quotas be supported as simply ensuring an exporting country its "fair share" of the market?

5. Consider the nature of "competition" and "market disruption."

a. Should the policy toward import competition be different when the competition is in terms of price, instead of quality, product innovations, or marketing competition?

b. Is there a real economic distinction between "disrupted trade" and other kinds of competition?

c. Did the GATT market disruption decision suggest that the exporting country was doing anything improper? Or did it simply question the principle of comparative advantage itself?

6. Compare the effects of quotas, tariffs, and measures-of-adjustment assistance.

    a. Are quotas more undesirable than tariffs?

    b. Can adjustment assistance distort trade as much as a quota?

7. Other United States imports subject to quotas include petroleum, steel, sugar, meat, certain dairy products, and wheat. Would you draw any distinction as to the merits of quotas for different commodities?

8. What do you think will be the economic effects of textile quotas in the United States? Japan? the other Asian exporting countries? third countries?

9. a. Can it be said that the textile industry has become a relatively inefficient and declining industry that should be phased out of the United States? In this connection, consider McGeorge Bundy's comment (before the International Chamber of Commerce, Nov. 28, 1967). "If our [the United States] standard of living had stayed low—and if there were not so many interesting things for capital to do right now, I think we could still manage to compete in steel and textiles. It is our general success that makes us vulnerable in special fields. . . . As a general proposition it is inescapable that as we get richer there should be some things—and important things—that we are too rich to do cheaply."

    b. Is not the impact of the series of American restrictions on imports of Japanese textiles (first on cotton goods, and then on synthetic and woolen textiles) simply pushing Japan along the path of evolving comparative advantage—that is, recognizing that Japan too should make way for the production of textiles by the late-developing countries that are joining the industrialization process?

    c. If it is argued that the textile industry should be phased out of Japan, would American import quotas on Japan, but not the other Asian exporting countries, be the best way to accelerate this?

10. If a domestic industry suffers dislocation because the government lowers tariffs and imports rise, do you think it is legitimate to argue that the industry should receive adjustment assistance because the injured had invested and operated in reliance upon a certain governmental commercial policy?

a. Would a similar argument apply to injury as the result of a change in monetary policy or fiscal policy? If you take a different view for commercial policy, why?

b. If imports should rise—not because of a reduction in governmental protection, but simply because the imports become competitive—should relief in the form of governmental assistance still be given?

c. Should adjustment be broadened to provide assistance to workers and firms engaged in production for export when there is a decline in the market for particular exports?

d. If adjustment assistance does not take the form of an increase in tariffs or the imposition of quotas, does a foreign nation have any basis for objecting to the adjustment assistance?

e. When the Lockheed Aircraft Corporation faced a financial crisis in 1971, the Congress voted to provide government backing for loans to Lockheed. The Congress rejected, however, a broader bill that would have authorized Government guarantees of loans to companies whose failure would "adversely and seriously affect the economy of the nation."

Would you have supported the guarantee for Lockheed? the broader bill?

Is there a parallel between Lockheed and the textile industry? between the number of quotas introduced in the Trade Bill of 1970 and the broader bill for guarantees of loans?

Problem III
Regional Integration:
European Economic Community

A. The Context

The European Economic Community (EEC)—first, in its formation and then in its enlargement—has proved to be one of the most far-reaching developments of the postwar world economy. The EEC exercised a decisive role in determining the outcome of the Kennedy Round, as already shown in Problem I. With its expansion to ten countries, the EEC is bound to be an even stronger—perhaps the single strongest—force in the future ordering of international trading arrangements. The materials in this problem are designed to help assess the impact of the EEC, both on its own members and on outside countries. There are several overriding questions. Will the increasing strength of the EEC act to ease or exacerbate the trade problems of the world? Will an enlarged EEC promote outward-looking or inward-looking policies? Will the goals of an integrated international economic system be more readily achieved, or will it become more difficult to pursue policies of international cooperation?

1. AN "ATLANTIC PARTNERSHIP"

In the past, the United States actively supported the European Common Market and attempted to strengthen it. The expansion of trade with the Common Market has been a major component of

American foreign economic policy. And an "Atlantic Partnership" with a politically integrated Western Europe has also been an essential objective of American security policy. As recently as February 1971, President Nixon reaffirmed in his State-of-the-World message that "we welcome cohesion in Europe because it makes Europe a sturdier pillar of the structure of peace." American support for European integration has assumed that the elimination of trade barriers among the member countries of a Common Market would strengthen the economies of the participating countries, that economic interdependence would promote political unification, and that European integration could have an outward-looking character promoting the expansion of freer world trade. Now, however, these assumptions no longer go unchallenged. The dominant official policy position may still be based on these assumptions, but there has been increasing concern that the EEC might become an inward-looking rival to the United States and that it might provoke other regional trading blocs that would tend to restrict international trade.

2. POST-KENNEDY ROUND OPTIONS

In the post-Kennedy Round era, the United States has had essentially four options open to it for negotiations on trade liberalization. These four alternatives provide the general context for this problem.[1] If it is to counteract the new forces of protectionism, the United States may advocate one of the following.

i. A Second Kennedy Round. Another round of tariff negotiations could be organized, based on the same ground rules of a targeted percentage linear reduction of tariff rates as in the Kennedy Round. This would be in accord with established lines of multilateral bargaining in GATT, but—in view of the nature and consequences of the Kennedy Round, as discussed in Problem I—it might be argued that "the Kennedy Round seems to represent 'the end of the road,' for traditional GATT bargaining, at least for a period of years." [2]

1. For a detailed elaboration of these alternatives, see H. G. Johnson, "World Trade Policy in the Post-Kennedy Round Era," *The Economic Record,* June 1968, pp. 154–67; G. Curzon and V. Curzon, *After the Kennedy Round: What Trade Policies Now?* (Atlantic Study Group, London, 1968).

2. Johnson, *op. cit.*, p. 159.

ii. The Sector-by-Sector Approach. An alternative approach could be the reduction of tariffs on particular industrial products or product groups, on a nondiscriminatory multilateral basis through GATT-type negotiations. Depending on the criteria used for the selection of sectors, however, the sector-by-sector approach may prove of little consequence. The attempt to achieve free trade on a sectoral basis would also be a step back from the Kennedy Round approach: there would be no urgency about negotiating tariff reductions, and the advance toward free trade could be blocked by the unwillingness of a major industrial country to participate in the multilateral negotiations.[3]

iii. The Conditional Most-Favored-Nation Approach. In contrast with the unconditional most-favored-nation principle of GATT that any trade concession made by one member to another is extended to all, the conditional most-favored-nation treatment would be a discriminatory approach to trade liberalization. Under this approach, tariff reductions arrived at by bilateral or multilateral bargaining would be extended to other nations that had not been party to the original bargaining only on condition that they offered equivalent reductions of their own tariffs. This would reintroduce discriminatory tariff policy and run counter to all the efforts of the past half-century to strengthen multilateral tariff reductions on a nondiscriminatory basis.

iv. Preferential Arrangements. For a group of countries that want to force the pace of trade liberalization among themselves, the GATT provisions regarding customs unions or free trade areas allow the formation of preferential arrangements among these countries—provided that the freer trading arrangement covers "substantially all trade" among the participating countries (Article XXIV of GATT). The EEC and European Free Trade Association (EFTA) were formed under this provision. Of much concern now to outside nations is the realignment between an enlarged EEC and EFTA. As an alternative to enlargement of the EEC or as an extension of the EEC to a wider area, attention has been given also to the possibilities of. forming a new Atlantic or Multilateral Free Trade Area. As a preferential trading group—but short of a customs union or economic union—this free trade area could be composed

3. Johnson, *op. cit.*, p. 161.

of EFTA countries, the United States, Canada, and possibly New Zealand, Australia, Japan, and other countries. This area might be open-ended in its membership, and it might serve to refocus the thrust of American commercial policy.

Some understanding of the actual and potential impact of the EEC is necessary before these alternatives can be appraised. And the impact must be considered in a context wider than simply that of exports and imports: also important are the repercussions of the EEC on foreign investment, the role of multinational enterprises, problems of the international monetary system, and the development of the Third World.

The materials below first set forth some major provisions of the Treaty of Rome that established the EEC, in order that the nature of the Community's commitments might be recognized. The evolution of Community policy is then outlined in three significant areas: common commercial policy, common agricultural policy, and proposed monetary union. In considering these policies, we should note how domestic political and economic interests of member countries may conflict with the Community's interests and how the Community's interests may conflict with those of nonmember countries. The "Great Debate" on Britain's entry into the Common Market provides an excellent opportunity to assess the progress of the Common Market and consider its future form. The last section then gives specific attention to the impact of the EEC on the United States.

3. ECONOMIC INTEGRATION

Interpretation of these materials can be enhanced by an understanding of the theory of economic integration.[4] There are, of course, various degrees of economic integration. The highest degree is a complete economic union which provides a supranational au-

---

4. For more detailed expositions of the economic theory of integration, see J. Viner, *The Customs Union Issue* (1950); J. E. Meade, *The Theory of Customs Unions* (1955); T. Scitovsky, *Economic Theory and Western European Integration* (1958); Bela Balassa, *The Theory of Economic Integration* (1961); P. P. Streeten, *Economic Integration* (2nd ed., 1964); J. Tinbergen, *International Economic Integration* (1965); Kiyoshi Kojima, "Towards a Theory of Agreed Specialization: The Economics of Integration," in *Induction, Growth and Trade: Essays in Honour of Sir Roy Harrod*, W. A. Eltis *et al.* (eds. 1970), pp. 305–20; R. G. Lipsey, *The Theory of Customs Union: A General Equilibrium Analysis* (1970).

thority with the power to remove forms of discrimination among member nations, to support a common market among the members, to co-ordinate monetary and fiscal policies, and to create a common currency. Short of a complete economic union, there are the following possibilities.

i. A common market, which institutes a customs union and eliminates barriers to the movement of capital and labor so that factors as well as goods are free to move among member nations;

ii. A customs union, in which the members reduce or eliminate tariffs among themselves, while imposing a common tariff level for third countries;

iii. A free trade area, in which the members agree to the mutual reduction or elimination of tariffs, but each member country retains its own separate tariffs against third countries.

It became apparent during negotiations in the early 1950's that the United Kingdom was in favor of a free trade area arrangement, while the formation of a customs union was advocated by the "Europe of the Six"—France, West Germany, Italy, and the three Benelux countries (Belgium, Netherlands, Luxembourg). These differences ultimately led to the withdrawal of the United Kingdom representatives in 1955 from the discussions about the creation of a general common market—discussions which subsequently led to the Treaty of Rome for the "Inner Six." In 1956, the Organization for European Economic Cooperation (OEEC), with strong British support, undertook a study of the proposal that the OEEC countries should create an enlarged European Industrial Free Trade Area which would embrace the customs union of the Six. These negotiations, however, broke down when Britain insisted on retaining her tariff preferences on industrial exports to Commonwealth countries and desired to exclude agriculture from any agreement. These difficulties remained obstacles to Britain's entry into the EEC, as will be seen below, pp. 221–28.

In 1971, however, Britain finally accepted the principle of joining the EEC. Norway, Denmark, and Ireland also applied for membership. In January 1972, these countries signed the Treaty of Brussels, joining the EEC.

Although the wider negotiations were abandoned in 1958, some identity of interest had developed among the United Kingdom, Norway, Sweden, Denmark, Austria, and Switzerland. Joined later by Portugal, these countries—the "Outer Seven"—established the EFTA in 1960. Western Europe was thus divided into two trade blocs—the EEC and EFTA, while Eastern European countries formed another trade bloc behind the iron curtain.

Unlike the EEC, the EFTA arrangement is purely a trading arrangement, with no objective of political unification. Each country sets its own external tariff, while emphasizing free trade in industrial goods among the member countries. The Outer Seven agreed to achieve complete free trade in nonfarm products by the end of 1966. Agriculture is outside the agreement, with each member deciding its own agricultural support policy. There is slight effort to harmonize other economic policies and little institutional machinery.[5]

The EEC has proved most effective in establishing a customs union, although some progress has also been made in liberalizing factor movements, and an agreement was reached in 1971 to undertake a five-year trial period of intensified economic and monetary co-operation (see below, pp. 214–20). Aside from any political objectives, the economic purpose of the customs union has been to increase the economic welfare—the real income—of its members by reducing trade barriers. A customs union raises, however, some hard questions as to what are the gains for the union as a whole; what are the gains or losses to individual members; and what are the gains or losses for nonparticipating countries. Within the union itself, it is possible for some members to gain while others lose, or for some members to gain more than others—and this can be a highly sensitive issue, determining the ultimate success of the union.

The gains to members are expected to be of three kinds: (i) an increase in the static gains from trade, (ii) an increase in the gains resulting from sharper competition among established firms, and (iii) gains from growth in the national income of member countries. The gains from trade for member countries may be increased through an improvement in the region's terms of trade and through more efficient allocation of resources based on increased specialization in accordance with comparative advantage within the customs union

5. See Hugh Corbet and David Robertson (eds.), *Europe's Free Trade Area Experiment* (1970).

and through "trade creation" (that is, through a switch from a higher real-cost source of supply in one member country, which had formerly been protected by a duty, to a lower real-cost source of supply in another member country).[6] As foreign competition intensifies with the lowering of protective trade barriers and the creation of a single market, the high-cost firms will be forced to increase their efficiency or must eventually exit from the more competitive industry. As the size of the market expands, there are expected also to be gains from the exploitation of potential economies of scale, additional investment, entry of new firms, promotion of technological change, and realization of external economies—effects which raise the rate of economic growth for members of the customs union. The gains from competition and growth are often referred to as the "dynamic" effects of membership in a customs union, and these cumulative effects are likely to be more significant than the more conventional "static" gains from trade that are likely to be limited to the once-for-all or "impact" effects of membership.

The strength of a customs union and its prospects for continued success also depend on the avoidance of too unequal a distribution of benefits among the participating nations. If some countries gain at the expense of others, some provisions are then necessary to compensate for the losses or the uneven distribution of benefits; otherwise, the forces of nationalism and domestic autonomy in economic policy-making will reassert themselves and diminish the overall gains from regional integration. With regional integration, some industries will be relocated as specialization occurs in the member country that acquires a comparative advantage; direct private foreign investment may be attracted to one of the participating countries; resources may be reallocated from less efficient to more efficient firms; and marginal firms will have to reduce costs or leave the industry. The relocation of industry and concentration of invest-

---

6. In contrast, the effects of "trade diversion" occur when, as a result of the external tariff, there is a transfer of trade from a lower real-cost source outside the customs union to a higher real-cost source of supply within the union (which only appears cheaper because it does not confront the external tariff).

It was the possibility of trade diversion that originally gave rise to the formulation of the "theory of the second-best." See R. G. Lipsey and K. J. Lancaster, "The General Theory of Second Best," *Review of Economic Studies*, 1956–57, pp. 11–32.

ment may constitute a polarization within the customs union, and some safeguards may be needed to retain the allegiance of the weaker countries.

Further, some member countries may gain more than others through changes in the terms of trade, consumption effects, agricultural policies, and balance-of-payments effects. Depending on their patterns of production and consumption, one country may experience an improvement while another suffers a deterioration in its terms of trade. This is most likely to occur under conditions of trade diversion. There also can be adverse consumption effects within some of the member countries as demand is diverted from a low-cost outside source to the high-cost supplier within the union, because of the external tariff. When countries have pursued different agricultural support programs before the union, the institution of a common agricultural policy might also cause production and consumption losses to some countries. The alteration of a country's pattern of trade after the formation of a customs union also will affect its balance of payments. In short, if the overall gains from a customs union are to be realized, the creation of the union will necessitate a series of adjustments within the member countries. To the extent, however, that a country has only a limited capacity to transform, or the benefits become highly polarized within the union, supplementary remedial measures must be adopted to safeguard or compensate the weaker members. These measures can range from regional investment programs, the provision of capital by a regional development bank, or a common exchange rate policy, to policies of fiscal redistribution among member countries.

Beyond the distribution of benefits within the union, we are also concerned with the impact of the EEC on nonparticipating countries. The impact on nonmembers must be evaluated if we are to answer a major question that runs through this problem: what should be the United States policy toward the EEC? Our answer will vary depending on whether we believe that only the insiders— or both insiders and outsiders—benefit from the Common Market. If only the member countries benefit, at the expense of economic losses for the United States, then the United States will tend to reduce its support of European integration. This is especially likely if there will be an economic cost to the United States at the same time as the American objective of promoting political unity in Western Europe is no more a likelihood today than it was when the Treaty of Rome was signed in 1957.

On July 4, 1962, President John F. Kennedy could say:

> "We do not regard a strong and united Europe as a rival but a partner . . . capable of playing a greater role in the common defense, of responding more generously to the needs of poorer nations, of joining with the United States and others in lowering trade barriers, resolving problems of commerce and commodities and currency, and developing coordinated policies in all economic and diplomatic areas. . . . The United States will be ready for a declaration of interdependence. . . . We will be prepared to discuss with a united Europe the ways and means of forming a concrete Atlantic partnership . . . between the new union now emerging in Europe and the old American union founded here 175 years ago." [7]

More recently, however, a former Assistant Special Representative for Trade Negotiations in the White House has summarized a contrary view that has gained wide acceptance: "There is no longer any reason to pay a commercial price for non-existent political unity in Europe. . . . We must change our views about some fundamental parts of our foreign policy." [8] And a knowledgeable international economic observer has noted that "Of all the grand and sad dreams of American foreign policy in the past 20 years, one of the two or three grandest and saddest is 'European unity,' as represented principally by the European Economic Community. We bought a pig in a poke. We have been taken." [9]

This problem calls for re-examination of the earlier presumptions of American foreign economic policy with respect to the EEC: Are there costs to the United States and to third countries that outweigh the gains from the EEC? What will be the possible consequences of an enlargement of the EEC? Is there a danger that the world economy will disintegrate into regional blocs, with adverse effects on trade liberalization, international monetary order, and economic development? These questions should now be confronted

7. Independence Day Address, Philadelphia, Pa., July 4, 1962.
8. Harald B. Malmgren, quoted in *Times* (London), Sept. 24, 1969, p. 25.
9. Edwin L. Dale, "The American Dreams That Went Wrong," *Times* (London), Sept. 24, 1969, p. 25.

with empirical—and judgmental—considerations of the benefits and costs of alternative trading arrangements. Some of these considerations may be prompted by the following materials.

B. The Issues

4. TREATY OF ROME

The vision of European unification has a long history—reaffirmed by Winston Churchill when he urged formation of a "United States of Europe" after World War II. The first major institution supporting the movement for European unity was the Coal and Steel Community. Of all the European developments of the past quarter-century, this has been judged the most original. "Its originality lay in its combination of economic proposals, bold enough in themselves, with longer-range political objectives, the creation of a framework which could provide the prototype for a future European federation and at the same time contain the revival of German power." [10] The European Coal and Steel Community began operating in 1952 and was soon joined by the formation of the European Atomic Energy Community (Euratom) and the European Economic Community (EEC). The Treaty of Rome, establishing the Common Market of the EEC, was signed in March 1957, and the Commission of the EEC—the Common Market's permanent executive body—began operating January 1, 1958.

As analyzed in an early Report of the Joint Economic Committee, [11] the driving forces behind European integration have been both political and economic:

> i. A key motive was to end the historic France–German enmity. The aim was to forge bonds firmly tying Germany to Western Europe by offering her a place as an equal member in a united Europe and a challenging outlet for the vital energies of her people. . . .
> ii. By 1950 many in Europe had come to see that even countries as large as France and Germany were too small to assure

10. Alan Bullock, "Europe Since Hitler," *International Affairs*, Jan. 1971, p. 16.

11. Robert R. Bowie and Theodore Geiger, *The European Economic Community and The United States*, Joint Committee Print, Subcommittee on Foreign Economic Policy of the Joint Economic Committee, 87th Congress, First Session, 1961, pp. 4–5.

a dynamic economy and the full benefits of technology, scientific advances, and research necessary for industrial efficiency and growth. Moreover, in France and Italy especially, it appeared that stagnation due to the lack of competition and enterprise could best be overcome within a larger framework. Competition from outside might strike a spark which could not be ignited from within.

The idea of a wider European market had great appeal. On the experience of the United States, it appeared to offer the prospect of stimulating economic dynamism which would raise living standards and enable industries to compete better on the world markets.

iii. The European nations, once their shattered economies had begun to recover, naturally wished to have a greater part in shaping their own destiny. Yet the rise of the United States and of the Soviet Union as superpowers now dwarfed even the major nations of Europe. A larger European entity was needed to mobilize and use the potential of Europe.

The persistence of the European integration movement over the past quarter-century—despite periodic setbacks and some long pauses—can be seen in a summary chronology of major steps in European co-operation.

EUROPE SINCE 1945 [12]

1945

At the end of the Second World War, Western Europe lay in ruins. It faced two fundamental questions. One was economic: how could the material destruction be repaired? The second was political: how could Europe recover political strength and stability?

1946

A response to the political question was heard in 1946 when, in Zurich, Winston Churchill stressed the need to build a "United States of Europe."

1947

The promise of economic recovery for Europe came from the United States with the Marshall Plan proposal in 1947. The only condition attached to American aid was that Europe itself organize the recovery. To do this, European nations formed the Organization for European Economic Cooperation (OEEC), and later the European Payments Union.

12. Reprinted from *European Community*, No. 134, May 1970.

1948

At a meeting held at The Hague in 1948, Europe's political leaders advocated the establishment of a European Parliament as a step to the political union of Europe. Ten European countries in 1949 agreed to form the Council of Europe. Despite ambitious aims, the Council of Europe lacked an institutional structure with decision-making powers. It soon became merely a diplomatic sounding board for its members.

1950

On May 9, 1950, Robert Schuman, French Foreign Minister, read to representatives of the world press a proposal from his Government, a proposal described by Walter Lippman as the most audacious and constructive since the war. This blueprint for the future integration of Europe, drafted by Jean Monnet only a few days earlier, became known as the "Schuman Plan." Its aim was to reconcile France and Germany within a European Federation. Its method was to create *de facto* economic solidarity among Europeans by pooling basic production, beginning with a European authority for coal and steel.

1951

On April 18, 1951, less than one year after Schuman's declaration, six European countries—Belgium, France, Italy, Luxembourg, and the Netherlands—signed the European Coal and Steel Community (ECSC) Treaty in Paris.

1952

The parliaments of the six countries ratified the Treaty and thus created the first European institutions with federal characteristics. The executive branch of the ECSC was independent of governments, and its decisions not subject to veto. It established a "common market" for coal and steel, administered Europe's first effective anti-trust law, carried out Europe's first labor resettlement and "trade adjustment" policy, and levied the first European (as opposed to national) tax on coal and steel production.

1954

After unsuccessful attempts to establish a European Political Community and a European Defense Community in 1954, Europeans turned back to the economic road to integration. Europe's economic weakness contrasted vividly with the economic strength of the two continental giants, the United States and the USSR, whose political policies largely dominated the world.

1955

Next step toward unification was taken at Messina, in June 1955, when, under the chairmanship of Belgian Foreign Minister Paul Henri Spaak, a committee was instructed by the six Community countries to examine the possibilities for general economic union and joint development of the peaceful uses of atomic energy.

1956

As a result of the Spaak Committee Report, negotiations for drafting two treaties opened in Brussels.

1957

The Treaties were signed on March 25, 1957, in Rome, where the ministers of the six countries formally established the European Economic Community (Common Market) and European Atomic Energy Community (Euratom).

1958

Provisionally located in Brussels, the Community's institutions began their work, consisting of setting up a customs union and shaping common economic policies for the whole Community.

1959

On the first of January, the first cuts in the custom duties for goods traded between the member countries were carried out.

1960

In 1960, the Six took the first steps towards bringing national tariffs on imports from non-member countries into line with a common external tariff.

1961

In the course of 1961, steps were made to free the movement of men, firms, and services throughout the six member states. The Community also moved into the more difficult phase of working out common policies, especially in the spheres of agriculture, competition, transport, and trade with the rest of the world. Hand in hand with the internal development of the Community, external affairs loomed larger in its activities: the first association agreement was signed, with Greece; applications for full membership in the Community were presented by Britain, Ireland, Denmark, and Norway.

1962

President Kennedy proposed the Trade Expansion Program and an "Atlantic Partnership."

1963

Formal association links for aid and trade were forged with 18 independent African countries and with Turkey. The Community signed its first trade agreement, with Iran. A sudden veto by France in January 1963 ended membership negotiations with Great Britain and precipitated the Community's first political crisis.

1964

On May 4th, negotiations opened in Geneva under the General Agreement on Tariffs and Trade (GATT) aimed at cutting tariffs by 50 per cent on goods traded among the GATT member countries. The Six adopted the first Community plan to combat inflation and, to secure growth equilibrium, drew up its first five-year economic program. The free movement of workers throughout the Community became effective with the abolition of the priority given to national workers on the national employment markets.

1965

In the first half of the year 1965, the customs union was well under way, agricultural policy was making progress, the merger of EEC, Euratom, and ECSC Community Executives was decided, and other decisions were being taken in a number of fields. At midnight on June 30, 1965, a second major crisis broke. France sought to modify the role of the Commission and abandon majority voting on matters which a government considered vital to national interests. The other five members refused. Consequently, France boycotted the Council of Ministers and other Community institution meetings for seven months.

1966

On the 28th and 29th of January 1966, the Foreign Ministers of the Six, after "agreeing to disagree" on disputed issues raised by France, decided to resume normal work in Community institutions. In July, the six agricultural ministers adopted the basic principles and fixed common prices to be applied throughout the Community for major agricultural products.

1967

On May 11, 1967, Britain renewed its application for Community membership. Four days later, the Kennedy Round—wherein the European Community spoke with one voice on trade affairs—was concluded.

1968

On July 1, 1968, a full customs union was established, providing free trade for agricultural and manufactured products throughout the Community.

1969

The Community's partnership with Africa was confirmed through renewal of the second Association Treaty with 18 independent African countries. Following a summit meeting in The Hague between the Governments of the Six in early December, the Community was given a new impetus. Main objectives were fixed and a timetable set for: monetary union, full economic union, and the strengthening and enlargement of the Community.

1970

The Council of Ministers further developed The Hague meeting proposals, including a decision to strengthen the budgetary role of the European Parliament.

A landmark in the foregoing chronology is the Treaty of Rome, under which the Six agreed to create an Economic community during a transition period of twelve years. The Principles underlying the EEC Treaty are set forth in its first four Articles:

TREATY ESTABLISHING THE EUROPEAN ECONOMIC COMMUNITY

PART ONE   PRINCIPLES

ARTICLE 1
By the present Treaty, the HIGH CONTRACTING PARTIES establish among themselves a EUROPEAN ECONOMIC COMMUNITY.

ARTICLE 2
It shall be the task of the Community, by establishing a Common Market and gradually approximating the economic policies of Member States, to promote throughout the Community a harmonious development of economic activities, a continuous and balanced expansion, an increased stability, an accelerated raising of the standard of living and closer relations between its Member States.

ARTICLE 3
For the purposes set out in the preceding Article, the activities of the Community shall include, under the conditions and in accordance with the timing envisaged in this Treaty:
(a) the elimination, as between Member States, of customs duties and of quantitative restrictions in regard to the importation and exportation of goods, as well as of all other measures with equivalent effect;
(b) the establishment of a common customs tariff and a common commercial policy towards third countries;
(c) the abolition, as between Member States, of the obstacles to the free movement of persons, services and capital;
(d) the inauguration of a common agricultural policy;
(e) the inauguration of a common transport policy;

(f) the establishment of a system ensuring that competition in the Common Market shall not be distorted;

(g) the application of procedures permitting the coordination of the economic policies of Member States and the correction of disequilibria in their balances of payments;

(h) the approximation of their respective municipal laws to the extent necessary for the orderly functioning of the Common Market;

(i) the creation of a European Social Fund in order to improve the possibilities of employment for workers and to contribute to the raising of their standard of living;

(j) the establishment of a European Investment Bank intended to facilitate the economic expansion of the Community through the creation of new resources; and

(k) the association of overseas countries and territories with the Community with a view to increasing trade and to pursuing jointly their efforts towards economic and social development.

ARTICLE 4

1. The achievement of the tasks entrusted to the Community shall be ensured by the following institutions:

an Assembly,
a Council,
a Commission,
a Court of Justice.

Each institution shall act within the limits of the powers conferred upon it by this Treaty.

2. The Council and the Commission shall be assisted by an Economic and Social Committee acting in a consultative capacity.

Other important Articles in the Treaty of Rome follow—on the formation of the customs union, agricultural policy, factor movements, commercial law, and balance-of-payments policy. These may be referred to again in connection with the summary of Community Policy below (pp. 207–21).

Chapter 1   The Customs Union

Section 1: The Elimination of Customs Duties as Between Member States

ARTICLE 12

Member States shall refrain from introducing, as between themselves, any new customs duties on imports or exports or charges with equivalent effect and from increasing such duties or charges as they already apply in their commercial relations with each other.

ARTICLE 13

1. Customs duties on imports in force between Member States shall be gradually abolished by them during the transitional period under the conditions laid down in Articles 14 and 15.

2. Charges in force between Member States having an effect equivalent to customs duties on imports shall be gradually abolished by them during the transitional period. The Commission shall. by means of directives, determine the timing of such abolition.

ARTICLE 14

1. For each product, the basic duty which shall be subject to the successive reductions shall be the duty applied on 1 January 1957.

2. The timing of the reductions shall be determined as follows:

(a) during the first stage, the first reduction shall be made one year after this Treaty comes into force; the second reduction shall be made eighteen months later; the third at the end of the fourth year after this Treaty comes into force;

(b) during the second stage, a reduction shall be made eighteen months after the beginning of that stage; a second reduction eighteen months after the preceding one; a third reduction shall be made one year later; and

(c) the reductions which still remain to be made shall be carried out during the third stage; the Council, by a qualified majority vote on a proposal of the Commission, shall determine their timing by means of directives.

Section 2: Establishment of the
Common Customs Tariff

ARTICLE 18

Member States hereby declare their willingness to contribute to the development of international trade and the reduction of barriers to trade by entering into reciprocal and mutually advantageous agreements directed to the reduction of customs duties below the general level which they could claim as a result of the establishment of a customs union between themselves.

ARTICLE 19

1. Subject to the conditions and within the limits laid down below, the duties in the common customs tariff shall be at the level of the arithmetical average of the duties applied in the four customs territories covered by the Community.

2. The duties taken as the basis for calculating this average shall be those applied by Member States on 1 January 1957.

Chapter 2   The Elimination of Quantitative
Restrictions as Between Member
States

ARTICLE 30
Quantitative restrictions on imports and all measures with equivalent effect shall, without prejudice to the following provisions, be prohibited between Member States.

ARTICLE 31
Member States shall refrain from introducing as between themselves any new quantitative restrictions or measures with equivalent effect.

ARTICLE 32
Member States shall, in their mutual trade, refrain from making more restrictive the quotas or measures with equivalent effect in existence at the date this Treaty comes into force.

Such quotas shall be abolished not later than at the end of the transitional period. During this period, they shall be gradually abolished under the conditions specified below.

TITLE II   AGRICULTURE

ARTICLE 38
1. The Common Market shall extend to agriculture and trade in agricultural products. Agricultural products shall mean the products of the soil, of stock-breeding and of fisheries as well as products after the first processing stage which are directly related to such products.

2. Except where there are provisions to the contrary in Articles 39 to 46 inclusive, the rules laid down for the establishment of the Common Market shall apply to agricultural products.

3. The products subject to the provisions of Articles 39 to 46 inclusive are listed in Annex II to this Treaty. Within a period of two years after this Treaty comes into force, the Council, acting by a qualified majority vote on a proposal of the Commission, shall decide what products should be added to that list.

4. The functioning and development of the Common Market in respect of agricultural products shall be accompanied by the establishment of a common agricultural policy among the Member States.

ARTICLE 39
1. The objectives of the common agricultural policy shall be:
(a) to increase agricultural productivity by promoting technical progress and by ensuring the rational development of agricultural production and the optimum utilization of the factors of production, particularly labor;

(b) to ensure thereby a fair standard of living for the agricultural population, particularly by increasing the individual earnings of persons engaged in agriculture;

(c) to stabilize markets;

(d) to guarantee supplies;

(e) to ensure the delivery of supplies to consumers at reasonable prices.

2. In working out the common agricultural policy and the special methods which it may involve, due account shall be taken of:

(a) the distinctive nature of agricultural activities, arising from the social structure of agriculture and from structural and natural disparities between the various agricultural regions;

(b) the need to make the appropriate adjustments gradually;

(c) the fact that, in the Member States, agriculture constitutes a sector which is closely linked with the economy as a whole.

ARTICLE 40

1. Member States shall gradually develop the common agricultural policy during the transitional period and shall establish it not later than at the end of that period.

2. In order to achieve the objectives set out in Article 39, a common organization for agricultural markets shall be established.

This organization shall take one of the following forms according to the products concerned:

(a) common rules concerning competition;

(b) compulsory co-ordination of the various national marketing organizations; or

(c) a European marketing organization.

3. The common organization established in accordance with paragraph 2 may include all measures necessary to achieve the objectives set out in Article 39, in particular, price controls, subsidies for the production and marketing of various products, arrangements for stock-piling and carry-forward, and common agreements for stabilization of common imports and exports.

The common organization shall confine itself to pursuing the objectives set out in Article 39 and shall exclude any discrimination between producers or consumers within the Community.

Any common price policy shall be based on common criteria and on uniform methods of calculation.

4. In order to enable the common organization referred to in paragraph 2 to achieve its objectives, one or more agricultural orientation and guarantee funds may be established.

TITLE III THE FREE MOVEMENT OF PERSONS, SERVICES AND CAPITAL

Chapter I Workers

ARTICLE 48

1. The free movement of workers shall be secured within the Community not later than by the end of the transitional period.

2. This shall involve the abolition of any discrimination based on nationality between workers of the Member States as regards employment, remuneration, and other working conditions.

3. It shall include the right, subject to limitations justified by reasons of public policy (*ordre public*), public safety and public health:

(a) to accept offers of employment actually made;

(b) to move about freely for this purpose within the territory of Member States;

(c) to stay in any Member State in order to carry on employment in accordance with the legislative and administrative provisions governing the employment of nationals of that State;

(d) to remain, on conditions which shall be the subject of implementing regulations to be laid down by the Commission, in the territory of a Member State after having been employed there.

4. The provisions of this Article shall not apply to employment in the public service.

Chapter 3   Services

ARTICLE 59

Within the framework of the provisions set out below, restrictions on the free supply of services within the Community shall be gradually abolished during the transitional period in respect of nationals of Member States who are established in a State of the Community other than that of the person to whom the services are supplied.

The Council, acting by unanimous vote on a proposal of the Commission, may extend the provisions of this Chapter to cover services supplied by nationals of any third country who are established within the Community.

ARTICLE 60

Services within the meaning of this Treaty shall be deemed to be services normally supplied for remuneration, to the extent that they are not governed by the provisions relating to the free movement of goods, capital and persons.

Services shall include in particular:

(a) activities of an industrial character;

(b) activities of a commercial character;

(c) artisan activities;

(d) activities of the liberal professions.

Without prejudice to the provisions of the Chapter relating to the right of establishment, a person supplying a service may, in order to carry out that service, temporarily exercise his activity in the State where the service is supplied, under the same conditions as are imposed by that State on its own nationals.

Chapter 4   Capital

ARTICLE 67

1. Member States shall, during the transitional period and to the extent necessary for the proper functioning of the Common Market, gradually abolish between themselves restrictions on the movement of capital belonging to persons resident in Member States and any discrimination based on the nationality or place of residence of the parties or on the place in which such capital is invested.

2. Current payments connected with movements of capital between Member States shall be freed from all restrictions not later than the end of the first stage.

ARTICLE 68

1. Member States shall, in respect of the matters referred to in this Chapter, be as liberal as possible in granting such exchange authorizations as are still necessary after this Treaty comes into force.

2. Where a Member State applies its domestic rules governing the capital market and the credit system to the movements of capital liberalized in accordance with the provisions of this Chapter, it shall do so in a non-discriminatory manner.

PART THREE   POLICY OF THE COMMUNITY

TITLE I   COMMON RULES

Chapter 1   Rules Governing Competition

*Section 1: Rules Applying
to Enterprises*

ARTICLE 85

1. The following shall be prohibited as incompatible with the Common Market: all agreements between enterprises, all decisions by associations of enterprises and all concerted practices which are apt to affect trade between the Member States and which have as their object or effect the prevention, restriction or distortion of competition within the Common Market, in particular those consisting in:

(a) the direct or indirect fixing of purchase or selling prices or of any other trading conditions;

(b) the limitation or control of production, markets, technological development or investment;

(c) market-sharing or the sharing of sources of supply;

(d) the application of unequal conditions to parties undertaking equivalent engagements in commercial transactions, thereby placing them at a competitive disadvantage;

(e) making the conclusion of a contract subject to the acceptance by the other party to the contract of additional obligations, which, by their nature or according to commercial usage have no connection with the subject of such contract.

2. Any agreements or decisions prohibited pursuant to this Article shall be null and void.

3. The provisions of paragraph 1 may, however, be declared inapplicable in the case of:

—any agreements or groups [*catégorie, Gruppen*] of agreements between enterprises,

—any decisions or groups [*catégorie, Gruppen*] of decisions by associations of enterprises, and

—any concerted practices or groups [*catégorie, Gruppen*] of concerted practices,

which contribute to the improvement of the production or distribution of goods or to the promotion of technological or economic progress while reserving to consumers an equitable share in the profit resulting therefrom, and which:

(a) neither impose on the enterprises concerned any restrictions not indispensable to the attainment of the above objectives;

(b) nor enable such enterprises to eliminate competition in respect of a substantial proportion of the goods concerned.

ARTICLE 86

Any abusive exploitation by one or more enterprises of a dominant position within the Common Market or within a substantial part of it shall be deemed to be incompatible with the Common Market and shall be prohibited, in so far as trade between Member States could be affected by it.

Such abusive exploitation may, in particular, consist in:

(a) the direct or indirect imposition of any inequitable purchase or selling prices or of any other inequitable trading conditions;

(b) the limitation of production, markets or technological development to the prejudice of consumers;

(c) the application of unequal conditions to parties undertaking equivalent engagements in commercial transactions, thereby placing them at a competitive disadvantage.

(d) making the conclusion of a contract subject to the acceptance by the other party to the contract of additional obligations which by their nature or according to commercial usage have no connection with the subject of such contract.

ARTICLE 87

1. Within three years after this Treaty comes into force, the Council, acting by unanimous vote on a proposal of the Commission and after the

Assembly has been consulted, shall issue the necessary regulations or directives to put into effect the principles set out in Articles 85 and 86.

If such regulations or directives have not been adopted within the specified time-limit, they shall be laid down by the Council acting by a qualified majority vote on a proposal of the Commission and after the Assembly has been consulted.

TITLE II ECONOMIC POLICY

Chapter 1 Policy Relating to Economic Trends

ARTICLE 103

1. Member States shall consider their policy relating to economic trends as a matter of common interest. They shall consult with each other and with the Commission on any measures to be taken in response to prevailing circumstances.

2. Without prejudice to any other procedure provided for in this Treaty, the Council may, by unanimous vote on a proposal of the Commission, decide on measures appropriate to the situation.

3. The Council, acting by a qualified majority vote on a proposal of the Commission, shall, where appropriate, issue any necessary directives necessary to carry out the measures decided upon under the terms of paragraph 2.

Chapter 2 Balance of Payments

ARTICLE 104

Each Member State shall pursue the economic policy necessary to ensure the equilibrium of its overall balance of payments and to maintain confidence in its currency, while ensuring a high level of employment and the stability of price levels.

ARTICLE 105

1. In order to facilitate the achievement of the objectives stated in Article 104, Member States shall co-ordinate their economic policies. They shall for this purpose institute a collaboration between their appropriate administrative departments and between their central banks.

The Commission shall submit to the Council recommendations on how to achieve such collaboration.

ARTICLE 107

1. Each Member State shall treat its policy with regard to exchange rates as a matter of common interest.

2. If a Member State alters its exchange rate in a manner which is incompatible with the objectives laid down in Article 104 and which seriously distorts the conditions of competition, the Commission may, after consulting the Monetary Committee, authorize other Member States to take for a strictly limited period the necessary measures, the conditions and details of which it shall determine, in order to deal with the consequences of such alteration.

ARTICLE 108

1. Where a Member State is in difficulties or is seriously threatened with difficulties as regards its balance of payments as a result either of overall disequilibrium of its balance of payments or of the kinds of currency at its disposal and where such difficulties are likely, in particular, to prejudice the functioning of the Common Market or the gradual establishment of the common commercial policy, the Commission shall without delay examine the situation of such State and the action which, in making use of all the means at its disposal, that State has taken or may take in accordance with the provisions of Article 104. The Commission shall indicate the measures which it recommends to the State concerned to adopt.

5. COMMUNITY POLICY

Although the features of the customs union are spelled out in some detail in the Treaty of Rome, the Treaty expresses only broad goals and leaves the elaboration of policies to the Community's central institutions for such matters as transport, competition, mobility of labor and services, state aids and state trading, capital movements and capital transfers, agriculture, and general commercial law.

It can be said that the Rome Treaty is in its detail strongly biased in the direction of "negative integration"—that is, it emphasizes the removal of trade restrictions, but shies away from "positive integration"—that is, it neglects the collective pursuit of broader economic and social policies by the members. Article 3 of the Treaty illustrates this by emphasizing in a definite and mandatory fashion the removal of discrimination and distortions, but the Article remains vague and imprecise when it considers such crucial elements of positive integration as economic policies and balance-of-payments problems. The history of the Common Market has certainly demonstrated that member states have found it easier to integrate negatively than to harmonize policies positively.

By the beginning of 1970, the transition period for integration of the EEC had ended on schedule.[13] Many goals—especially those in

13. The literature on the EEC is quite extensive. For many insights on the economic and political relationships within the EEC and EFTA and the kind of European arrangements that may evolve over time, see the *European Series of Papers* (Chatham House/PEP). The *Journal of Common Market Studies* also provides numerous articles of interest. Some useful books are: Randall Hinshaw, *The European Community and American Trade* (1964); L. B. Krause, *European Economic Integra-*

support of a viable customs union—have been achieved. In other respects, however, full economic integration remains distant—notably the attainment of harmonization of national monetary and fiscal policies.

5.1. Common External Tariff. The final stage of establishing the European customs union was reached eighteen months ahead of schedule, as duties disappeared within the Common Market on July 1, 1968. At the same time, the separate tariffs of the six member nations gave way to a single tariff—the Common External Tariff (CET). The Treaty of Rome contemplated (in Article 19) that the CET would be established as an arithmetical average of the customs duties of the member nations. A single import tariff would then be applied equally to all imported goods, with future alterations by Common Market authorities. By being an average of members' duties, the CET initially resulted in lower tariffs for France and Italy but higher tariffs for Germany and Benelux countries.

The crucial question to be asked with respect to the CET is whether it constitutes an inward-looking or outward-looking policy for the Common Market. Does the external tariff result in benefits for the member countries at the expense of outsiders? Does the CET constitute trade discrimination in favor of the members without promoting trade liberalization vis-à-vis the rest of the world?

5.2 Common Agricultural Policy. Much controversy over a common agricultural policy (CAP) has persisted in the European Community. Not only did the national agricultural programs of the original Six members differ markedly at the outset of the Common Market, but the agricultural trade of the Six also accounted for a large portion of total world trade. In the United States, agricultural producers are more dependent on foreign markets than are other

tion and the United States (1968); A. Spinelli, *The Eurocrats: Conflict and Crisis in the European Community* (1968); I. Walter, *The European Common Market: Patterns of Trade and Production* (1967); T. M. Franck and E. Weisband (eds.), *A Free Trade Association* (1968).

The political aspects of the EEC are discussed in W. Hallstein, *United Europe* (1962); Leon N. Lindberg, *The Political Dynamics of European Economic Integration* (1963); E. B. Haas, *Beyond the Nation-State* (1964); U. W. Kitzinger, *The Politics and Economics of European Integration* (1965); Miriam Camps, *European Unification in the Sixties* (1967); Leon N. Lindberg and Stuart A. Scheingold, *Europe's Would-Be Polity* (1970). Theoretical analyses of integration are critically surveyed in *International Organization*, Jan. 1971.

American producers, and Western Europe has historically been the major importer of American agricultural goods. The Community's agricultural policy was also a major hurdle in the United Kingdom's bid for membership in the EEC, insofar as the United Kingdom is the world's largest agricultural importer and has pursued agricultural support policies different from the Community's common policy.

During the first four years of the Community's existence, no agreement on agricultural policy could be reached. A major dispute revolved around the common grain price issue, and a direct conflict emerged between France and West Germany. West Germany is relatively inefficient in the production of wheat, and the German national price level was the highest in the Six. Finally, a Common Agricultural Policy formally took effect on July 1, 1962—even though it was initially limited to cereals, and each member was still to be allowed to fix its own internal "target price" for each agricultural product, with the differences among members' prices to be reduced only gradually until a common Community target price for the product might be achieved at some future date. In order that the higher price countries, such as Germany, might be protected from the pressure of unrestricted agricultural imports, these countries were authorized to impose a variable levy on their imports—that is, a duty equal to the difference between the country's target price and the "c.i.f. price" of the import, and a duty that could increase whenever the c.i.f. price fell. The important features of the variable levy are discussed in the next selection.

EUROPEAN COMMON MARKET IN AGRICULTURE [14]

[I]ntegrating agriculture requires the positive steps of coordinating and then fusing six disparate regulatory systems. The consequence will be regulation of a major portion of the member states' economy by an international agency (or, to follow the mode, by a "supranational institution") which can bypass the legislatures and administrations of the member states at nearly every critical point. This achievement alone—which is without precedent in the history of international law and organization—makes the regulatory mechanism and the process of

14. Excerpts from Kenneth W. Dam, "The European Common Market in Agriculture," *Columbia Law Review*, Feb. 1967, p. 209ff. Footnotes eliminated. Reprinted by permission.

bringing it to fruition worthy of study. But quite aside from questions of international organization, the Common Agricultural Policy, as it is called in Community circles, raises some major questions of regulatory policy and technique. Finally, the agricultural common market must be understood since it lies at the heart of several current issues of international trade, including the fate of the Kennedy Round. . . .

Among the six national support programs in existence before the move toward integration, an observer could have identified almost every protective device known to the cereals trade: tariffs, quantitative restrictions, internal taxes, import monopolies, mixing regulations (requiring millers to use a specified minimum proportion of local wheat) and so forth. The EEC decided to replace these with a single protective device which would gradually disappear from intra-Community trade while providing permanent protection for the EEC as a whole against imports from third countries.

1. *The Price Support System.* It is important to note that the fundamental decision to aid agricultural incomes by supporting cereals prices rather than granting direct subsidies was not a break with the past. It was the technique used to support prices which introduced the element of novelty. In a price support system, whatever the technique used, the consumer pays a large portion of the income supplement through higher food prices. Such a system is to be contrasted with a "deficiency payment" system in which food prices are allowed to find their level in competition with imports from the world market and the "deficiency" in agricultural incomes is made up by direct cash payments to farmers. Under this latter system the burden of the aid falls entirely on the taxpayer. Moreover, unlike the price support system, it is possible to know with some precision what this form of aid costs.

Whether it is a good thing to know how much a subsidy costs depends on one's perspective. European farmers, just as any subsidy recipients, prefer to keep the subsidy free from budgetary control and review. The EEC position was simply that legislatures would never appropriate sufficiently large sums for agriculture to meet what was taken to be the income needs of farmers; therefore the income aid had to be taken from the pockets of unsuspecting, or at least helpless, consumers. Taxation hidden in food prices is, of course, considerably more regressive than income taxation. What is perhaps more serious is that the price support system, by raising food prices, lowers consumption—an unfortunate consequence for consumers and producers alike. . . .

Once a price support rather than a deficiency payments system is chosen, the question of technique becomes crucial. In spite of the multitude of protective devices available, there are essentially only two ways to support domestic agricultural prices. One is to keep out imports; the other is to remove from the market that portion of the supply which cannot be sold at the price sought. The two methods can be used singly or in combination, and the extent to which one or the other is used depends essentially on the country's degree of self-sufficiency. In the case of a deficit country—that is, a country not fully self-sufficient—it will normally suffice to restrict imports, thereby limiting supply, to bring the price up to the desired level.

In the case of a surplus country, the operation can be viewed, for the sake of simplicity, as the purchase by the government of the surplus; what is then done with the surplus is a secondary question. A surplus country which wants to maintain its domestic price above the world market level must supplement its purchasing operations with import controls, but these restrictions have a somewhat different function from the import controls of a deficit country. For the surplus country, the import restrictions spare the government the cost of supporting the entire world market through its buying operations above the world market price. The controls are used to exclude supplies which would otherwise flow into the country once the government commenced its purchasing operations.

A deficit country could also use government purchasing to support prices, but most governments prefer not to do so, since purchases require budgetary expenditures while import restrictions throw the burden of support on the consumer. Since most forms of import controls are clumsy and cannot be depended upon to let in no more and no less than the proper quantity of foreign supplies at precisely the time needed, however, even deficit countries need some form of government purchasing as a secondary measure.

2. *The Variable Levy.* The EEC, in its attempt to support prices in a deficit area, uncovered a technique of controlling imports, called the variable levy (*prélèvement*), which avoids certain limitations of traditional forms of protection. It would perhaps be too much to say that the variable levy is to protection what the wheel was to transportation, but the ease with which it arrives at precisely the level of protection desired is striking. The essential idea is to set in advance the desired internal price which, in the EEC, is called the target price (*prix indicatif*). The import levy is then varied as often and as much as necessary to make up the difference between the lowest price on the world market and the target price. Any change in the world price is thus reflected immediately in the amount of the levy. So long as the local market price is below the target price, the levy excludes all imports because purchasers will not find it advantageous to buy imported products (excluding quality and other special factors). The moment the local market price rises above the target price, the levy becomes insufficient to keep out imports. Imports then flow in until domestic demand is no longer sufficient to keep the local market price above the target price, at which time imports once again cease. The variable levy has some dramatic economic effects for a deficit area. It places the entire burden of adjustment to variations in local supply and demand on third-country suppliers. No matter what quantity is produced (short of a surplus) or demanded locally, domestic

suppliers receive the promised prices. Furthermore, third-country suppliers have no incentive to reduce prices so long as the domestic market price is below the target price; any price reduction would always be absorbed by the levy. Under the variable levy, in contrast to the tariff, third-country suppliers thus become only residual suppliers; the levy tends to isolate domestic markets in compartments of unprecedented impermeability. The variable levy is also attractive to deficit areas because it discourages export subsidies by governments of surplus countries. It is pointless for exporting countries to engage in competitive subsidization because as long as the importing country's domestic price is below the target price, the variable levy soaks up the effect of the subsidy.

Overcoming formidable problems, the major policy achievement of the European Community has been the creation of the agricultural Common Market. When individual member countries have domestic farm policies, a product is likely to have a low price because its production is subsidized; member countries will then react against the "unfair competition" represented by imports of some foodstuffs from another member country that are cheaper than the domestic products simply because they are more heavily subsidized. The only alternative, therefore, is to stop managing the markets for such products or to manage them in common. The Community chose the latter course with respect to agricultural products. French agriculture has been in a strong competitive position, and it might be concluded that the European Community has been for France a bargain in which a risk was taken for French industry in exchange for a great and certain gain for French agriculture. If this bargain had not been kept, General De Gaulle would have broken the Community by withdrawing France from it. The Germans, as well as the other members, knew this and therefore agreed to the Common Agricultural Policy after difficult and prolonged sessions in the Council of Ministers.[15]

The breakthrough for a Common Agricultural Policy emerged with what became known as the Mansholt Plan—a proposal to improve the structure of agricultural production along with the common pricing policy. Recognizing that prices could not be raised to a level which would allow farm incomes to achieve parity with other sectors, without creating large surpluses for many products, the

15. See John Pinder, "Positive Integration and Negative Integration," *The World Today*, March 1968, pp. 100–101.

Mansholt Plan concluded that there should be community regional planning of agricultural production. In 1968, the Community adopted the Mansholt Plan which specified a number of longer-term structural goals for agriculture, the gist of which amounted to increasing the size of farms and reducing the total number of farms, so that the agricultural labor force would be reduced by 1980 to only half of that in 1970.[16]

5.3. *Plan for Economic and Monetary Union.* A major event in the history of the EEC occurred in October 1970, when a committee headed by Pierre Werner, Finance Minister of Luxembourg, presented to the Council and Commission of the EEC a "phased plan" for the development of an economic and monetary union by 1980. The Werner Plan sets forth three stages of monetary integration. During the first three to five years, fluctuation among the exchange rates of the EEC members is to be narrowed, and there are to be more consultations for co-ordinating economic policies. During the second stage, policy recommendations by the Council of Ministers would become binding on member governments. Finally, in the third stage, to be reached after ten years, the then-existing exchange rates would be frozen and there would be de facto and de jure a single European currency.

The Commission approved the Werner Report in February 1971; in so doing, the Commission's President declared: "Perhaps since the signing of the Treaty of Rome no choice has been of greater importance for the future of the peoples and countries of the European Community." The economic and monetary union would be especially significant in requiring major economic policy decisions to be taken at a Community level and in transferring the necessary powers from the national to the Community plane. The economic and monetary union is therefore claimed to be indispensable for the emergence of political union. Critics, however, contend that political union is necessary prior to economic union in order to achieve fiscal integration (not simply harmonization) through a Community government that can assume responsibility for expenditures now provided by the national governments and finance them by taxes.

The main proposals contained in the Werner Report are that the

16. For a detailed consideration, see John Marsh and Christopher Ritson, *Agricultural Policy and the Common Market* (Chatham House/PEP, 1971).

monetary union would include freely convertible currencies, irrev-
ocably fixed parities of exchange rates, which could not fluctuate
among the member states, free capital movement, and a central
body to administer community monetary policy, such as the United
States Federal Reserve System.

Economic union would involve common decision-making for
budget policy and short- and medium-term tax policies, a common
tax system, and harmonized policies regarding financial and capital
markets. The Report avoids the dispute of whether or not the economic union should precede monetary action, by devising an integrated program involving parallel developments toward an economic and monetary union. Some aspects of the Werner Report are
summarized in the following.

THE WERNER REPORT [17]

The group has not attempted to construct an ideal system in abstract
terms. Its aim has rather been to define those elements which are essential to the existence of complete economic and monetary union. This
union, as described here, represents the minimum which needs to be
done and is one point in a dynamic development which the pressures of
fact and political will may shape differently.

Economic and monetary union will enable a zone to be created inside
which goods and services, persons and capital will circulate freely and
with no distortion of competition without however causing structural or
regional imbalances.

The implementation of such union will entail a lasting improvement to
well-being within the Community and will strengthen the latter's hand in
contributing to world economic and monetary balance. This supposes
joint efforts on the part of various economic and social agents so that, by
means of the combined effect of market forces and of policies conceived
and consciously applied by the authorities concerned, an adequate
growth rate, a high level of employment and stability will all be simultaneously achieved. In addition to this, Community policy should be aimed
at reducing regional and social disparities and at ensuring the conserva-
tion of the environment.

Monetary union implies that, within it, there should be total and irreversible convertibility of currencies, no margins of fluctuation in the rates of
exchange, irrevocable establishment of parity relations and total freedom

17. Council–Commission of the European Communities, "Report to the Council
and the Commission of the Realization by Stages of Economic and Monetary Union
in the Community," Luxembourg, Oct. 1970. Supplement to EEC Bulletin, No. 11.

of capital movement. It can be accompanied, either by the retention of national currency symbols, or by the introduction of a single Community currency. From a technical point of view, there might seem to be very little to choose between these two solutions, but human and political considerations clearly favour the adoption of a single currency which would bear witness to the irreversible nature of the enterprise.

In such a union, the only balance of payments that would matter would be that of the Community as a whole *vis-à-vis* the outside world. Equilibrium within the Community would thus, at this stage, become a reality, in the same way as within national territory, because of the mobility of the factors of production and because of financial transfers from the public and private sectors.

If the cohesion of economic and monetary union is to be guaranteed, it will be essential that responsibility is transferred from the level of the individual country to that of the Community. This will only be done in so far as it is necessitated by the effectiveness of Community action, and will be essentially concerned with those policies which determine the achievement of a general equilibrium. In addition, it will be necessary to standardise the instruments of economic policy in various fields.

Quantified medium-term objectives, drawn up in the form of forecasts compatible both with one another and with the finalities of the Common Market, will be set at Community level as regards growth, employment, prices and external balance. These forecasts will be periodically updated.

Medium-term economic policy will be determined in outline at Community level. To this end, and so as to assess and set the conditions for intervention on overall supply and demand—notably by means of economic and budgetary policy—it will be necessary each year to establish normative and inter-compatible economic budgets and to supervise their realisation.

It is essential that the main *monetary policy* decisions should be taken centrally, whether these are concerned with liquidity, interest rates, exchange market intervention, management of reserves or fixing exchange parities with respect to the rest of the world. The Community will have to have at its disposal the full range of necessary instruments, although the use of such instruments might, within certain limits, vary from country to country. Finally, there must be Community policy and Community representation in financial and monetary relations with third countries and international organisations of an economic, financial and monetary nature.

Budgetary policy has major significance in the general development of the economy. As the Community enters the final stage, its budget will obviously be larger than it is today, but its economic weight will remain slight in comparison with the national budgets; standardised management of these will constitute an essential factor in giving cohesion to the union.

The margins within which the major budget items should come, both as regards the annual budget and for longer-term planning, will be decided on at Community level with reference to the economic situation and the special structural elements of each country. The basic elements will be the determination of the variation in volume of the budgets, of the size of the positive or negative balance and of the methods of financing any deficits or absorbing any surpluses which may occur. To enable rapid and effective reaction to economic developments it would be of value to have, at national level, budgetary and fiscal instruments which could be used in accordance with Community directives.

In this field, efforts should be made to avoid any form of excessive centralisation. Power should only be transferred to Community bodies in so far as this is necessary to ensure that the union functions smoothly; otherwise, a variegated budgetary structure at several levels—Community, national, etc.—should be respected.

If fiscal frontiers are to be abolished without damaging the degree of elasticity necessary for fiscal policy to operate at the various levels, there will have to be an adequate degree of *fiscal harmonisation,* particularly with regard to the value added tax, taxes liable to influence movement of capital, and certain excises.

The removal of various obstacles should make it possible to achieve a genuine *common market for capital* without any form of distortion. The financial policy of the member States will have to be sufficiently unified to enable this market to operate smoothly.

The achievement of overall economic equilibrium may be seriously threatened by differences in structure. Cooperation between the partners of the Community on *structural and regional policy* will help to overcome these difficulties, and will at the same time enable distortions in competition to be eliminated. The solution of the major problems in this field will be made easier by financial compensatory measures. In a state of economic and monetary union, structural and regional policies will not be able to be the exclusive prerogative of national budgets. What is more, the environmental problems posed by industrial expansion and urban development will have to be dealt with at Community level in their technical, financial and social aspects. Finally, the continued development of intra-Community trade will find a fresh stimulus in an adequate transport policy.

Another way of guaranteeing the cohesion of economic and monetary union will be to consult *management and the unions* prior to the drafting and implementation of Community policy. Procedures will need to be developed to ensure that such consultations are systematic and continuous. In this context, wage developments in the various member countries will be observed and discussed at Community level, and management and the unions will take part in these discussions.

To sum up, economic and monetary union implies the following main consequences:

—Community currencies will be guaranteed complete reciprocal convertibility, with no fluctuation in rates and with inalterable parity relations or, preferably, will be replaced by a single Community currency;

—the creation of liquidities throughout the zone will be centralised, as will be monetary and credit policies;

—monetary policy towards the rest of the world will be the responsibility of the Community;

—member states' policies with regard to the capital market will be unified;

—the essential, overall factors of Government budgets, and in particular the variations in their volume and the means of financing or utilising any positive or negative balances, together with the size of such balances, will be decided on at Community level;

—regional and structural policies will not be the exclusive prerogative of the member states;

—permanent, systematic consultation of management and the unions will be guaranteed at Community level.

Resulting from this is the fact that, as far as *institutional reforms* are concerned, the achievement of economic and monetary union will necessitate the creation or transformation of a certain number of Community bodies which will be responsible for things hitherto the responsibility of national authorities. These transfers of responsibility represent a process of fundamental political significance implying the progressive development of political cooperation. Economic and monetary union would thus seem to be a catalyst for the development of a form of political union which it will not ultimately be able to do without.

The group does not feel bound to formulate detailed proposals as to the institutional form which the various Community bodies should take; it does, however, feel it should point out the main requirements to be met by two bodies which it considers essential for the control of economic and monetary policy within the union: a decision-taking centre for economic policy, and a Community system of central banks.

The *decision-taking centre for economic policy* will, as a representative of the Community's interest, independently exercise a decisive influence on the general economic policy of the Community. Given that the role of the Community budget will be inadequate as a means of medium-term economic policy, the Community decision-taking centre will have to be in a position to influence national budgets, notably with regard to the size and the positive or negative nature of any balances, as well as the means of financing deficits and absorbing surpluses. In addition, any changes in the parity of the single currency or in the national currencies as a whole will be the responsibility of this centre. Finally, so as to ensure the necessary links with general economic policy, its responsibility will extend to other areas of economic and social policy which have been transferred to Community level. It is essential that the decision-taking centre for economic policy be in a position to take swift and effective decisions along lines to be determined, notably with regard to the participation of the member states in its actions.

The transference to Community level of powers previously exercised by national bodies will go hand in hand with the transfer of a corresponding parliamentary responsibility from national to Community level. The decision-taking centre for economic policy will be politically responsible to a European Parliament, and this latter will have to be equipped with a statute corresponding to the extended scope of Community responsibilities, not merely from the point of view of wider powers, but also from that of the way in which its members are elected.

The introduction of a *Community system of central banks* might well be based on bodies such as the Federal Reserve System which operates in the United States. This Community institution will, when the economic situation so requires, be empowered to take internal monetary policy decisions concerning liquidity, interest rates and the granting of loans to the public and private sectors. As far as external monetary policy is concerned, it will also be empowered to take action on the exchange market and in the management of the Community's monetary reserves.

The Six's Council of Ministers also expressed strong support of an economic and monetary union in February 1971. As observed by *The Economist*, "The resolution . . . does not carry the weight of a full decision, and much of its wording is free of the supranational idealism with which the whole subject of monetary union was invested during the heyday of the Werner Plan last year. But its actual provisions, in contrast to the gentle wording phrased for France's benefit, are as likely or unlikely to lead to eventual monetary union as Werner." [18] A portion of the Council's Resolution follows.

COMPROMISE PLAN FOR ECONOMIC AND MONETARY UNION [19]

The Council of the European Communities and the representatives of the Governments of the Member States, . . . adopt the following resolution.

I. In order simultaneously to ensure satisfactory growth, full employment, and stability within the Community, to correct the structural and regional imbalances that exist in the Community and to increase the Community's contribution to international economic and monetary cooperation and thus achieve a Community of stability and growth, the Council and the representatives of the Governments of the Member States ex-

18. *The Economist*, Feb. 13, 1971, p. 64.
19. Text of Resolution of the Council of the European Communities, in Press Release No. 304/71 (Press II), Brussels, Feb. 9, 1971.

press their political will to build, over the next ten years, an economic and monetary union following a stage-by-stage plan, beginning January 1, 1971.

As a result of the actions to be taken, at the end of this program, the Community must:

1. create a zone within which persons, goods, services, and capital will move freely and without distortions of competition, without, however, bringing about structural and regional imbalances, and under conditions that will enable businesses to carry on their activities at the Community level;

2. form a monetary entity having its own identity within the international system and characterized by the total and irreversible convertibility of currencies, the elimination of fluctuation margins for exchange rates, the irrevocable fixing of parity relationships, which are necessary conditions for the creation of a single currency and involve an organization of the Central Banks at the Community level;

3. in the economic and monetary field, have powers and responsibilities that will permit its institutions to assume the management of the union. To this end, the necessary economic policy decisions shall be taken at the Community level and the necessary powers shall be given to the Community institutions.

The allocation of powers and responsibilities among the Community institutions, on the one hand, and the Member States, on the other hand, shall take place in consideration of what is needed for the union to be cohesive and Community action to be effective.

The Community institutions shall be placed in a position to carry out their responsibilities in economic and monetary matters effectively and promptly.

The Community policies applied within the framework of the economic and monetary union shall be submitted to the European Parliament for discussion and review.

The Community organization of Central Banks shall assist, within the framework of its own responsibilities, in the realization of the objectives of stability and growth of the Community.

The principles set forth above shall be applied in the following areas:

—the monetary and internal credit policy of the union;

—monetary policy vis-à-vis the outside world;

—the policy concerning a unified capital market and capital movements to and from third countries;

—budgetary and fiscal policy as related to the policy of stability and growth; for the budget policy proper, the margins within which the principal headings of all the national budgets must remain will be determined at the Community level, in particular as regards changes in their total size, the amount of the balances, and the methods used to finance such balances and apply them;

—the actions required at the structural and regional level within the framework of a Community policy shall be supported by appropriate means, so that they too may contribute to the Community's balanced development and in order to resolve the most important problems. . . .

III. In order to attain these objectives, the Council and the representatives of the Governments of the Member States have agreed to set in motion, starting on January 1, 1971, a series of actions to be completed in a first, three-year stage.

1. The Council will establish, on a proposal of the Commission, such provisions concerning a strengthening of the coordination of short-term economic policies as can ensure that such coordination will really be effective, this mainly by intensifying and generalizing the mandatory prior consultations. This coordination of short-term economic policies will take into account the guidelines for the medium-term economic policy. . . .

5. In order to tighten coordination in the area of the Member States' monetary and credit policy, the Council has agreed that:

—prior mandatory consultations will be intensified within the Monetary Committee and the Committee of Governors of the Central Banks;

—the Central Banks will, within the limits of their powers and within the framework of their own responsibilities, be invited to coordinate their policies within the Committee of Governors of the Central Banks, with due regard for the general economic policy guidelines which the Council will define;

—the Monetary Committee and the Committee of Governors of the Central Banks in close collaboration will continue the work on the harmonization of the instruments of monetary policy.

6. The Council has agreed that the Community must gradually adopt common positions in monetary relations with third countries and with international organizations and particularly must not, in exchange relations between member countries, invoke any provisions that might permit a weakening of the international exchange system.

7. The Council and the Member States shall ask the Central Banks of the member countries to keep, from the beginning of the stage and on an experimental basis, the fluctuations in rates between Community currencies within narrower margins than those resulting from the application of the margins in effect for the U. S. dollar, and to do so by concerted action with respect to that currency.

The Council has agreed that in light of the circumstances and of the results in the harmonization of economic policies, new measures could be taken consisting in a transition from a de facto to a de jure system, in the interventions in Community currencies and in successive reductions of fluctuation margins between Community currencies. The Committee of Governors of the Central Banks will report twice a year to the Council and the Commission on how the concerted actions of the Central Banks operate on the exchange market, as well as on the advisability of taking new measures in that area.

The capability to adopt common positions in monetary relations, as emphasized in the preceding resolution, will be necessary for the implementation of any economic and monetary union. The Ministers and Governors of the central banks set June 15, 1971, for the entry and application of the first important monetary measure: a reduction in the fluctuation margins between the Community currencies, which were to go from 0.75 to 0.60 per cent, in both directions. After President Nixon's New Economic Policy on August 15, 1971, which severed the dollar's link to gold and caused the dollar to float in relation to other currencies, each Community country actually reacted in dispersed order. No joint float could be agreed upon by the Common Market countries, and instead of being able to narrow the margins among exchange rates, the float actually appreciated the German mark considerably more against the French franc. In September 1971, at the International Monetary Fund's meeting, the European countries did present a united front against the United States, urging the United States to devalue the dollar against gold. Finally, on December 15, 1971, President Nixon, after meeting with France's President Pompidou, announced that the dollar price of gold would be raised. After this announcement it still remained to be seen whether future developments in international monetary arrangements would allow the Community to move toward a genuine common currency. The fate of monetary union is very much dependent upon the future course of international monetary reform.

6. COMMUNITY ENLARGEMENT: THE BRITISH ENTRY

Some additional perspective of the European Community may be gained by summarizing the long series of negotiations culminating in Britain's entry into the Community. These negotiations point up a number of sensitive issues of regional integration and provide an indication of how the European Community might affect the way nations will deal with the longer-term trade problems of the world.

6.1. Background. After two earlier vetoes by France, in 1967 the British government reactivated its application to join the Community. Some background to Britain's application is given in the following statement.

BRITAIN'S APPLICATION [20]

Her Majesty's Government decided on 2nd May, 1967 to make an application under Article 237 of the Treaty of Rome for membership of the European Economic Community (EEC), and parallel applications for membership of the European Coal and Steel Community (ECSC) and EURATOM. The Government's decision was debated by both Houses of Parliament, and at the end of a three-day debate in the House of Commons the decision was approved by a majority of 426, one of the largest majorities in a vote in the House of Commons in peacetime. Her Majesty's Government thereupon applied for membership of the Communities on 10th May, 1967.

2. The Prime Minister's statement on the Government's decision was presented as a White Paper (Cmnd. 3269) which set out the reasons underlying the decision to apply for membership of the Communities, and the issues which it would be necessary to resolve during the negotiations for that purpose. On the economic side, the White Paper spoke of "the long-term potential for Europe, and therefore for Britain, of the creation of a single market of approaching 300 million people, with all the scope and incentive which this will provide for British industry, and of the enormous possibilities which an integrated strategy for technology, on a truly Continental scale, can create." On the other side of the account Parliament was also informed that, while all calculations were necessarily extremely speculative, the effect of adopting the EEC's common agricultural policy as it stood might be to bring about a rise in the cost of living of 2½–3½ per cent (reflecting a 10–14 per cent rise in the cost of food) and to create a cost to the balance of payments of between £175 million and £250 million a year. The overall cost to the balance of payments of entry, including the agricultural element, was estimated to require the redeployment of resources from present home use to exports, or to import substitution, of the order of about £100 million each year over a period of perhaps five years.

3. The political reasons for applying for membership of the European Communities were summarised in the White Paper as follows: "But whatever the economic arguments, the House will realise that . . . the Government's purpose derives above all from our recognition that Europe is now faced with the opportunity of a great move forward in political unity and that we can—and indeed we must—play our full part in it. We do not see European unity as something narrow or inward-looking. Britain has her own vital links through the Commonwealth, and in other ways, with other continents. So have other European countries. Together we can en-

20. Reprinted from *Britain and the European Communities*, Cmnd. 4289, HMSO, London, Feb. 1970, paragraphs 1–4.

sure that Europe plays in world affairs the part which the Europe of today is not at present playing. For a Europe that fails to put forward its full economic strength will never have the political influence which I believe it could and should exert within the United Nations, within the Western Alliance, and as a means for effecting a lasting *détente* between East and West; and equally contributing in ever fuller measure to the solution of the world's North-South problem, to the needs of the developing world." Her Majesty's Government consider that events since the statement was made, and particularly the outcome of the Summit Conference of the Six on 1st and 2nd December, 1969, reaffirm the validity of the statement.

4. Following approval by Parliament of the Government's decision to apply for membership of the Communities, the then Foreign Secretary on 4th July, 1967, made a statement on behalf of Her Majesty's Government to the Council of the Western European Union (Cmnd. 3345), in which, after elaborating the political and economic and industrial reasons indicated above which underlay Britain's application to join the Communities, he set out the issues which Britain would seek to deal with in the course of negotiations for entry into the Communities. The major issues included the inequitable burden which the then existing financial arrangements for agriculture would place on Britain; the need for a transitional period or periods to permit a gradual adaptation to the circumstances of an enlarged Community; the need to make provision for the interests of the developing countries and territories whose economies are dependent on the Commonwealth Sugar Agreement; and the need to make provision for New Zealand's dairy products. On 4th December, 1969, the Prime Minister in the House of Commons confirmed that this statement by the Foreign Secretary remained the basis for our negotiations for membership.

6.2. The Negotiations. Beginning in July 1970, there followed a series of complex negotiations on the specific terms for Britain's entry into the EEC. The decisive part of the negotiations concerned the establishment of the stages and precise measures by which Britain would become integrated into the Community over a transition period. In his opening statement at the first negotiating session, the Chairman of the Council of Ministers of the European Community made clear the Community's position.

THE COMMUNITY'S POSITION [21]

We must now describe to you the position and procedures which the Community has decided upon for the purpose of the negotiations.

21. Extract from the opening statement, in Luxembourg on June 30, 1970, made by Monsieur Pierre Harmel.

A. We assume in principle that your states accept the treaties and their political objectives, all the decisions of every type which have been taken since the treaties came into force and the choices made in the fields of development.

These decisions also include the agreements concluded by the Community with third countries.

B. Under these conditions, the Community wishes at the opening of the negotiations, to state a certain number of principles it intends to apply:

1. The rule which must necessarily govern the negotiations is that the solution of any problems of adjustment which may arise must be sought in the establishment of transitional measures and not in changes in the existing rules.

2. The object of the transitional measures will be to allow for the adjustments which prove to be necessary as a consequence of the enlargement. Their duration must be restricted to that required to achieve this aim. As a general rule, they must incorporate detailed timetables and must commence with an initial significant mutual tariff reduction on the entry into force of the accession treaties.

3. The transitional measures must be conceived in such a way as to ensure an overall balance of reciprocal advantages. With this in mind, it will be necessary to ensure an adequate synchronisation of the progress of freedom of movement of industrial goods with the achievement of the agricultural common market. This consideration must be taken into account in respect of the durations of the transitional measures in the industrial and agricultural sectors.

4. In the field of trade, the duration of the transitional period should be the same for all the applicants.

5. In other fields in which transitional measures prove to be necessary, the duration of such measures could, if possible and desirable, be varied according to their subject matter and the applicants involved. These questions will be examined during the negotiations.

6. The various accession treaties should come into force on the same date.

The main problems of British entry, as will be evident in the following selections, focused on Britain's contribution to Community finance, Community preferences, Commonwealth sugar, New Zealand dairy products, and the timetable of tariff reductions.

On each transitional measure there was to be extensive negotiations in an attempt to reconcile the different views on the benefits and costs of each measure. Concerning the adoption of the common external tariff, for example, Britain originally wanted a three-year transition period beginning in 1973. Britain also wanted a six-year period in which to adopt the higher farm prices of the Community.

The Community insisted on the same transition period for both industry and farming, which was finally settled at five years.

On another major issue—that of Britain's payments to the Community's budget—the negotiating was also keen.

THE BATTLE IS JOINED [22]

It is a good time to be a sceptic in Europe. The newspaper stories on Wednesday of a collision in Brussels between Britain and the six common market countries should be taken with a good pinch of salt. The talks are not on the verge of breakdown. Certainly Mr. Rippon's meeting with the European community's ministers on Tuesday left Britain and the Six far apart on what Britain should pay into the community fund during the transitional period after it goes into Europe. The Six themselves are at odds over how much to ask for; they agree only that it should be more than Britain wants to pay. The gap may take time to bridge. It might just possibly prove unbridgeable, and then Mr. Rippon will be right when he says that "they, we and all Europe will lose the ultimate goal." But we doubt it.

Mr. Rippon has shown his teeth in the negotiating room before, but never over something as important as finance. Britain wants its way on several key points in return for the very large concession it has already made—its acceptance, lock, stock and barrel after a transition period, of the community's rules for financing its budget. The main virtue of Britain's finance proposal, ever since it was tabled on December 16th, is that it confronts the Six, especially the French, with their own rhetoric about wanting Britain in. The weakness of Britain's case is unfortunately just as obvious. Britain has offered to pay so little by the end of the transition period that it will face a jump (which might cost an extra £150 million–£400 million in a single year) when it eventually moves over to the community's automatic finance system. And it has offered to pay so little in the first year of the transition period that it finds itself involved in a maze of contradictory figuring with the European commission and the Germans over whether this will in fact be enough to cover the net outflow needed to look after farmers in two other new members hoping to join together with Britain—Denmark and Ireland. As it is, the Germans pay much the largest share of the bill for subsidising European farming, and they are understandably reluctant to add to that bill.

Such pulling and shoving were predictable. Something would have been curiously wrong if this had not happened when the heart of Britain's application was at last reached. Since the argument about figures was bound to come, and since it will probably get even shriller, the only useful question is how the compromise will eventually be struck. Britain has bravely—or rashly—committed itself to a hard line. Now it will dig

22. Reprinted from *The Economist*, Feb. 6, 1971, p. 13.

in on its low opening figure of a contribution of around 3 per cent of the community's budget in the first year of transition. It may be more ready to change the figure which it has suggested for the end of the transition (13–15 per cent of the budget). It will stick out for some sort of formal statement by the community that it will not let the financial price of entry drive a new member broke. And it will go for at least two extra years (it has asked for three) at the end of the five-year transitional period during which Britain's contribution will have a ceiling while the British get ready for the final jump into the automatic system.

Getting ready for the final jump is what the transitional period is all about in British eyes. British industry will need some years to take advantage of joining the larger European market; it would be unfair, Britain argues, for Europe to demand too much at the start when Britain will be getting few industrial advantages and when it will already be paying a higher price for European food. Though dismayed by the figures Britain is suggesting, the usual pro-British quarters in Europe—Holland, Italy, Luxembourg and Germany—have at least some sympathy for its argument. The temptation is to drive France into a corner on this and then reach a compromise with Britain by haggling over figures.

To give in to this temptation would be a mistake. France wants Britain in, but will not let it in from a corner. President Pompidou has carefully left his escape routes clear; other European politicians should be clear in their own minds that France's president has as much to lose in France if he is seen to let Britain in on concessionary terms, and under pressure from outside, as if he keeps Britain out for no better reason than General de Gaulle used to offer.

To reach agreement with another man it is important to know his mind. France is asking a stiff price from Britain because the common farm policy is central to its interests. And if the price cannot be met France is bursting with solutions which are not nearly so loaded against Britain as the British Treasury claims they are. If Britain, unlike Germany, cannot pay much during the transitional period it will be because Britain's balance of payments is weak. This is something, France argues, which a Europe groping towards a common monetary identity should be able to cope with, either by medium-term credits to Britain or by allowing its payments to the fund to be frozen in London during difficult transitional years; the community would then borrow the money for its budget instead. France would also back any scheme to take the sterling area liabilities off Britain's back provided the privileged access to the London market now enjoyed by the richer Commonwealth countries—Australia, Canada and New Zealand—no longer applied. It is an extraordinary sign of how far ahead France now looks that such imaginings are commonplace among the senior French officials dealing with British entry. Britain is right to go for easy figures if it can get them. If it cannot get them, it should understand the alternatives are at hand—and that it does not have to turn its back on the whole enterprise.

Finally, almost a year after the first session of "real negotiations" had begun, the various delegations were able to agree on definite terms.

COMMON MARKET OPENS THE DOOR [23]

LUXEMBOURG, June 23—Through the long day and night Geoffrey Rippon, Britain's Chief negotiator in the talks with the European Economic Community, sat in his delegation room in the organization's skyscraper offices here.

Down the hall the Foreign Ministers of the Six talked among themselves in their council chamber, dispatching Jean-François Deniau of the Economic Community's Commission to Mr. Rippon with new proposals.

Under the extraordinary negotiating procedure they use, they did not want to meet formally with the British until everything had been worked out in private.

Finally, shortly before 5 this morning, Mr. Rippon walked down the corridor. When he entered the chamber the assembled diplomats and Eurocrats spontaneously broke into applause. As one said groggily later, "I had no idea I was going to do it until I suddenly found myself clapping."

That reaction among a group of tough professionals was about as dramatic testimony to the significance of what happened here as could be imagined. It was a tribute not so much to Mr. Rippon personally, of course, as to the end of the 10-year estrangement between Britain and the Common Market.

The sentiment of that moment was not allowed to overwhelm reality. Foreign Minister Maurice Schumann of France, when he met the press a few minutes later, referred to the problem that still lies ahead— ratification by the British House of Commons.

It will be difficult, he said, though he did add: "I have confidence in Providence and in a nation which, in the last 30 years, has become dear to me among all."

Since the negotiations began in the Luxembourg skyscraper just a year ago, they have consistently had a dual focus. Their object has been not merely to accommodate the differing interests of Britain and the six members of the bloc but to meet the needs of British politics.

A participant on the Common Market side related that ideas were brought up and then discarded again and again last night on the ground that they would not satisfy British public opinion.

The terms actually agreed on went much further than almost anyone would have predicted a year ago to quiet the concerns of the Briton on the street. Perhaps the most telling example is New Zealand.

23. Special report by Anthony Lewis to *New York Times*, June 24, 1971.

The logic of the Economic Community certainly seems to make a special relationship with a prosperous country 12,000 miles away a doubtful notion. It is a European community, designed to create an integrated geographical market in industrial and agricultural products.

On the New Zealand issue, therefore, France has always had considerable support from her five partners for a negative view. The French position has been that the privileged access of New Zealand dairy products to the British market had to be ended during the five-year transitional period after Britain joins the Economic Community.

The actual terms that Mr. Rippon won will allow New Zealand to keep 71 per cent of the British market after five years, and there will be a further review by the members, including Britain, with no commitment ever to end the special treatment.

Any mildly dispassionate observer would regard that outcome as a triumph for Britain and her New Zealand kith. It is a measure of the passionate opposition in some British quarters that the terms were promptly denounced.

"A miserable, inadequate, bogus settlement for New Zealand," said John Silkin, former Labor party chief whip.

The fact is that Mr. Silkin and others like him are against the European venture for historical, patriotic or emotional reasons that hardly can be affected by any terms.

Aside from New Zealand, the agreements mark considerable gains on what Britain was first offered.

In 1970 the Government, then headed by Labor, estimated that the net cost of Britain's contribution to the bloc's budget could run as high as $1.37-billion a year. This morning a British spokesman said the agreed terms would cost up to $528-million after the five-year transition.

The six members agreed to put aside their fishing policy of free access to each other's waters and let the new members reserve their grounds for their own fishermen. That again was designed to meet public opinion, as was an undertaking to adopt special measures for hill farmers, mostly in Scotland.

With a long list of negotiating achievements in one night, one might have expected an atmosphere of electric excitement. Despite the usual theater of the all-night session—plus champagne at the end this time— there was more of a sense of satisfaction than of drama.

The reasons are clear enough. For one, the real drama occurred in Paris last month, when President Pompidou and Prime Minister Heath showed the political will that ended the 10-year stalemate and made agreement possible. For another, as the diplomats know so well, they must now give way to the politicians for one last act in the drama of Britain and Europe.

6.3. *White Paper on Entry into EEC.* The terms negotiated for entry were published by the British Government in a White Paper on July 7, 1971. "Every historic choice involves challenge as well as opportunity," stated the White Paper. "Her Majesty's Government are convinced that the right decision for us is to accept the challenge, seize the opportunity and join the European Communities."

THE WHITE PAPER [24]

In the White Paper, *The United Kingdom and the European Communities,* the British Government assesses the terms which have been negotiated as "fair and reasonable" and states that it "will seek the approval of Parliament in the autumn for a decision of principle to take up full membership of the Communities on the basis of the arrangements which have been negotiated with them." The United Kingdom's geographical, military, political, economic, and social circumstances are so similar to those of the Six, and it has so many objectives in common, that its best interests would be served by joining forces with them in the creation of a wider European Community of free nations.

Selected excerpts from Part One of the Paper are given below.

(1) "We shall be required to pay a contribution to the Community budget which—after allowing for our estimated receipts from the budget—will involve a net cost to our balance of payments of some £100 million in the first year, [and] if the structure of the budget were to remain unchanged [of] some £200 million in the fifth year."

(2) "Gradual adoption of the common agricultural policy will stimulate British farm output and open Community markets to [U.K.] food exports, but at the same time will raise food prices in the United Kingdom and the cost of [U.K.] food imports; . . . it is estimated that the rise in average retail food prices during the transitional period . . . will amount to about 2½ pence in the £ each year. As a result the cost of living will increase by about half a new penny in the £1 each year, but at the same time tariff reductions should lead to lower prices for manufactures which will go some way to offset this increase."

(3) The United Kingdom will "be asked to subscribe £37.5 million in sterling to the paid-up capital of the European Investment Bank; it is expected that the greater part of this sum will remain in the United Kingdom. [The United Kingdom will also be expected to] subscribe £24 million to the reserve funds of the European Coal and Steel Community; this would be primarily if not wholly spent in this country."

(4) "The effects of membership on British industry will stem principally from the creation of an enlarged European market by the removal of tariffs between the United Kingdom and the Community countries . . . at

24. *International Financial News Survey,* Vol. XXIII, No. 28, July 21, 1971, pp. 220–21. Condensed from original sources: *The United Kingdom and the European Communities* (Cmnd. 4715), July 1971, and *Financial Times,* July 8, 1971, London.

the end of the transitional period . . . manufacturers will be operating in a 'domestic market' perhaps five times as large as at present, in which tariff barriers cannot be put up against them however well they do. There will in consequence be a radical change in planning, investment, production, and sales effort. [The Government does] not believe that the overall response of British industry to membership can be quantified in terms of its effect upon the balance of trade [but is] confident that this effect will be positive and substantial, as it has been for the Community."

(5) "In the light of the experience of the Six themselves, and their conviction that the creation of the Community materially contributed to their growth, and of the essential similarity of our economies, [the U.K. Government is] confident that membership of the enlarged Community will lead to much improved efficiency and productivity in British industry, with a higher rate of investment and a faster growth of real wages . . . this belief is shared by a substantial majority of British industry, whose own interests are at stake, and who are in the best position to judge."

(6) "These improvements in efficiency and competitive power should enable the United Kingdom to meet the balance of payment costs of entry over the next decade as they gradually build up. The improvement in efficiency will also result in a higher rate of growth of the economy."

Part Two of the White Paper sets out the terms of entry arrived at in negotiations with the EEC. In summary, the main terms are as follows:

Participation and Voting in the Communities' Institutions. It has been agreed from the start that the United Kingdom should have a position in the institutions equal to that enjoyed by France, Germany, and Italy— with 10 votes (out of a total of 61) in the enlarged Council and 2 seats (out of a total of 14) on the Commission.

Transitional Arrangements for Industry. Assuming U.K. entry on January 1, 1973, the progressive introduction of a customs union between the Six and the United Kingdom will consist of five reciprocal tariff reductions of 20 per cent each on April 1, 1973, January 1, 1974, January 1, 1975, January 1, 1976, and July 1, 1977. The United Kingdom's move to the Community's common external tariff (which is rather lower than the U.K. tariff) will be carried out in four stages, as follows: 40 per cent on January 1, 1974, and 20 per cent each on January 1, 1975, January 1, 1976, and July 1, 1977.

Transitional Arrangements for Agriculture. The transitional period for agricultural products will be precisely five years, with the United Kingdom making its sixth and final move toward Community price levels at the end of 1977. For those agricultural commodities for which the Community has a common external tariff instead of, or in addition to, levies, the transitional arrangements will take the form of tariff adjustments similar to those agreed for industry.

Contribution to the Community Budget. The arrangements agreed are illustrated in Table I below. The first entry sets out the nominal "key" which has been agreed. The second entry shows the proportion of this nominal key which the United Kingdom will in practice be required to pay. The third entry gives the resulting U. K. share of the Community budget in each year. The fourth entry sets out the possible size of gross U. K. contributions on the assumption that the budget amounts to £1,400 million in 1973 and rises to £1,600 million by 1977. The fifth entry shows the estimated buildup of U. K. receipts from the budget. The final entry gives the resulting estimates of net U. K. payments.

Table I. United Kingdom Contribution to the Community Budget

	1973	1974	1975	1976	1977
			Per cent		
"Key" (share of budget)	19.19	19.38	19.77	20.16	20.56
Per cent of key to be paid	45.0	56.0	67.5	79.5	92.0
Contribution as share of budget	8.64	10.85	13.34	16.03	18.92
		Prospective contribution (million pounds sterling)			
Gross	120	155	195	245	300
Receipts	20	40	55	75	100
Net	100	115	140	170	200

After the first five years there will be a further period of two years during which the size of the U.K. contribution will continue to be limited. In 1980 and subsequent years the United Kingdom will be required to contribute 90 per cent of its agricultural levy and customs duty receipts and such value-added tax (VAT)—not exceeding the yield of a 1 per cent VAT—as is necessary.

The Commonwealth. Provision has been made to safeguard New Zealand exports of dairy products by arrangements acceptable to the New Zealand Government. . . . For all British dependent territories with the exception of Hong Kong and Gibraltar, and for all independent Commonwealth developing countries with the exception of those in Asia, arrangements have been made which provide the opportunities of Association— or for the independent developing countries, the alternative of a trade agreement—with the enlarged Community. Independent Asian Commonwealth countries not only will benefit from the generalized preference scheme of the enlarged Community, but will be assured that the Community's continuing objective will be to expand and reinforce existing trade relations and that the Community will be ready to examine trade problems which might arise in the future with a view to finding appropriate solutions.

The Commonwealth Sugar Agreement will continue until 1974, after which arrangements for sugar imports from developing Commonwealth producers will be made within the framework of an association or trading agreement with the enlarged Community. It has further been agreed that the enlarged Community will have as its firm purpose the safeguarding of the interests of the developing countries concerned whose economies depend to a considerable extent on the export of primary products, particularly sugar.

Sterling. The United Kingdom has stated that it is prepared to envisage an "orderly and gradual" rundown of official sterling balances after its accession; that, after accession, the United Kingdom will discuss measures by which a "progressive alignment of the external characteristics of sterling with those of other Community currencies might be achieved"; and that, in the meantime, the United Kingdom will manage its policies with a view to "stabilizing" the official sterling balances.

Fisheries. The United Kingdom and other applicant countries have made clear that they do not consider the common fisheries policy to be appropriate to the needs and circumstances of an enlarged Community, particularly in respect of access to fishing grounds. The Community has agreed that the arrangements governing access to coastal fisheries will have to be reconsidered in the perspective of enlargement, and further discussion will be held in the near future.

6.4. The Great Debate. Publication of the White Paper signaled the start of a great debate between pro- and anti-Marketeers. Initial editorial comment was generally favorable. *The Financial Times,* for example, adopted this position.

THE DEBATE BEGINS [25]

The main importance of yesterday's White Paper is that it will enable an informed public debate to begin about the Government's decision to seek Parliamentary backing for entry into full membership of the European Communities. It contains no revelations. It consists of a detailed account of what has been agreed in the course of negotiations between Britain and the Six and a forceful statement of the case for entry. This statement, however, is a good deal more colourful in its use of language than is usual in official documents. Whatever civil servants may have contributed to it, and the Cabinet Office seems to have contributed a good deal more than the Treasury, the final version evidently owes a good deal to Ministers, and especially to Mr. Heath himself.

No attempt has been made on this occasion to quantify the total effect of entry on the balance of trade, for the good reason that any such at-

25. *Financial Times,* July 8, 1971.

tempt would be misleading. Not only could an estimate be readily falsified by relatively small movements in, say, the relative level of wages but the psychological reaction of British industry to the opportunity of operating in a much larger home market is likely to count for more than tariff changes as such. The Government may be going too far in stating that there *will* be a radical change in planning, investment, production and sales effort, but there certainly may be.

What the White Paper does try to estimate (though only for the years immediately after entry) is the cost of contributions to the Community Budget—rising from £100m. in the first year to £200m. in the fifth if the proportion spent on agriculture remains unchanged—and the effect of higher food prices on the cost of living—a rise of about half a new penny in the £ each year. Both these changes are small in relation to those which are likely to take place in the balance of payments and the cost of living in any case. To offset them, there must be set down the chance of achieving greater efficiency and faster growth in a larger market and the insurance which membership of a wider trading block provides against the risk of a resurgence of protectionism.

The economic case for entry here begins to merge into the political case, which the White Paper deploys at length. Its arguments are similar to those which have persuaded the Financial Times that the future of Britain lies in Europe. Briefly, the world balance of power has changed out of recognition since 1939 and the Six, helped by circumstances, have been quicker than Britain to realise that in the new conditions differences between the countries of Europe are much less significant than what they have in common. Alone, our political influence will inevitably continue to decline, and there is no alternative grouping to which to attach ourselves.

Whether it be in the field of defence, or of international trade, or of strengthening the international monetary system, or of aiding the underdeveloped countries of the world, or even of keeping up with the competition in a time of advanced technology and transnational corporations, we shall be much better placed to achieve our national objectives as a member of the Communities. The Six are now anxious for us to join and help to complete the work they have begun so successfully. To refuse membership at this stage would be a retreat into isolation which would leave them without obligation or cause to consider our interests in future.

These arguments will be familiar to those who have followed the long negotiations: the value of the White Paper is that it sets them out effectively before a wider audience. At the same time, by setting out the facts about what has been agreed in detail, it will help to reassure the doubtful, force the waverers to make up their minds, and deprive the committed opponents of entry of some of their ammunition. The heavy stress played on the retention of sovereignty is understandable in this context. The assurance that the British legal system, the English language and the National Health Service will be unaffected is less unnecessary than it may seem. It is right to point out that the essential interests of Commonwealth countries have been looked after and to promise that pensions and other social security benefits will be protected against the price effect of joining the Community.

It is right, too, to point out as frequently as the White Paper does that it has been the policy of Labour as well as Conservatives to enter the EEC if the terms were acceptable, and that the present terms are better than Labour expected to obtain. It refers constantly to what successive Governments have sought to achieve. It quotes tellingly from statements made by Mr. Wilson as Prime Minister in 1967. And it rubs in the fact that the present Government merely "picked up the hand which their predecessors had prepared for the negotiating table." This is a national and not a party issue.

A decision not to join the Communities when at last we have the power to do so, the White Paper concludes, would be a rejection of an historic opportunity and a reversal of the whole direction of British policy under successive Governments during the last decade. "Her Majesty's Government believe that the terms which have been negotiated are fair and reasonable and provide this country with an opportunity which may never recur." We agree wholeheartedly.

Although the White Paper unreservedly recommended British membership in the European Community, it did so only on the broadest political and economic grounds—not on the basis of extensive economic analysis. No attempt was made to quantify either the indirect short-term benefits for the balance of payments or the long-term economic advantages. Among economists, the central issues in the debate narrowed down to what would be the "impact effects" and "dynamic effects," and whether the positive dynamic effects would outweigh any adverse impact effects.

It was recognized generally that Britain's balance of payments would initially be affected adversely by these impact effects: (i) the tariff changes (affecting exports as Britain moved out of preferential trade areas in the Commonwealth and EFTA in exchange for freer access to the Common Market); (ii) the working of the Common Agricultural Policy (which would raise agricultural import prices and in turn affect the general cost structure of the economy and the competitiveness of exports through the effects of the higher prices for imported agricultural products); and (iii) the contribution that Britain would have to pay to the Community budget. There were considerable differences of judgment as to the magnitude of these impact effects, and whether the burden of the impact effects—as the price of entry—would be outweighed over the longer period by the gains from the dynamic effects. The following two selections highlight these differences.

THE TRUTH ABOUT THE "DYNAMIC EFFECTS" [26]

It is generally agreed that the initial effects of joining the Common Market are likely to be unfavourable to Britain, mainly owing to the heavy cost of assuming the obligations of the common agricultural policy. It is argued however that these unfavourable impact effects are likely to be more than offset by the long-term advantages—the so-called "dynamic effects" of membership. Last year's White Paper on *Britain and the European Communities* (Cmnd. 4289, February 1970) described the nature of these advantages in the following terms:

> For industry and trade, the main consequences of United Kingdom membership of an enlarged community would be that we should then form part of a Customs Union of up to 300 million people stretching from Scotland to Sicily and from the Irish Republic to the borders of Eastern Europe. Within this vast area, industrial products would move freely—without tariff or quota restrictions—as soon as any transitional period had been completed. And over the years ahead it would be the intention to convert this Customs Union into a full economic union by the progressive alignment and harmonisation of commercial policy, i.e., trading relations with third countries; of economic and fiscal policy; of company and patent law; of standards for industrial products . . . etc. The creation of such an enlarged and integrated European market would provide in effect a much larger and a much faster growing "home market" for British industry. It would provide the stimuli of much greater opportunities—and competition—than exists at present or would otherwise exist in future. There would be substantial advantage for British industry from membership of this new Common Market, stemming primarily from the opportunities for greater economies of scale, increased specialisation, a sharper competitive climate and faster growth. These may be described as the "dynamic effects" of membership on British industry and trade. It has not been found possible to measure the likely response of British industry to these new opportunities nor, therefore, the effects on our economic growth and balance of payments. (Paras. 52–53.)

26. Nicholas Kaldor, "The Truth About the 'Dynamic Effects,' " *New Statesman*, March 12, 1971, pp. 329–36. Reprinted by permission.

In the concluding section the White Paper strikes an even more confident note about the "dynamic effects" resulting from membership of a 'much larger and faster growing market':

> This would open up to our industrial producers substantial opportunities for increasing export sales, while at the same time exposing them more fully to the competition of European industries. No way has been found of quantifying these dynamic effects but, if British industry responded vigorously to these stimuli, they would be considerable and highly advantageous. *The acceleration in the rate of growth of industrial exports could then outpace any increase in the rate of growth of imports* with corresponding benefits to the balance of payments. Moreover, *with such a response,* the growth of industrial productivity would be accelerated as a result of increased competition and the advantages derived from specialisation and larger scale production. This faster rate of growth of productivity would, in turn, accelerate the rate of growth of national production and real income. (Para. 77, my italics.)

The same argument has been repeated in other documents but without adding anything of substance to the case as presented in these quotations. There are frequent references to the fact that the countries of the EEC have experienced much higher growth rates than has Britain since the war, with the implication that if Britain formed part of the Community, its own growth rate would be assimilated to that of the other members. Since the rate of economic growth of Britain has been so much lower than that of the countries of the Common Market—around 3 per cent a year, in the period 1958–69, as against 5.4 per cent for the Six–this in itself would establish a strong presumption in favour of joining the Community

But whether any such tendency can be presumed to exist or not is a matter that requires closer analysis of the causes of high and low growth rates, and of the effects of increased competition on growth. It cannot be taken for granted as a self-evident matter that the intensification of competition between different industrial regions brought about by a customs union will automatically enhance the rate of growth of *each* of the participating regions taken separately. Indeed, as the italicised passage in the White Paper indicates, the favourable effects on our growth rate depend on the hypothesis that opportunities created by the Common Market will lead to an acceleration in the rate of growth of industrial exports which will "outpace any increase in the rate of growth of imports."

But what if the response were the other way round, with an acceleration in the rate of growth of imports that "outpaced" any increase in our exports? Or, if exports, instead of rising, fell in consequence? It could not then be maintained that the rate of growth of national production and real income would be higher as a result; on the contrary, the effect would be to make our rate of economic growth lower than it would be otherwise, or even to make it negative. The question, in other words, is not only one of "quantifying" the magnitude of these "dynamic effects" but of discovering, in the first place, whether they should be entered on the credit side or the debit side.

The White Paper is certainly correct in suggesting that the "dynamic effects" on our growth rate are likely to be far more important over a run of years than the "impact effects," however large the latter may be. An increase in our growth rate by 1 per cent—that is, from, say 3 to 4 per cent a year—is likely to compensate for the initial cost of entry in three years even if the latter is as much as 3 per cent of our national income, or £1,200m. a year. Conversely, a 1 per cent diminution in our growth rate is likely to double the annual cost of membership in three years, treble it in six years, and so on.

The basic question therefore is whether entry into the EEC is likely to have a favourable effect on our growth rate or an adverse one.

There is a substantial amount of evidence in favour of the view that causes of high and low rates of productivity growth of various countries or regions are closely bound up with the rates of growth of manufacturing production. There are two main reasons for this. The first is that economies of large-scale production, due to ever-increasing differentiation and subdivision of processes, are peculiar to manufacturing ("processing activities") as distinct from either primary production (agriculture or mining) or tertiary production (transport, distribution and miscellaneous services). The second is that in the sectors other than manufacturing (chiefly in agriculture but also in services) there is in most countries a considerable surplus of labour (some kind of "disguised unemployment") so that when the manufacturing sector expands and draws more labour from other sectors, these other sectors are not forced to curtail their output; on the contrary, their output will also tend to increase if they provide goods or services that are complementary (or ancillary) to manufacturing activities. Hence the faster manufacturing output expands, the faster productivity will rise, both in the manufacturing sector and in the non-manufacturing sectors.

Added to these is the fact that in "capitalist" economies at any rate the increase in industrial capital necessary for an expansion of output is largely self-generated: the more production expands, the greater is the inducement to invest in the expansion of capacity, and the higher are the profits which provide the finance for such investment.

Under these conditions the economic growth of particular industrial regions will largely be determined by the growth of demand for the products of those regions which emanates from outside the region, i.e., the growth of its exports. A faster rate of growth of exports will induce a faster rate of growth of production, an acceleration in industrial investment, and these will lead to a faster growth of consumption. . . .

Britain's rate of productivity growth has been relatively slow in rela-

tion to other "developed" countries mainly because the rate of growth of
its manufacturing output was slow; the latter was slow because the rate
of growth of its exports was low; and the latter in turn was low because
owing to its relatively slow productivity growth, it was steadily losing
ground to its competitors.

The remarkable feature . . . is that our losses in EEC markets (where
we faced growing tariff discrimination in relation to EEC producers)
were only slightly larger than in EFTA markets (where the discrimination was increasingly in our favour) and in both cases were much smaller
than in other foreign markets.

The rapid fall in our market shares . . . was not unavoidable. It could
have been largely, if not entirely, prevented if we had taken more
prompt and more frequent steps to offset the effects of our growing loss
of competitiveness by devaluation. . . .

The benefits to be gained from "export-led" growth are long-term:
they require an adaptation of the economic structure to a higher growth
rate of demand for manufactured goods; a change in both the volume
and the structure of capital investment which would come about gradually, as a result of a steady and sustained stimulus. They require in
other words small and frequent adjustments in the exchange rate (such
as could be secured by a free market rate subject to market intervention
by the Central Bank); it would be hopeless to expect that the long-term
"dynamic benefits" of greater competitiveness could be brought about
permanently by a single act of devaluation, however large.

But can they be brought about by joining the EEC? In the light of
our large losses of trade in overseas markets in the post-war period, the
idea of a "secure home market of 300m. people" sounds very tempting at
first sight as a long-term solution to our problems. But a closer analysis
of the likely magnitude of both the costs and the benefits, and the restraints on our freedom of action which would follow from membership
of the Community, does not sustain the favourable first impression.

As the issue is a complex one, it is best to tackle its various aspects
one by one.

(a) First, what are the benefits of a "larger home market" and what
precisely does a "home market" mean in this context? The only tangible
gain is free access to the markets of the other members of the Community, in exchange for giving free access to Community producers in the
British market. The meaning of "free access" in this connection is the abolition of import duties on British goods which, under the Community's
new common external tariff, amount to only 7 to 7.5 per cent *ad valorem*, and the abolition of British customs duties on manufactured imports from the Community the level of which is estimated at 10 to 11
per cent *ad valorem*. Since the EEC market now takes about 25 per cent
of our exports, the benefit gained is the same as a 7.5 per cent reduction
of prices on one-quarter of our exports, in return for a 10 to 11 per cent
reduction in prices in the British market on rather more than one-quar-

ter of our imports of manufactures. So long as the Community's tariff remains a moderate one, the creation of a customs union cannot in itself make a great deal of difference. We shall derive benefit from a fast-growing Community whether we are inside the Common Market or not —as indeed is shown by the fact that our exports to EEC countries have increased much faster (despite the tariff discrimination) than our exports to other areas. Furthermore the extraordinary new evidence which emerges from the recent OECD study shows that in competition with individual EEC exporters (Belgium-Luxembourg, France, Germany, Italy and the Netherlands) we fared better, in relation to each of the EEC producers in the "internal" market of the EEC than in "neutral" markets.[27] While the mutual abolition of tariffs is bound to increase the share of each trading partner in the market of the other, in the longer term the growth of our exports to the Community would be subject to much the same competitive influences (both from inside and outside competitors) as if we remained outside. And if the experience of other EEC countries is any guide, we could not hope for more than a modest increase in our share of the EEC market as a result of being part of the customs union. . . .

(b) On the other hand, by joining the Market we should lose the benefit of the existing preferences in favour of British goods in the Commonwealth markets, in EFTA and in the Irish Republic. In the case of those EFTA members which also join the Common Market, we shall retain the benefit of duty-free entry, and lose only the benefit of the existing tariff discrimination in relation to EEC producers. But in the case of the Commonwealth and those EFTA members (such as Switzerland or Sweden) which are not likely to join EEC we shall lose the benefit of the present preferential treatment altogether. Since these preferential markets account for a much larger share of our total exports than the EEC, the net effect on our exports will be adverse; the White Paper estimates that there will be a net loss of exports of £75m. to £175m. in consequence. At the same time the net effect on our imports of manufactures are also likely to be adverse, since the abolition of duties on EEC goods will have a greater impact on our imports than the abolition of preferential treatment to Commonwealth goods and to goods imported from those EFTA members which remain outside. The White Paper estimates the net increase in imports of industrial goods at £50m. to £100m., so that the net demand for British manufactures will be adversely affected to the tune of £125 m. to £275m.

(c) This is before taking into account the adverse effects on real income and on the balance of payments of assuming the obligations of the Community's common agricultural policy. The EEC is a relatively low-tariff area for manufactures but a highly protected area for agriculture.

27. Cf. "An Empirical Analysis of Competition in Export and Domestic Markets," *OECD Economic Outlook, Occasional Studies,* Dec. 1970.

While the tariff on industrial goods (as a result of the Kennedy round) is only 7 to 7.5 per cent, the average level of effective protection accorded to agriculture—the excess of Common Market prices over the world prices—is 45 per cent. By joining the Common Market we therefore face a large adverse change in the relationship of the prices of industrial goods to agricultural goods. There will be a loss on our "external" terms of trade of at least £400m. a year—i.e., our food imports will cost that much more, in terms of our industrial exports—and there will be a similar shift in our 'internal' terms of trade, in that payments to our own farmers (after allowing for the withdrawal of present subsidies) will cost about £300m. more for the same output as now. The present level of EEC agricultural prices is around 27 per cent higher than British *guaranteed* prices. The real income generated by the industrial sector at any given level of physical productivity will be reduced on both counts: each unit of manufactured goods produced in Britain will buy 20 to 30 per cent *less* in foodstuffs than now.

(d) In addition to the loss due to the unfavourable change in price relationships, we shall face the further loss on account of the net contribution to the Community's agricultural fund in excess of the receipts from the agricultural levy (which have already been included in the above calculation). This will come to a further £230m. to £470m., depending on the scale of Community expenditure in the support of European agriculture but, whether the Mansholt Plan is adopted or not, it is unlikely that the contribution we shall be called upon to make will be much below the maximum that we shall be committed to pay.

(e) This means that in terms of balance of payments cost in current account, (apart from the change in the export-import balance of industrial goods referred to above) we shall start off (after the transitional period) with a debit of between £530m. to £820m. (£400m. a year on account of the additional cost of imported food; £230m. to £470m. in further contributions to the agricultural fund, *less* £50m. to £100m. in receipts from the agricultural fund) which will have to be covered by additional net exports if a deterioration in the balance of payments on current account is to be avoided. To obtain these additional exports inside or outside the Common Market, we should have to lower our labour costs in terms of international currency in relation to our competitors (depending on the size of the cost) by 5 to 10 per cent. This would require an additional devaluation (at the present relationship of our productivity and of our industrial wages to the industrial productivity and wages of our competitors) of 10 to 15 per cent, which, in terms of the further resources that we would have to transfer from domestic consumption to the balance of payments means an additional burden of £205m. to £340m. (It was a deplorable omission of the White Paper that it failed to take any account of the additional resource cost of the adjustment process in the balance of payments.) Hence in terms of total resource cost, the requirement for the balance of payments adjustment is the equivalent of £735m. to £1,160m. This estimate also allows for the resource cost of making good the initial reduction in net exports of manufactures. . . .

(f) However, this takes no account of the deterioration in our competitiveness on account of the rise in money wages that is bound to result from the rise in the cost of living. The counterpart to the deterioration in the terms of trade is a rise in food prices of 18 to 26 per cent (on the White Paper's estimates) which would cause a cut in real wages of 4 to 5 per cent for the higher-paid workers, and 6 to 8 per cent for the lower-paid. . . . If past (and present) experience is any guide, the rise in food prices and in indirect taxes will cause a rise in wages which will call for *more* devaluation if adverse effects on our exports are to be avoided.

(g) But once we are inside the Common Market, it will be more difficult to regain competitiveness through adjustments in the exchange rate. One reason for this is that under the Community rules, the prices paid for both imported and home produced food are fixed in terms of "international units" so that whenever the exchange rate is altered, domestic food prices will be raised by the full extent of the adjustment. This increases the real resource cost of achieving any given improvement in the balance of payments; and it means that the rise in the cost of living resulting from devaluation is greater than it would be now. On both these grounds it will be harder to regain competitiveness by devaluation. The second and more fundamental reason is that the possibility of offsetting adverse trends in competitiveness through exchange rate adjustments will itself become impossible as the Community proceeds with its current plans for full economic and monetary union. . . .

The long-term benefits to Britain of joining the Common Market depend entirely on attaining a higher rate of growth of productivity. But we could only hope to achieve this if the rate of growth of our industrial production is accelerated which in turn presupposes, as the White Paper recognises, a faster rate of growth of exports. For all the reasons listed, this would require a large *initial* cut in the level of our real wages and salaries—of the order of 10 per cent, if both the adverse change in the terms of trade, the adjustment in the tax structure, and the need to cover the cost of our net contribution to the Community fund by additional exports is taken into account—and this in turn is unlikely to be achieved—in any industrial community, not just Britain—by a straightforward reduction in money wages: it will require a succession of downward adjustments in the exchange rate.

But owing to the Common Market agricultural policy, any act of devaluation will have a greater resource cost in terms of real income and both generates greater inflationary consequences internally and makes the necessary reduction in real wages that much greater; and as the Community proceeds towards a full monetary union, the possibility of devaluation will be ruled out altogether.

If we failed to reduce real wages initially (or failed to reduce them to the extent required) the "dynamic effects" of membership would not be favourable but increasingly adverse. Industrial production and employment would fall, both on account of the deterioration of the trade balance, and on account of the restrictive policies we would be forced to adopt in order to restore the balance of payments and to finance our contribution to the Community. This would be aggravated by an increased capital out-flow as domestic industrial investment became unprofitable owing to the fall in domestic demand, and full transferability of capital funds was introduced under EEC rules; and this would necessitate further restrictive fiscal and monetary measures to avoid a balance of payments crisis. In those circumstances Britain would become the "Northern Ireland" of Europe—an increasingly depressed industrial area, with mass emigration the only escape.

The critical assumptions which lead to this gloomy prognosis are: (a) that we can enter the Community only by assuming the obligations of the common agricultural policy and the relation of EEC agricultural prices to world prices remains much the same as now; and (b) that we shall not be able to offset the adverse initial effects on our *industrial* export-import balance by devaluation.

If we could enter the EEC on the same terms as we entered EFTA, and also made sure—by repeated devaluations if necessary—that our industry benefited from entry from the beginning we might gain considerably through greater industrial specialisation as well as through a higher rate of growth of total output. For the labour-releasing effects of sharper competition (due to the abolition of British import duties on EEC products) would then serve to enhance the growth of our more efficient industries, and the growth of these industries would more than compensate for the decline of the others. On the vital issue of long-term "dynamic benefits" it all depends on whether one starts off on the right foot or the wrong one.

The overwhelming probability is however that just because of the heavy initial cost of entry we shall start off on the wrong foot, and the "impact effects" will then be aggravated by adverse "dynamic effects," not offset by beneficial ones. In that event, entry into the Common Market, if it were really irreversible, would be a national disaster. In reality, this will never happen. Nations do not commit *hara-kiri* for the sake of international treaties, however solemnly and sincerely entered into. But in addition to incurring the odium of default, we would be blamed for the break-up of Community arrangements, even though this would have happened anyway. . . .

REPLY TO KALDOR'S ARGUMENT [28]

Professor Nicholas Kaldor has long made practice runs at the economic case against British entry into the common market which he fi-

28. *The Economist*, March 13, 1971, pp. 29–30.

nally published in the *New Statesman*. . . . His nine-page article is to be circulated among anti-marketeers as the formal, received economic argument against entry. . . .

The starting point is the 1966 Kaldor theory which explained Britain's slow growth rate. . . . This is the tautology that "low rates of productivity growth are closely bound up with the rates of growth of manufacturing production." The sort of self-generating dynamism characteristic of Europe and Japan is stimulated by outside demand for their industrial goods—it is therefore often export-led. The only way for a country like Britain, which is slow to expand productive capacity and so fails to keep its share of export markets, is to lower its efficiency wages by periodic devaluations. But Europe's rules, Professor Kaldor thinks, would prevent Britain from devaluing. Since "relatively fast-growing areas tend to acquire a cumulative competitive advantage over relatively slow-growing areas," Britain would find itself locked in as the Northern Ireland of Europe, "an increasingly depressed industrial area, with mass emigration the only escape"; since Europe has no effective central government, Britain could not expect from it the subsidies and social security transfers which Ulster at least gets from London.

The argument is meant to tackle pro-marketeers on their own favourite economic ground—"the dynamic effects" of entry. Professor Kaldor agrees that the effects will be dynamic all right. Indeed, he emphasises that his table shows "that the potential of the EEC market for Britain is very large, provided only that British products are competitive with other community producers"; this is because British exporters' present "share in the EEC market is very small—the same as that of Belgium-Luxembourg which only has one-seventh of Britain's output." But if Britain gets off on the wrong foot, his thesis is that it will be Britain's imports of manufactures that will grow dynamically, not its exports. And Britain has little chance of starting off on the right foot, he argues, because it will be carrying a balance-of-payments cost as a result of entry, which he computes (using figures from last year's discredited white paper) at between £530 million and £820 million a year. He then says that the 5 per cent to 10 per cent devaluation necessary to cope with this would cost Britain, on assumptions "too tedious to set out," another £205 million to £340 million in domestic resources.

In addition, Professor Kaldor argues that entry will cause an outflow of capital. Higher food prices will be socially regressive and will depress domestic demand for manufactures, thus further damaging productivity. And even if devaluations were permitted, their impact would be reduced by the farm policy rules which compel members to adjust farm prices immediately to a common level.

All this is, in fact, an amalgam of the conflicting cases that were put forward in 1958 to say that both Germany and France would be ruined through the burdens put upon each by the other after entry into the EEC. It was said then that Germany's balance of payments would be permanently weakened by the cost of having to support France's surplus peasant agriculture; that has been shown to be rubbish because, of course, Germany has expanded its industrial exports to other EEC members even though it started off with a potential for expansion smaller than Britain has now.

It was also said in 1958, sometimes by the same people, that France would be condemned to backwardness through partnership with a more dynamic Germany and also be prohibited from letting the exchange rate take the strain. But what happened was that France, far from being prevented from devaluing the franc, was for much of 1968–69 being pressed to do so by its European partners, chief among them Germany itself. The only political resistance to devaluation was in Paris. Political reality also meant that the farm rules were not enforced immediately at the time of the French and German parity changes as Professor Kaldor says they would be on Britain; the full impact of the parity changes was allowed to take place, only diminishing slowly thereafter as farm prices and yields were brought back into line.

So Mr. Kaldor has chosen to ignore common market politics. This may be an academic practice, but it happens to destroy his central conclusions. It also involves him in glossing over the political prescience which has actually gone into the making of Europe's monetary union policy: the policy which he believes will be the chief instrument for locking Britain into fixed parities. He quotes the Werner report at length, although Werner is now a museum piece which all the Six—bar Holland—regret ever having allowed to assume the importance it briefly did. In its place the Six have embarked on a series of monetary and economic experiments. Judgments on these will specifically be deferred until after Britain joins, and the process will only advance towards a common currency if there is unanimous agreement that the trial period has been a success.

The whole thesis that the cost of entry might be allowed to ruin Britain runs against the Six's reasons for wanting Britain in. By the time the community's finance system becomes automatic in 1978, the Six will have given themselves 18 years to make sure that the farm policy has not prejudiced Germany's balance of payments. The Treaty of Rome includes safeguards for members anyway. The Six have officially told Britain that the finance rules would not be allowed to impose an intolerable burden on its balance of payments; as Mr. Kaldor concedes at one point, it would not be practical from the Six's point of view to let them do so.

Two economic assumptions in Professor Kaldor's paper look to be just plain wrong. On the farm policy he says: "It would be prudent to reckon that [spending on farm subsidies] will continue to rise at least at half the rate of the previous four years." It would be most imprudent to reckon any such thing. The past four years have been ones during which the farm policy has been virtually completed so that spending has risen automatically from a low level. More important, the assertion that the Six are politically unable to reduce farm prices—and what Mr. Kaldor seems to be talking of here is farm prices relative to all other prices—is simply untrue. By pegging their common farm prices for the past three years at a time of rising inflation the Six have caused growing unrest among their farmers, a drastic reduction in real farm incomes and an equally drastic shakeout from farming. Professor Kaldor does not refer to the aim of Europe's farm policy, protectionist though it is, which is clearly being achieved; namely, a fairly civilised flight from the land which will halve the Six's already much reduced farm labour force to below 5 million by 1980. Only in footnotes does he refer to a growing feeling among farm economists that Europe's surpluses are likely to diminish as the effect of this exodus exceeds the effect of higher efficiency. In his text Mr. Kaldor maintains the reverse.

Second, Mr. Kaldor assumes a common industrial tariff rate in the EEC of 7 per cent to 7½ per cent and a British industrial tariff of 10 per cent to 11 per cent. The unpublished median tariff rates actually calculated for the purposes of bargaining between Britain and the Six are about 8½ percent for the Six and 9.9 per cent for Britain, a narrower tariff gap than Professor Kaldor assumes Britain is about to lose. Little of the statistical sleight of hand practised in the recent study on the common market by the National Institute of Economic and Social Research is used by Professor Kaldor. But the conclusions which he reaches from an OECD study of export market shares in fact beg many of the questions which he claims they answer. Britain has lost less of its market share in the markets of the Six than it has elsewhere in the world. Britain's exports have grown much faster to the Six than elsewhere, yet British manufacturers have lost most ground in their own market and in markets outside the Six to common market producers. France's foreign minister last week drew the conclusion from this which seems clearly right: that while France has not increased its market share inside the Six, the competitive experience of being a member of the market had helped it increase its exports outside. The same, M. Schumann said, should be true for Britain.

Professor Kaldor draws a different lesson. He ignores the fact that Britain's declining performance in markets other than Europe has been largely because of the slower growth in our unfortunately favoured market of the Commonwealth. He concludes, instead, that Britain's record in doing relatively less badly in the common market than in slower growing areas is proof that it can continue to do so, inside the EEC or out. He agrees that a great deal could be gained if Britain entered in good competitive fettle; but his figuring of the costs and his notion that sterling's exchange rate would be pegged by entry for good and all persuade him that Britain is nothing like fit enough to take the shock. In which case, God help Britain if it has to stay outside.

While Kaldor's argument (above) represented the position held by many British economists that the economic terms of entry were unfavorable, the other anti-Market arguments of a noneconomic character were essentially that entry would affect adversely Britain's democracy and independence, and that Britain should not link up with Europe at the expense of surrendering its looser association with many other countries and continents.

THE CASE AGAINST ENTRY [29]

The main objective of any British Government must be to safeguard the security, the prosperity and the effective democratic self-government of the United Kingdom and its people. In our generation, as in previous periods, we have to consider these objectives in the light of major changes in the world outside. In particular, since 1958, we have had to consider these aims against the emergence of a new grouping, the European Communities in Western Europe.

Our security has long been bound up with that of our European neighbours. Since the days of the Armada, no Government in these islands has been able to ignore for more than a short time the course of events on the Continent of Europe. Britain, has, however, successfully maintained her security over the centuries both by her own endeavours and with the help of allies in Europe and outside, according to the needs of the time. For the past twenty-five years, the maintenance of our security, together with that of the rest of Western Europe, has been bound up with the Western Alliances, in which the United States of America and Canada, the countries of the Six, many other European countries as well as our own, are all partners. Although in the last twelve years the Six have come more closely together in economic and other matters, no separate defence arrangements have been made. With the exception of France, who has pursued distinctive and nationalistic policies, the nations of the Six have accepted that their security is far more strongly based in NATO than in any conceivable arrangement among themselves. Whatever the future holds, it is obvious that a military alliance that includes both Western Europe and North America is bound to be very much stronger than one based upon Western Europe alone. Clearly then, there is no question of our membership of the European Communities leading to greater security for the British people than the arrangements of which we are already a part. It must be judged on other grounds.

The prosperity of the United Kingdom depends partly on the efforts of its people and partly on the economic conditions prevailing in the world outside. We live and have long lived by manufacturing for and trading with the world. The conditions under which we manufacture and trade are of vital national interest to us. But we have to consider

29. *New Statesman,* "*The Case Against Entry: The Answer to the White Paper*" (Statesman & Nation Publishing Co., Ltd., 1971), paragraphs 1–9, 33–41.

not only the trade opportunities which membership of the European Communities might offer, but the consequential effects of our membership on the great bulk of our trade, which is transacted outside the Continent of Europe. What we have to judge is whether the preferences and advantages that we now enjoy in the Commonwealth and in EFTA are worth abandoning for the trading advantages that we would get by joining the EEC.

Events of recent years, revaluations, devaluations and the emergence of new economic powers, have shown that international monetary and trade arrangements need to be adapted from time to time to meet changing circumstances. Hitherto we have played a full part as an independent nation in these crucial international decisions. We have now to consider whether our influence on future changes in these arrangements will be greater if we become part of the European Communities, which will increasingly speak with one voice for all their members, or whether we can do better for ourselves and our friends by retaining our independent voice outside.

Democratic self-government in Britain is of immense value to our people and has provided a stimulus and example to other nations. Moreover, the practice of democracy in Britain has been both a consequence and a cause of our continued and unequalled ability over the centuries to maintain our security and our prosperity. Membership of the European Communities would limit the powers of British Governments and of the British people in many areas of policy. We should moreover in signing the Treaty of Rome be bringing ourselves for the first time within the ambit and the disciplines of a written Constitution. The question we now have to consider is whether the loss of democratic power at the national level in Britain will be compensated for by the extension of democratic power at the level of the Community.

Not our security, but our influence, our prosperity and our democracy will thus be greatly affected by the decisions we now have to make about our accession to the European Communities. Nor will our decision affect ourselves alone. Our membership would have an enormous effect upon the whole Commonwealth system, upon the sterling area, upon EFTA and upon those international organisations such as GATT and the IMF which play so large a part in expanding world trade. The entry of the United Kingdom into the European Communities is therefore an issue of historic importance not only for us and Europe but for the Commonwealth and the world.

Our first round of discussions with the six member countries of the Communities about arrangements for entry between 1961 and 1963 made considerable progress but many important matters were still unsettled when General de Gaulle ended the negotiations with his veto. The second round in 1967 never proceeded beyond the opening British speech, and it too was vetoed by the French Government in the autumn of that year. The third round of discussions began in Luxembourg on 30

June 1970 and have continued to the summer of this year. From the start of this round, when M. Harmel stated the demands of the Community on 30 June 1970, it has been clear that the political will necessary to make those changes and compromises, without which no responsible British Government could join, has been absent from the negotiating table. The arrangements which the Six have sought to impose upon us as conditions of entry are now known and clearly stated. They are set out in detail in Part II of this document. The opportunity to join the Communities is open to us—if we accept their demands. We have now to decide whether or not to do so.

As this paper shows, our democracy will be more effective, our country will be more secure, our influence greater, our economy stronger and our industries and people more prosperous if we stay out of the European Communities than if we join them on the terms that they now demand. We are also convinced that a decision not to join will enhance the security and prosperity of both EFTA and the Commonwealth, will serve the causes of world trade and trade expansion and will in no sense be injurious to the interests of the Six themselves.

We urge therefore Parliament this autumn to reject membership of the Communities. . . .

There can be no doubt that Britain would be weakened and reduced by joining the European Communities on the terms now available. While we must expect substantial disadvantage from the unequal trading effects of membership, the main burden on the United Kingdom would arise from the agricultural and financial policies of the Six. As we have seen, these arrangements cannot now be changed from within. Consequently we should be forced, not later than the end of the five year transitional period, into a serious debtor position with painful consequences to our own people and with an inevitable loss of influence within the Community itself.

In particular, we should have a continuing anxiety about the consequences of the two major and open-minded commitments to phase out the sterling balances and to achieve an Economic and Monetary Union by 1980. The former could well impose upon us still greater burdens of payment while the latter, if a common currency or permanent parities were agreed, would deny us even the possibility of remedial measures.

The terms are moreover such as to involve the immediate destruction of the European Free Trade Area, which today provides us with a single home market of 100 million people.

The Commonwealth will also be disrupted. Its trade preference system will have to be phased out within five years and in its place we should have to impose upon our major Commonwealth partners the common external tariff of the Six. Similarly, the present preferences accorded to the Commonwealth in the Sterling Area in terms of access to the London capital market and virtually unrestricted capital investment from Britain, will have to be discontinued. For Britain cannot sustain a free movement of capital to both the Commonwealth and the European Community. We would henceforth be obliged to give preference to the latter. Some Commonwealth countries, those in Africa and the West Indies, will be able to become associated overseas territories of the European Community, as former French and Dutch territories have already become. But all the Commonwealth countries in Asia, India, Pakistan, Ceylon, Malaysia and Singapore, as well as Canada, New Zealand and Australia, will be excluded. It is hardly likely that, deprived of its preferential arrangement with Britain and divided into associated and non-associated territories, the Commonwealth would long survive Britain's membership of the EEC.

Since the break-up of EFTA and the Commonwealth are inevitable consequences of British membership, it is clear that even if, in spite of all the obstacles, we were able to hold our own in Common Market trade, our influence upon international events would be seriously reduced. True, in matters of economic policy generally, we would have a voice on new policies inside the European Community as well as on new Community policy towards the world outside. But while our influence within the Common Market should not be under-stated, equally it should not be exaggerated. Britain would be—on the assumption that Norway, Denmark and Eire also join—1 of 10 nations, 55 million people out of a total of 250 million. In so far as the Rome Treaty decision-making procedures are followed, we should have 2 Commissioners out of 14 at Brussels, 10 votes out of 61 on the Council of Ministers, 36 seats out of 208 in the European Parliament. In so far as the rule of unanimity works, we too would have a veto on new policies, but would have to prepare for a process of endless bargaining with other member states. In short, we should have a minority influence in shaping Community affairs. But where the Community acted on behalf of its members in dealing with outside nations in trade negotiations and other matters, there would no longer be a separate British voice. Britain would not be there.

It is sometimes said that Britain has no choice: that she must accept the terms however disadvantageous, in order to escape the perils of semi-isolation that exclusion would impose upon her. Such fears, which have been deliberately excited, have little substance. Far from being isolated in either the economic, the political or military sense, Britain is a full member of virtually all the large and powerful organisations that exist in the world today. In Europe itself, if we reject the Common Market, not one of our EFTA partners would join without us. EFTA would continue—taking as it does almost as much of our trade as the Common Market itself—and its membership could well be extended. Outside of Europe, we have the influence that goes with our position in the Commonwealth and the support that this gives us in the General Assembly of the United Nations, in all its many agencies and in the Security Council where we remain one of the five permanent members. As for our military security, we are members not only of NATO but of numerous other alliances covering a large part of the globe. Indeed, far from being on our own, it might be argued that we are in too much company.

So far the case against entry into the EEC has been presented in terms of its existing structure. It must now be considered in the perspective of the future development of what is admitted by its supporters as well as by its critics—to be a hybrid organism which can only resolve its own inconsistencies by developing into a full-scale European superstate. Today, despite the growth of supernational bureaucracy under the Commissioners in Brussels, the EEC is still basically an alliance of nation states united by a common tariff and by their agreement to renounce certain economic powers; and the only full supranational organisation now in operation is the Common Agricultural Policy. The most recent evidence of the instability and transitional character of the present structure was, of course, the discord caused by the German Government's attitude to revaluation and the complete failure of the Six to achieve any common attitude to currency problems. We must anticipate therefore, an ever-mounting volume of pressure from inside the EEC for effective central control of currency, economic policy and probably also of defence. Pressure will come from the avowed Federalists in each of the member countries who are eager to achieve a United States of Europe as soon as possible. But just as strong will be the demand of those who, for non-ideological reasons, regard the present compromise as unviable and realise, therefore, that the choice for Europe is between a rapid advance to full federalism or the successive abandonment of all their ambitious plans for unification.

At present, however, there is no escape from the impasse because the European Communities can advance only by the slow crawl of unanimity. Developments needed to give substance even to the limited aim of achieving a common currency and overall economic policy would be the creation of a democratic European Parliament and the signature of a new treaty giving to this Parliament and the Government which emerged from it, specific federal powers. Under such a treaty the national veto would of course disappear. None of this, we need scarcely add, has been even remotely touched on during the recent negotiations in Brussels. If it had been, the negotiations would have collapsed. Formally an advance towards federalism is excluded both by the conditions laid down for our entry and by British Government policy. Yet to sign the Treaty of Rome in the belief that the road to federalism is effectively barred by our national veto would be to blind ourselves to the logic of events. There can be no doubt whatsoever that within a few years of our entry we should come under the most powerful pressure to accept an advance towards full federalism as the only alternative to the complete collapse of the EEC. Those whose support for entry has been won by assurances that no sacrifice of national sovereignty will be involved, should remind themselves how often in history the most solemn assurances have been invalidated by economic necessity. Whatever is now

said to the contrary the EEC, if it is to overcome its financial and economic problems, will have to be transformed from an alliance of national states, limited by common rules, into a European superstate.

We consider later the grave inroads on our democratic freedoms
which entry to the EEC, even with its present incomplete supranational
structure, would involve. While they are in our view too serious to be
acceptable, they are as nothing compared with the sacrifices involved in
making this country a province within a federal Europe. We see no special virtue in becoming part of a large and populous superstate. Of
those which exist today, two are tyrannies faced with all the internal
and external strains that tyranny presents to its practitioners, and the
third is racked by the abuse of its own power, by dissidents within and
by the inability to the point of paralysis of its democratic institutions to
cope effectively with the great problems that its scale and diversity present. Indeed twentieth-century experience so far suggests that wherever
it is tried on a very large scale, Federal Government proves to be re-
mote government, bad government, and doomed to failure. We should
have no part in it. Instead we should reassert the principle that the
forms of concerted action evolved for defence purposes in NATO and
for economic purposes in EFTA are likely to prove the surest basis for
the unity of Europe.

Perhaps the final word may be left to Mr. Sieber:

THE "UNFAVOURABLES" [30]

Britain in the last half of October was going through the final stages
of what inevitably was called a "great debate," the issue being British
entry into the European Common Market. The issue was political as
well as economic, of course, but this tale will be limited to the economic, which was crucial in the debate.

About a week before the climactic vote in Parliament, there appeared
in *The Times* of London a pair of rather remarkable letters. They ran
side by side, and at first glance they appeared very long.

In fact, however, each was very short. The first said this:

"Sir: The undersigned, being full-time teaching officers of economics
in British universities, believe that the economic effects of joining the
Common Market, taking both short and long term effects into account,
are more likely to be unfavourable than favourable to Britain."

The letter was then followed by 154 signatures, which is why it appeared so long.

The one adjacent read as follows:

"Sir: The undersigned, being full-time teaching officers of economics

---

30. Report by Edwin L. Dale, Jr., *New York Times*, Nov. 7, 1971.

in British universities, believe that the economic effects of joining the Common Market, taking both short and long term effects into account, are more likely to be favourable than unfavourable to Britain."

There followed 142 signatures.

Thus did the informed British public receive the verdict of the "experts," following about 10 years of erudite discussion and a mass of written material (including statistics) that probably equaled the entire literary output of the productive eighteenth century.

A few days later in *The Times* one of history's unsung heroes, a man named Peter Sieber, produced the following letter:

"Sir: The undersigned, being full time in business, believes that the economic effects of economists, taking both short and long term effects into account, are more likely to be unfavourable than favourable to Britain."

There was more. *The London Economist* intoned about "The descent in reputation of British economics."

Above all—possibly unfairly—we have had a rise in skepticism about what economists can tell us.

As the mountain of literature grows, and the mathematical equations become more impenetrable, and the predictions become more suspect, it is fair to ask a cruel question: are we seeing the decline and fall of the economists' empire?

6.5. *The Free Trade Area Option.* Prior to the Great Debate, a major group of critics of Britain's entry into the Common Market had already founded the Atlantic Trade Study [ATS] in 1966 as a research group to study the implications for Britain of participating in a broadly based free trade association as possibly the next phase in the liberalization of international trade. Professor Harry Johnson is Director of Studies. A brief description of the purpose and scope of the program follows: [31]

> As a basis on which to proceed with research, the proposed free trade association was defined as initially embracing the United States, Canada, Britain and other member countries of the European Free Trade Association; open to the European Communities and to Japan, Australia and New Zealand, as well as other industrially advanced nations; and affording less developed countries greater access to their markets.
>
> Several proposals along these lines had already been receiving serious attention at academic, business and official levels in North America. The ATS was in fact a British response to a new trade strategy proposed in May, 1966, by the Canadian-

31. See Hugh Corbet (ed.), *Trade Strategy and the Asian-Pacific Region* (1970).

American Committee, a non-official group sponsored by the Private Planning Association of Canada and the National Planning Association in the United States.

With the expiry on June 30, 1967, of President Johnson's authority under the Trade Expansion Act of 1962 to negotiate trade agreements with other countries, and the completion of the so-called Kennedy Round of multilateral tariff negotiations, made possible by the Act and conducted under the auspices of the General Agreement on Tariffs and Trade, the United States Administration and Congress was expected to embark upon a thorough reappraisal of trade policies and practices with a view to formulating a fresh negotiating authority. The proposal for a multilateral free trade association initiated by North Atlantic countries has been one of the policy options to have subsequently come under consideration.

Meanwhile, the British Government had made a second application for United Kingdom membership of the European Communities. But whether Britain gained admission or not, the concept of a potentially world-wide free trade association was deemed, in either eventuality, as likely to prove of large significance. For in the event of membership being negotiated it was considered that the United Kingdom would then require an informed policy for the development of closer commercial and political relations between Western Europe and North America. If on the other hand the European Communities rejected Britain again, even if only temporarily, it would be important to have examined beforehand whether there exists a viable alternative.

The first Atlantic Trade Study publication, *The Free Trade Option,* concluded that the most promising future for British trade lay in the North American market.[32]

PROPOSAL FOR A NORTH ATLANTIC FREE TRADE AREA [33]

The various NAFTA proposals were originally a response to the challenge President de Gaulle presented to the West when he vetoed Britain's 1961 application to join the EEC. At that time it appeared that the

---

32. See also G. Curzon and V. Curzon, *op. cit.;* T. M. Franck and E. Weisband (eds.), *op. cit.;* David Robertson, *Scope for New Trade Strategy* (1968).

More recent studies carried out under the Atlantic Trade Study Program also deal with Britain's extra-European relations and more particularly with economic and politico-strategic issues involving the countries of the Asian-Pacific region.

33. Maxwell Stamp Associates, *The Free Trade Area Option* (Atlantic Trade Study, 1966).

Common Market would be an inflexibly protectionist bloc in world trade and that those other countries desiring freer world trade would have to pursue that objective by negotiating special arrangements among themselves. The unexpectedly successful conclusion of the Kennedy Round has dispelled the worst of these earlier fears, but at the same time it has opened up the possibility of a further substantial move towards full free trade among industrial nations. Whether the members of the EEC would be prepared for this further step is at present extremely problematical; consequently, contemporary exponents of the NAFTA scheme see it as a means whereby those nations that wish to move ahead may do so without being blocked by the unwillingness of the Common Market countries to join in and yet without jeopardising the chance of their eventual participation.

Why a free trade area? If North Atlantic countries want free or freer trade why is it necessary to use this form of economic organisation? First, as already mentioned, it would seem unlikely that another multilateral negotiation like the Kennedy Round can again be mounted. In GATT negotiations the rate of progress has been determined by those major trading nations least willing or able to offer meaningful concessions. . . .

The success of the Kennedy Round means that another multilateral negotiation would be confronted with the hard-core problems such as textiles and the question of non-tariff barriers. Indeed, the Kennedy Round may well have made non-tariff barriers more significant obstacles to trade than tariffs themselves. Like the mountains at the bottom of the sea, non-tariff barriers have not been so important while trade has had to navigate against a raging sea of tariff protection, but as the level of the sea comes down, the peaks of non-tariff barriers are likely to show more above the surface. It is highly probable that non-tariff barriers will be resorted to more and more by governments as tariffs are removed under the Kennedy Round agreement. The GATT, however, has never had a very strong mandate in the field of non-tariff barriers and it is unlikely that negotiations in the GATT will be able to deal with them adequately. A free trade association, on the other hand, would be well placed to adopt measures to control the discriminatory effects of regulations and practices that affect the free flow of goods and services. Even EFTA, for example, which intentionally limited the degree of economic integration among its members, found it necessary to establish some "rules of competition" in order to prevent tariffs being replaced by non-tariff barriers. . . .

This study has been written largely from a British point of view. We have been mainly concerned with trying to assess the effects on Britain of joining a broad free trade area as an alternative, or supplement, to joining the EEC. So far as can be seen, and provided export prices can be kept competitive, an Atlantic-based free trade area would have beneficial effects both on the volume of British trade and on the country's balance of payments. If there is no deterioration in the U K's relative position, Britain should be able to compete with other participants, even in the face of superior American technology, in a large enough proportion of trade to enable her, in all probability, to improve her position. Having the big, rich and homogeneous American market to "shoot at" would provide the stimulus and opportunity to enable British manufacturers to exploit to the full the economies of scale made possible in a large assured market. American competition in the U K market would, even more than European competition, administer the "salutary jolt" which would encourage or force British industry to improve productivity. But, as must follow if our trade balance with the U S improves, as we would expect, this "jolt" would be no more than Britain could healthily absorb.

Our examination of the figures and views expressed by the business economists who answered our questionnaire lead us to the conclusion that fears of American domination, either through takeovers or by beating British firms in competition, are much exaggerated. Indeed, it may be that American fear of British competition may be one obstacle to be overcome in persuading the U S A that a NAFTA arrangement would be in American interests.

Almost all the purely economic advantages put forward as reasons for British entry into the EEC apply with equal or greater force to participating in NAFTA. And Britain would not have to suffer the disadvantages of the EEC's agricultural arrangements, with the higher food costs involved and the promise of an inevitable rise in the British cost of living. Instead, the U K could continue to purchase food from traditional cheap suppliers. New "special arrangements" would not have to be negotiated to prevent damage to New Zealand and others.

These advantages are offset in many people's minds by the fear, already mentioned, that U S firms would buy up British industry, or, put another way, that Britain "would become the 51st State of the Union." When this last fear was heard after Bretton Woods, Lord Keynes replied: "No such luck!" One of the virtues of the free trade area system is that it is not necessary to surrender sovereignty. Neither Sweden nor Switzerland have become dependencies of Britain as a result of EFTA, despite discrepancies of size and population. If the U K, the U S A and Canada want to draw closer together politically, then clearly free trade between them will make the approach easier. But free trade does not make political domination inevitable.

There appears to be equally little reason to believe that the formation of NAFTA, or a wider arrangement, would produce a vast increase in the inflow of U S capital into the U K, with British industry becoming mainly American-owned. Of course if NAFTA increases the U K growth rate, as we think it may, then Britain will be a much better place to invest in and more attractive to foreign capital. Britain normally welcomes foreign capital. For her own savings are inadequate to finance all the investment required. American investment up till now has certainly been beneficial to the nation's balance of payments and to its overall efficiency. One of the factors holding back British growth would appear to be a low rate of investment. There accordingly seems to be no reason why this welcome for foreign capital should be reversed. In fact, the need for capital to take advantage of new opportunities would be greater if Britain was to enter NAFTA and therefore the welcome should be warmer. But if, in the event, the inflow of U S capital reaches "dangerous" proportions it should not be impossible, or incompatible with a free trade area (which in essence provides only for tariff free entry of goods and need not cover capital movements or the movement of labour), to control this flow. Britain would still have the choice, if she remains an attractive place to invest in, between more American capital, on the one hand, with more American ownership, and less investment, on the other, with slower growth and more "independence."

A major problem likely to be the subject of increasing attention concerns assistance to less developed countries. Of itself NAFTA would do nothing to help African, Asian and Latin American nations to expand their exports. Unless special arrangements are made it may even worsen their position. But it would be possible, within the NAFTA framework, to accord them temporary advantages over the next few years. Thus if the NAFTA agreement provides, as it probably would, for a long period, say 15 years, during which tariffs between members were to be gradually reduced, it would be possible to remove tariffs against the manufactured products of developing countries in a much shorter time, say 5 years. Developing countries would then enjoy a preferential rate for several years, during which time they could develop industrial production. NAFTA would, therefore, be a useful instrument for helping all developing countries, free from the complications of entrenched preferences for a few (the former French colonies) in the EEC.

NAFTA would hold advantages for Britain if it were confined to Canada, the U S A, the U K and other EFTA countries. It would hold even bigger advantages if it proves to be not the end of the road, but the first steps on a road towards a much wider free trade area to include Japan, Australia, New Zealand and eventually the EEC. The British interest lies in freeing trade on a permanent basis so that British industry obtains the benefits of the largest possible potential markets and in order that competition can work its usual beneficial miracles at home. To be excluded from a NAFTA-type arrangement, if one were formed, would certainly hurt Britain. The damage she would suffer could possibly be greater than any economic advantages obtained from joining the EEC. Hence even if the U K is successful in renewed negotiations with the Common Market it will be to Britain's economic advantage if the enlarged EEC becomes a member of an Atlantic-based free trade area to avoid being excluded from or discriminated against in the U S A and Canada. It must be a matter of judgement whether the chances of the

Community ultimately joining NAFTA would be greater if Britain was to join the EEC first or join NAFTA first.

This study has not been concerned with the economic advantages and disadvantages of NAFTA to the other prospective partners. Others are working on this. But because the share of foreign trade in the American GNP is so much less than in the case of Britain—because indeed the U S A already has a very large home market—it would seem probable that the U S A would gain less than Britain and Canada. That she would still gain is very likely. The U S A, moreover, does have an interest in, and a genuine concern for, the prosperity of others. She has a concern for helping developing countries, and NAFTA, as we have seen, could be adapted to those ends; she has, we hope, a concern also for the future of Britain; and she is concerned that Europe should not degenerate into a selfish, inward-looking trade bloc.

Free trade associations can be effective economic instruments, as EFTA has shown. By comparison with the EEC they do lack glamour. "Building Europe" has a fine ring to stir the imagination. "Building a free trade area" would mean little to the man in the street. A vision though of an economic community of the free world, with hope of sweeping away the trade barriers which do so much to prevent the world reaching its full economic potential, could all the same stir imaginations in Britain and in the U S A. And so to the final question: "Would the Americans accept the free trade area concept of a new Grand Design?"

6.6. The Vote: Britain Chooses Europe. After a final six-day debate in Parliament, the House of Commons voted on what *The Economist* called "the most momentous peacetime decision of its history" [34]—accession to the European Communities—by a majority of 112.

PARLIAMENT GIVES A RESOUNDING YES TO EUROPE [35]

The Government last night carried in the House of Commons by 356 votes to 244 their motion asking the House to approve in principle the United Kingdom's entry into the European Communities. The majority of 112 votes, as jubilant ministers lost no time in emphasizing, was equal to more than four times the Government's overall majority in the Commons and three times their majority over the Parliamentary Labour Party.

But in an important sense the size of the majority was deceptive. Large numbers who voted for the principle of entry last night will not

34. *The Economist*, Oct. 30, 1971, p. 11.
35. *Times*, (London), Oct. 29, 1971.

be able or willing to support the Government when it brings forward EEC legislation next session. Everybody at Westminster knows that within a few months the Government will be able to do no more than squeeze Britain through into the EEC by January, 1973.

In a statement from 10 Downing Street, Mr. Heath said:

> Parliament has now decided that Britain should, in principle, join the European Economic Communities on the basis of the arrangements which have been negotiated.
>
> Today's decision has been reached by a clear majority of the elected representatives of the people: men and women who, irrespective of party political differences, share the conviction that this decision is right for their country.
>
> This is the outcome of years of patient negotiation by governments of both parties. It marks the end of 10 years of debate. Now we stand ready to take our first step into a new world full of new opportunities.
>
> Our historic decision has been made: the British people accept the challenge. Let us show ourselves to that new world as we would wish it to see us: confident, proud and strong.

Mr. Francis Pym, Government Chief Whip, said: "It is a decisive verdict in this Parliament in favour of the Market."

PEERS VOTE FOR ENTRY [36]

The House of Lords last night approved British entry into the Common Market by an overwhelming majority. When the peers divided at 8:30 p.m. the vote was 451–58, in favour of accepting the terms negotiated by the Government.

Unlike the Commons, the Lords had a free vote, and the split in the Labour Party showed when Lord Shackleton, leader of the Labour peers, and a member of the "shadow" cabinet—voted with the Government. He was joined by a number of his front bench spokesmen.

The Lords vote came 90 minutes before the Commons also approved British entry by a decisive majority.

During the closing stages of the Commons six-day debate, Mr. Harold Wilson dismayed pro-Marketeers in all parties by outlining the circumstances in which a future Labour Government might leave the EEC.

The only consolation for the Government and for his own pro-Marketeers was that he did not suggest or imply that a Labour Government would actually take the initiative in "pulling out." But what he did say delighted his Left-wingers and other fervent anti-Marketeers.

Challenged by Mr. Duncan Sandys to state the position of a future Labour Government on the Common Market, the Labour leader said: "It

36. *Financial Times*, Oct. 29, 1971.

is a fact that one Parliament cannot bind its successor. On the other hand, we recognize what is involved in a Treaty signature.

> We would immediately give notice we could not accept the terms negotiated by the Conservatives, and in particular the unacceptable burdens arising out of the Common Agricultural Policy, the blows to the Commonwealth and any threats to our essential regional policies.

> If the Community then refused to negotiate or if negotiations were to fail, we would sit down amicably and discuss the situation with them. We should make it clear from that moment that our posture, like that of the French after 1958, would be rigidly directed towards the pursuit of British interests, and all other decisions and actions in relation to the Community would be dictated by that determination until we had secured our terms.

Then came the final sentence, which immediately had Labour anti-Marketeers cheering. "The Community," said Mr. Wilson, "could accept, or decide that we should agree to part. That would depend on them."

Mr. Reginald Maudling, the first Government speaker yesterday, commented that Mr. Wilson had in this statement gone "rather further than, on reflection, he would wish he had done."

Mr. Wilson rallied his anti-Marketeers again by saying that the fight against the Government's entry terms would continue. "To-day is not an end. It is a beginning," he said. He was clearly referring to the Opposition's coming attack on the Government's consequential legislation.

The Government is now confident that, in spite of the inevitable difficulties it will face, it will be able to carry the long and comprehensive legislation next year on a Tory vote.

Finally, on January 22, 1972, Britain signed the Treaty of Brussels, formally joining the EEC.

TREATY OF BRUSSELS [37]

Ten nations of Western Europe joined today to create a larger and more powerful economic community.

An elaborate ceremony marked what the sponsors hope will be seen in history as a great step toward the dream of a united Europe. Millions of Europeans watched on television as politicians and diplomats signed the Treaty of Brussels.

The new members must still ratify the agreement, and that will present difficulties. In Britain there will be a long struggle in the House of

37. *New York Times,* Jan. 23, 1972.

Commons. Ireland, Denmark and Norway will seek popular approval in referendums.

The enlarged community is to be formed on Jan. 1, 1973. It will be one of the great economic powers—though still lacking political unity and effective centralized institutions.

Britain is both the political and the economic key to the hopes for the greater Common Market. Prime Minister Heath, therefore, was the central figure in the ceremony. . . .

Mr. Heath particularly emphasized the need for Europe to look outward.

"It must be a Europe which is strong and confident within itself," he said, "a Europe in which we shall be working for the progressive relaxation and elimination of tension between East and West, a Europe alive to its great responsibilities in the common struggle of humanity for a better life.

"This ceremony marks an end and also a beginning: an end to divisions which have stricken Europe for centuries. A beginning of another stage in the construction of a new and a greater united Europe."

7. IMPACT ON THE UNITED STATES

At no time were the economic conflicts between the EEC and the United States more intense than at the time when Britain signed the Treaty of Brussels. The United States endorsed Britain's earlier attempts to enter the Common Market and strongly supported greater economic integration in Europe at the time of the Trade Expansion Act of 1962. A decade later, however, the tensions between the EEC and United States clearly had increased. Some of these differences surfaced in the Kennedy Round (see Problem I), in the rising protectionist sentiment associated with nontariff barriers (see Problem II), during the negotiations between Britain and the EEC, and in the bargaining over new international monetary arrangements since 1971.

The changes that had occurred in the world economy as a result of the Kennedy Round and the enlargement of the EEC, presented the United States with several trade policy options. It could support the EEC generally, but seek specific changes in EEC policies so as to be more favorable to United States interests; it could promote a North American regional arrangement for the United States and Canada; or, seeking to avoid polarization between the EEC and a North American regional bloc, it could promote some other form of multilateral free trade association combined with Japan, the EEC, and other countries that would want to join. A choice among these options must, of course, depend in large part on what are the expected economic consequences.

So far the greatest impacts of the EEC have been from the common external tariff, common agricultural policy, and effects on private overseas investment. After January 1973, the full membership of Britain, Ireland, Norway, and Denmark will add new significance to the EEC. Already in 1971, the new Community's population was about 257 million, larger than either the United States or the Soviet Union. In 1970, the GNP of the ten countries was approximately $637 billion—more than two-thirds that of the United States. The Community's share of world trade was more than 40 per cent, nearly double the share of the United States, Soviet Union, and Japan combined. And the ten had a larger share of world monetary reserves and a larger vote in the IMF than did the United States.

In considering the impact of the EEC, it is necessary to analyze how much is due to the change in tariff rates and how much is due to the growth of income within the Community. There has clearly been an increase in output in the EEC; but how much of this is because of integration? There has also been an increase in imports into the EEC; but again, how much of this is because of integration? Imports from the United States have also risen, but it is questionable whether the share of United States' imports in total EEC imports is being maintained. There has also been an increase in intra-EEC trade; but again, has this been due to a decrease in tariff levels or an increase in income within the Community? A major question is whether the increase in intra-EEC trade is deleterious to member trade—that is, whether it constitutes trade diversion and whether the trade-pattern effects of tariff changes accompanying the Common Market outweigh the expansionary effects of induced income growth in member countries? Another major question is how the common agricultural policy affects domestic production, consumer prices, and the volume of net imports into the EEC. Beyond these economic questions, there is the more subtle question of the political and economic power of a regional bloc, that by virtue of its large population, industrial production, and share of world trade has now acquired a leadership role in world affairs.

An earlier assessment of what could be the impact of the Common Market on the United States trade position was made as follows.

THE U. S. TRADE POSITION AND THE COMMON MARKET [38]

It is widely appreciated that the terms upon which the United States has participated in world trade during the past century have been favored by unique features of U. S. geography and economic structure. There is reason to fear that some of these past sources of strength may be eroding, owing partly to the continuing revolution in transportation and communication and partly to economic changes both in the United States and in other important industrial countries.

In particular, the economic structure of Western Europe has been moving closer to that of the United States. The United States thus is being made less unique; it is being confronted with keener competition and with a more nearly equal concentration of economic and political power.

The European Economic Community (EEC) or the Common Market has accelerated these developments—some more clearly than others. It may not be amiss, therefore, to try to assess the impact of the Common Market upon the United States against this general background of changing relative positions. This approach shifts attention somewhat from the usual emphasis on the dangers of trade diversion that are created by the rapid elimination of trade barriers within the Common Market and the establishment of a common tariff wall around it. Aside from the fact that trade diversion has already been so widely discussed, there are several reasons for favoring this line of attack.

In the first place, the extent of trade diversion itself will depend largely upon the policy choices made by the EEC and these will in turn be influenced by the whole constellation of political and economic power relationships between the EEC and other countries, particularly the United States. This is the more likely since the common external tariff itself cannot be regarded as unduly protective by American standards. Tariff comparisons are notoriously difficult, but it is probably significant that at the rates prevailing in 1960 the average U. S. duty was higher than the common external tariff for 47 out of 74 chapters of the Brussels classification for which data were calculated by the Committee for Economic Development. Taken in conjunction with the trade-creating effects of the fillip to economic growth given by the Common Market, adverse overall effects on U. S. exports to the Common Market countries will not necessarily follow *automatically* from the existence of the Common Market. Adverse ef-

---

38. *Factors Affecting the United States Balance of Payments* (1962), Joint Economic Committee Print, Subcommittee on International Exchange and Payments of the Joint Economic Committee, 87th Congress, Second Session, 1962, pp. 87–104.

fects may, however, result from the future commercial and economic policies of the Common Market.

Secondly, a discussion of the effects of the Common Market which is concentrated upon trade diversion stresses competition for EEC markets and may omit the important question of competition between EEC and U. S. firms for American and third markets. After all, U. S. exports to the six account for only about 15 percent of U. S. commodity exports, and they are, of course, small relative to total sales in the domestic market. Furthermore the more basic issues of relative competitiveness are important also in the contest for EEC markets.

The forces working against the U. S. trade position thus arise fundamentally from changes in the technology of transportation and communications and from basic changes in the economic structure of Western Europe. Western Europe has been the chief beneficiary of the enhanced geographical mobility of the elements that historically have been primarily sources of American advantage in international trade. Furthermore, Western Europe proceeds toward Americanization from an internal dynamic as well as from external effects flowing from the United States. As incomes rise, costly and high quality products begin to find domestic markets. Domestic industries arise to cater to these demands, and supplying industries develop to produce the improved materials and the new machines necessary to make the new goods.

These changes were flowing at full tide before the advent of the Common Market at the beginning of 1958, and the new organization has probably added to them only marginally. . . .

The real threat posed by the organization of the Common Market for the trade position of the United States is the greater concentration of economic and political power than had previously existed, particularly since there are built-in factors that may cause this power to be used in ways that will be harmful to American exports.

Before turning to these political aspects, however, let us examine briefly the respects in which the advent of the Common Market brings or accelerates economic changes that weaken the U. S. trade position.

In the first place, the Common Market institutions may have had some effect in producing more rational practices with respect to certain raw materials than might otherwise have been followed. The complete elimination of tariffs and other restrictions on intracommunity trade in coal and steel, achieved under the European Coal and Steel Community (ECSC), reduced transport costs by rationalizing channels of distribution. In coal, for example, mines near national boundaries began to serve areas determined by economic rather than political factors. There are some signs also that the European Communities (i.e., the ECSC, EEC, and Euratom) aided by pressure from the Italians (who have no coal and depend upon cheap oil from external sources), will hasten the process of relaxing restrictions against the import of oil so as to obtain cheap energy supplies despite unfavorable effects on coal.

Secondly, the Common Market has dramatized the European market and made it more attractive to American capital and enterprise. The Common Market thus has tended to accelerate the process by which American enterprise, technology, and capital rather than American goods move across the ocean.

Third, the formation of the Common Market seems to have provided a stimulus to the growth of large size firms. A wave of mergers, affiliations, and understandings has probably led to larger size and lower cost plants, and has increased the degree of product specialization in plants of a given size. It has led also to larger firms which are more strongly placed with respect to research, finance, and foreign marketing than the smaller ones they replaced. The extent and significance of merger movements in the Common Market are difficult to assess. It is conceivable that what is going on is merely an adjustment by business to the new situation created by the prospect of free trade within the Community. If so, the policy of live and let live, which seems to have characterized Western European business psychology to a greater degree than that of the United States, may soon reassert itself. It is possible that this attitude was as responsible as the inherent limitations of a market of the size of say England or France or Germany for the existence of smaller scale plants than in America. Of course, the EEC has taken steps to implement the anti-cartel provisions of the Rome Treaty, but whether European business will become imbued with a new competitive spirit either through self- or official-inspiration is far from clear. In any case, at the moment there has been a clear gain in efficiency from the rationalization movement that has taken place.

Fourth, the formation of the Common Market has made a contribution to the rate of growth, and thus created a greater market and a greater opportunity for the mass production of standard items and for the large scale production of more costly goods that were almost an American monopoly. In TV and radio, for example, the European market is already on a par with that of the United States in the quality of the product which it can absorb; in most other consumer durables, however, it is 10 to 30 years behind the United States. Of course, the expansion of the European market has been a boon to American exports thus far; it has offset any tendency for trade diversion to hurt U. S. exports. Indeed, U. S. exports to the Common Market have expanded more rapidly than U. S. exports as a whole since 1957 or 1958. However, the European boom can hardly last forever, and when the domestic absorption of European output slackens, U. S. producers may feel the full impact of the new capacities of European firms to produce goods in varieties, qualities, and quantities which formerly could be obtained only in the United States. Many American businessmen fear just this. They feel that their European competitors have been satisfied to follow the price leadership of American firms in the American and sometimes in other markets; this enables European firms, in view of their lower costs, to enjoy high profit margins on their foreign business at a time when their plants are occupied with domestic orders anyway. Of course, if the European countries succeed in maintaining full employment economies with only mild and infrequent recessions further European inroads on markets held by the United States will depend upon the longer run growth of European capacity.

Finally, the agricultural policy of the Common Market threatens to increase the degree of self-sufficiency of the area by stimulating the expansion of internal production. New export surpluses such as French wheat have already appeared, and if high internal prices are added to the system of variable levies giving preference to Community products, the United States which has been exporting over $1 billion of agricultural products to the Common Market may find itself reduced to the position of a residual supplier especially for grains. Unlike the other factors we have listed, this one involves competition between United States and European producers only for the markets of the Community itself. To the extent that it will affect competition for other markets, it will be unfavorable to the EEC because it will tend to raise the level of costs.

With the possible exception of the last factor, the adverse influences upon U. S. trade that we have discussed thus far have stemmed from economic changes. The most important consequences of the Common Market for the U. S. trade position are, however, likely to flow from a new political fact: For the first time in many decades the United States is faced in the Western World with an almost equal aggregation of economic and political power. The uncoordinated, sometimes conflicting, and often offsetting policies pursued by six governments are being replaced by coordinated decisions reached in Brussels. Even without the addition of new members, the decisions are taken on behalf of countries whose combined importance in world trade already equals or exceeds that of the United States and who provide a significant fraction of the U. S. export surplus. The bargaining power of the Common Market, already substantial, will of course be further increased if Great Britain and other new members and associates are admitted. As the geographical scope of the Common Market is expanded, it will embrace an increasingly diversified area and will become more self-sufficient and less dependent upon external trade than the individual member countries have been. Thus, like the United States, the new entity will have considerable leeway for deciding upon more or less liberal policies.

How will this power be used? Some parts of the answer seem clear. In the first place, the power of the Common Market is likely to be used to retaliate promptly and fully in response to any adverse actions taken in trade matters by another country, including the United States. This has recently been illustrated by the action of the Council of Ministers of the EEC in raising the common external tariff on a half dozen product groups in reprisal for U. S. increases under the GATT escape clause in the duties on carpets and glass. . . .

A second factor affecting the use of the power that the EEC has is the

inherent tendency of any large area composed of diverse interests to reconcile conflicts over the resolution of domestic difficulties by shifting as
much of the burden of adjustment to outsiders as possible. This is evident in U. S. commercial policy. For example, the extensive protection
accorded by the United States to its textile industry, including high tariffs
and new legislation authorizing the establishment of import quotas, reflects pressures arising from the failure of domestic consumption of textile products to expand as rapidly as productivity, with the result that employment levels have been declining. In the short history of the Common
Market, there are already a number of illustrations of this tendency to resolve difficulties by cutting off the outsider. . . .

Even if it seems reasonable to suppose that the Common Market will
retaliate when the occasion arises and shift the burden of adjustments to
third countries when internal difficulties develop, there remains a large
and important area of doubt about the way in which the Community will
wield the great power which its size and importance confers upon it. Although the Rome Treaty contains a clause stating that the member countries intend to follow a liberal commercial policy (art. 110), the commitment is quite general and could conceivably be subordinated to other
objectives of the Six. At the risk of some oversimplification, one might
say that there are two schools of thought within the Community on this
matter. One school, for which the French are the spokesmen on many issues, takes the view that the Community represents, among other things,
a club for the mutual benefit of the member countries at the expense of
outsiders. This position has been generally opposed by the Dutch and
also by the Germans, both of whom tend to prefer more liberal trading
policies for the Community. Of course, the difference is one of degree, al-
beit an important one, because some element of tariff discrimination in
favor of fellow members is the essence of a customs union. While it is
true that the conception of the EEC goes far beyond a mere customs
union, it is also true that the most immediate practical attraction of the
EEC to participants and would-be participants is its customs union
feature. . . .

There are a number of basic developments that seem to be reducing
the strength of the American position in international trade. The exhaus-
tion of some low-cost domestic sources of material supplies and economies in the use of natural raw materials have reduced the margin of advantage enjoyed by the United States from the availability of cheap
natural raw materials. The American comparative advantage in agriculture has been offset by governmental policies that limit increasingly the
ability of the United States to market its agricultural products commer-
cially. The greater geographical mobility of entrepreneurs and of capital
and the more rapid dissemination of new techniques and new products
have dispersed to many countries, especially those in Western Europe,
important elements of strength that formerly favored the United States.
The growth of income and wealth in foreign countries, particularly in Eu-

rope, have made it more possible for foreign producers to take advantage of the economies of mass production, and sizable foreign markets have begun to develop for high cost quality products which formerly could be marketed on a large enough scale to warrant domestic production only in the United States.

The advent of the Common Market has strengthened many of these adverse economic tendencies, but, more important, it has created a center of political and economic power that can retaliate against any increase in American protection and that may in any case be driven to use its power to exclude foreign competition. There are in the Common Market, just as in the United States, divided opinions on the choice between protectionism and liberalism. A distinct choice of one position or the other by either entity would undoubtedly have strong repercussions on the other's policy.

It is possible, of course, that these losses of advantage may be offset by a new flowering of innovations, particularly in various fields of application of atomic science, such as energy, medicine, and telecommunications.

Even if this does not occur or if its impact is too small to offset fully the other adverse effects, it does not mean that the United States would be left without a comparative advantage in a significant range of products. Indeed, the rapid growth in trade between the more nearly equal partners of the Common Market suggests that trade need not rest upon large differences in economic structure.

However, as far as the Atlantic Community is concerned, such trade would be trade between equals rather than trade between a technological leader and a number of other countries none of which has so high a per capita income or so extensive a market. The real terms of trade that can be maintained by a technological leader are superior to those that can be attained by one of a group of equals. The reason is that the leader's currency is placed at a premium as a result of its power to command goods that cannot be obtained elsewhere.

Even a sharp adverse movement in the terms of trade would hardly have severe effects upon the real income of a country such as the United States whose imports are equivalent to less than 3 percent and exports to less than 4 percent of its gross national product. The real problem would be to find the optimum means for the necessary adjustment in the terms of trade to take place.

If the United States has to accept less favorable terms of trade, there are two ways in which this can be accomplished. One way is to depreciate the exchange value of the dollar in terms of other currencies. This possibility has been receiving increasing attention recently both in terms of a one-time devaluation and in terms of establishing a free or floating rate of exchange. Either of these alternatives would tend to weaken the strength of the forces that are moving the world toward a higher degree of economic integration.

The other way is to increase the internal purchasing power of the dollar relative to that of other currencies while keeping exchange rates fixed. This used to be discussed entirely in terms of an absolute deflation of prices and wages, and in such terms it clearly is not politically feasible. In a world of rising prices, however, the same result can be achieved by confining the movement of the price level to a smaller rise than that which takes place in other countries. . . .

On the political side, the main implication that has to be drawn from the rise in the political and economic power of Western Europe and particularly the Common Market is that the United States is no longer able with impunity to adjust its tariff and trade measures unilaterally to meet difficulties arising for domestic industries. While the postwar trade record of the United States is no worse and in some respects better than that of most other industrial countries, there is a larger gap—which has been well publicized—between the trade philosophy consistently preached by all our postwar administrations and the invocation of quantitative restrictions on such things as dairy products, lead and zinc, and oil and the increases in tariffs on such products as watches, bicycles, and glass. The result is that the United States is not in a strong moral or political position to oppose the inherent tendency of the Common Market to act in a similarly protective manner when confronted with its own internal problems. Furthermore, more than two can play, and there are other—though less powerful—countries and blocs ready to enter the game.

During the period of negotiations between Britain and the Six, the prospect of an enlarged Common Market aroused more United States fears of adverse effects. The following commentary indicates some of the apprehension over the possible effects on American exports and firms operating abroad.

EUROPE VS. THE U.S. [39]

Ever since World War II, U. S. policy-makers have been promoting the dream of a united Europe. But now that an enlarging Common Market makes this much closer to reality, many officials are awakening to fears that the U. S. can ill afford the economic consequences.

They say that the surge toward a European Economic Community of 10 tightly knit nations instead of six loosely linked ones carries these important implications for the U. S.:

—A drop in such key U. S. exports as crops and computers that cross the common tariff fence into the EEC countries.

—Spawning of powerful, Europe-wide corporations that will compete

39. *Wall Street Journal*, Oct. 28, 1970. Reprinted by permission of the *Wall Street Journal*.

more keenly with U. S. companies in Europe, America and other markets.

—And, eventually, a common European currency to help the EEC challenge U. S. financial influence.

"It's difficult to see how the effect on us economically could be anything but adverse," confides one high Nixon Administration economic official. . . .

The American apprehensions go far beyond the present tensions over whether the textile and import restrictions pending in Congress might trigger a "trade war," though such a clash would clearly create a more hostile attitude on both sides. EEC authorities warned yesterday at a Luxembourg meeting that they are ready for "immediate action" to retaliate against U. S. goods if the Administration carries out protectionist measures. . . .

Despite their misgivings about the effects, top U. S. authorities insist they won't try to torpedo the unity movement. One good reason for not interfering, some U. S. aides say, is the prospect that initial export losses may be more than offset in the long run as a more prosperous Europe buys greater volumes of U. S. goods.

"We're only asking that your companies take a smaller share of a growing market instead of a larger share of a stagnant market," says a British official reassuringly. He expects more U. S. companies will profit, too, by building plants in Britain to serve all of Europe; some expansion-minded American firms have been holding back to see if the United Kingdom will gain EEC entry.

More important, U. S. policy-makers say, whatever happens to trade is secondary to much more sweeping considerations of international politics and Free World security. Thus, they stress, the basic U. S. policy remains as stated last February by President Nixon: "The possible economic price of a truly unified Europe is outweighed by the gain in the political vitality of the West as a whole." . . .

Among Nixon Administration economists, there's a growing undercurrent of skepticism about either political or economic benefits of EEC expansion. "Frankly, I'm very pessimistic," says a well-placed U. S. analyst, who fears the U. S. will face "the worst of both worlds"—a stronger "discriminatory customs union" that never evolves into true political unity.

Administration men are increasingly anxious to minimize the economic price of the European unity movement as the time to pay looms closer. "There is no reason today why we should incur short-term economic costs" from an enlarged Common Market, declares Nathaniel Samuels, Deputy Under Secretary of State for Economic Affairs. He reasons that Europe is already such an "economic giant" that it can well afford to avoid hurting U. S. trade.

While the shock of U. S. adjustment to EEC expansion may be neither massive nor long-lasting, it may be painful indeed for some

Americans heavily dependent on selling to Europe, and particularly to Britain. Once the United Kingdom can buy goods duty-free from other Common Market members, the U. S. may well lose some of its $2.3 billion annual exports to Britain temporarily, according to EEC trade experts.

Both EEC and British officials candidly concede that they will try to reduce their imports of "sensitive" U. S. items, such as aircraft and aircraft components. "To put it bluntly, we don't want to depend on Boeing forever," says one official in London. He figures that only under the EEC umbrella will the United Kingdom and Continental countries have a big enough market to specialize efficiently in making engines and other parts for "truly European" aircraft.

Computers are another high-technology product that the U. S. has been especially successful in exporting, to a point that hurts European pride. EEC members will welcome more injections of U. S. investment and technological know-how into their own computer industries, a British aide promises, but he adds, "What we don't welcome is U. S. takeover of such a vital industry." Europe's computer-building ambitions plainly bode ill for U. S. sales of the machines.

American exports of certain farm products, notably grains, are apt to suffer the most from Common Market enlargement, it's widely agreed. British conformity to the "common agricultural policy" of generous subsidies for members' farm output probably would mean reduced purchases of grain from the U. S., admits one analyst in Brussels, headquarters of the EEC, though he also foresees greater U. S. sales to the U. K. of soybeans and livestock feedstuffs that the EEC lets in duty-free.

Some U. S. aides worry, too, that it will be increasingly difficult for this country to sell to more than a score of smaller countries with which the EEC has "preferential" trade pacts, mainly in Africa and the Mediterranean area. "You look around," one Nixon aide says, "and they're fencing off a hell of a large part of the world." The EEC is starting to explore a "political" relationship with Latin America, its officials note, and a British official boasts that within a few years the EEC is likely to have the Communist market "all sewed up."

The more optimistic advocates of European integration argue that the direct export losses by the U. S. aren't apt to be massive. They would be no more than $100 million to $200 million annually after allowing for faster European economic growth, according to a confidential State Department study; that would be a fraction of the U. S. trade surplus of about $3 billion expected this year and a much thinner sliver of total U. S. exports of over $40 billion yearly.

But the depth of Washington concern varies sharply from one U. S. agency to another, with State Department men taking the EEC expansion pretty much in stride while those at the Commerce Department are closest to panic. Scoffing at the State Department arithmetic, a Commerce official contends the short-run losses would be "very high," adding that eventually such other nations as Austria, Greece, Turkey and Spain may join the EEC, too. If Spain and its oranges get behind the Common Market's tariff wall, "our citrus industry will take a real shellacking," he worries.

So far, Brussels officials assert, the unity moves among the six present EEC members have helped—not hurt—U. S. exports. Their decision in late 1957 to form the Common Market and start dismantling tariffs among themselves, EEC aides say, has triggered a boom that draws in more U. S. goods.

Common Market statistics show that between 1958 and 1969 annual U. S. exports to the six bulged by 182% to $7 billion, outstripping the 143% increase to other European countries and the 118% increase in exports to the rest of the world.

Whatever the future trend in U. S. exports, EEC men figure many more "multinational corporations" will be created by Continental and U. K. interests once "the 10" harmonize various policies and practices ranging from antitrust laws to driver's license tests. "Not many German companies think of putting a factory in France now," one planner says, but he expects that before long across-the-border mergers will produce more European corporations muscular enough to invest heavily in facilities in the U. S., too.

The most resounding impact on the U. S. from a bigger and stronger EEC, however, would be in the realm of monetary unity, officials on both sides agree. If member nations go along with the Brussels planners, by 1980 there will be no more exchange-rate fluctuation among EEC member currencies, and there might even be a single European money pumped out by one central bank, replacing pounds, francs and the like.

In contrast to this rigidity of exchange rates within Europe, Brussels experts hope their money could "float" in relation to the U. S. dollar as much as 5% either way from the official parity. "This way," one says, "if there are too many U. S. dollars coming our way their price would simply get cheaper." This loss of value, while aiding U. S. exports, would discourage American importers, investors and tourists from continuing to swell the stream of dollars to Europe.

"People in Europe are getting fed up" with the way massive flows of U. S. dollars to Europe cause inflation and sharp interest-rate swings and "keep us from being masters of our own economies," says one EEC source in Brussels. The Europeans "wish to resist the inflationary consequences of past U. S. political and economic policy decisions in which they did not participate," observes Eugene Birnbaum, Chase Manhattan Bank's vice president for international monetary affairs.

Even though the common-currency drive has an anti-American tinge, both U. S. and EEC experts generally agree that the world might be better off as a result. "A European currency would be fundamentally stronger and more secure than any of its separate national component currencies had ever been," Mr. Birnbaum says. An EEC official reasons that it would provide a "second pillar" helping the dollar shore up the entire international monetary system.

Not surprisingly, the views within the American business community were mixed, depending on how individual enterprises interpreted their own prospects. As predicted by one *Wall Street Journal* reporter, the Common Market could be expected to have at least these consequences:

—An increase in European economic power and a consequent relative downgrading of the U. S. dollar's role internationally.

—A loosening of Britain's special relationship with the United States.

—A chance for American companies to operate in a single, economically united market that would include nearly every major country in Europe. This could reduce duplication of effort and boost profits for some companies, but other concerns may suffer from strengthened European competition.

—A rough time for American farm exports to Britain, the world's largest export market for agricultural products.[40]

It also was reported that

A recent survey of 465 American companies operating in the present six-nation Common Market, conducted by U. S. management consultants Heidrick and Struggles, reflects a good measure of the Yankee enthusiasm over European unity.

According to the poll, 69% expect benefits from the Common Market enlargement. Only 6% saw any disadvantages, while 25% saw no effect on their business. A little over half the companies surveyed cite larger markets as the chief advantage to them, while 35% said lower costs would be the most favorable factor.

Nearly half the companies said they expected increases in sales volume ranging from 6% to 10% as a result of British entry into the EEC. Twenty per cent saw increases of 1% to 5% while another 20% expect increases of 11% to 20%.

Companies who discussed their European prospects in greater detail with *The Wall Street Journal* placed less emphasis on volume increases, which they said were hard to calculate in any case. But they did enthuse over "easier decision making," greater "planning freedom" and more efficient distribution.[41]

40. *Ibid.*, May 18, 1971.
41. *Ibid.*, Nov. 18, 1971.

Of special significance will be the effect on American direct investment in the Common Market. The book value of direct United States investments in the Common Market increased from $2.6 billion in 1960 to almost $12 billion by 1970.[42] The growing strength of American firms in Europe definitely has become a cause of considerable unease.[43] The widening of the European market undoubtedly will stimulate more investment by some American corporations or American equity interests in multinational enterprises operating in Europe. Continued progress in integrating European markets may, however, counteract formation of the "American Europe." If the enlarged Common Market improves the ability of European firms to compete with American firms, this can go against additional American investment. Especially important will be the increasing tendency for European-owned enterprises to view their market as European-wide, rather than national. Also important will be the extent to which a common EEC policy emerges toward foreign investment. The progress toward an economic and monetary union, the increasing number of mergers across national borders within Europe, and the development of European multinational enterprises will also have effects on American direct investments. Perhaps a fair summary is the following comment.

> During the first 20 postwar years the European firms have given first consideration to the internal rebuilding and to exports. They have left it to American firms to establish themselves in Europe without themselves being ready or willing to push across the Atlantic. . . . The danger that America and Japan will alone provide the leading world corporations during the next 20 years will continue to exist only if Europe is not successful in its economic integration and if the European firms have to rely on national partial markets which are too small a home base for their international expansion.[44]

7.1. Monetary Negotiations and Trade Concessions. With President Nixon's announcement on August 15, 1971, of several new measures to improve the United States balance of payments, the

42. U. S. Department of Commerce, *Survey of Current Business*, Oct. 1971, p. 28.

43. See, for example, J.-J. Servan-Schreiber, *The American Challenge* (1968); C. P. Kindleberger, *American Business Abroad* (1969), chap. 3; J. N. Behrman, *Some Patterns in the Rise of Multinational Enterprise* (1969), chaps. 2, 3; Rainer Hellman, *The Challenge to U. S. Dominance of the International Corporation* (1971), especially chaps. 3–5, 9–10; Raymond Vernon, *Sovereignty at Bay* (1971).

44. Hellman, *op. cit.*, p. 314.

economic grievances between the United States and the EEC were
forced into the open. Along with other policies, President Nixon imposed a 10 per cent import surcharge and suspended the dollar's
convertibility into gold with the intent of forcing a realignment of
exchange rates and bargaining for some trade concessions.

The mood of the immediate reaction is conveyed in the following
extract.

TRADE WINDS BLOW COLD [45]

There has been bad feeling between the Common Market countries
and the Americans over trade for some time, but President Nixon's 10
per cent import surcharge has made matters very much worse.

The Europeans are particularly angry about the increasingly high
price he wants for its removal, though until it was imposed, it was the
U S which complained most bitterly about unfair trading.

Early this summer a committee was set up to look at the problem,
after American pressure in the Organisation for Economic Cooperation
and Development, but it has been rather submerged. Now both sides are
feeling more aggrieved.

The Americans point to restrictions on agricultural imports to the
Common Market, while the Europeans stress that last year the Americans had a surplus of $2.4 billions in their trade with the Six. Their ex-
ports went up from $7.3 billions in 1969 to $9 billions in 1970.

The Common Market is going to be badly hit by the surcharge, for
over 90 per cent of its exports to the U S will be affected.

The steel industry is particularly angry when it has been observing a
voluntary quota which limited the increase in exports to 5 per cent a
year. Like the Japanese textile men, it sees no reason for being penalised
first by a quota and then by a surcharge.

It has offered the administration a choice between the two and says
that if there is no exemption, it will drop its voluntary limit.

Cars too, will be hit, though the abolition of the 7 per cent car duty
in the U S should offset part of the surcharge's impact. There are also
plenty of worries about heavy engineering. The new U S Job Development Act which the President announced, allows a 10 per cent tax credit
this year—with 5 per cent next year—for investment in plant, provided
that it is U S made.

This will hit Britain and Germany badly, and like the surcharge itself,
is against the trading rules. This is why there is now such resentment
about U S charges of discrimination.

The long-standing American complaint on the industrial front has

45. *The Manchester Guardian*, Sept. 9, 1971, p. 18.

been about the Community's acceptance of the value added tax where there is a rebate on exports including indirect costs.

Although VAT is allowed by the general agreement on tariffs and trade, the U S has always regarded it an export subsidy and one of the options discussed before Mr. Nixon took action was to impose a tax which would exactly counter VAT's benefit to Europe's exporters.

There are plenty of other disputes. Nontariff barriers, which cover most of the ways of keeping out exports for bogusly respectable reasons are a big area for negotiation.

Both sides have them in profusion, particularly in foods and pharmaceutical products. The American ban on broiler imports is matched by a French order prohibiting import of orange juice containing dextrose, for instance.

The biggest American bugbear has been the Six's common agricultural policy. Europe's market for U S grain this year is going to be much smaller than last. With a bad European harvest then U S grain exports had to supply 100 million tons more than they had exported in 1969. There is little prospect of that happening now, for forecasts suggest that harvest totals in the Common Market will be at a record level.

The U S wants massive changes in the methods of the Common Market's agricultural support. It says the aim should be to help the poorer farmer rather than pay all farmers a given sum for their produce. The present system leads to over production and helps the rich farmer more than anyone else.

There are now three separate rates—which could go up to four—with a series of rebates and subsidies to keep prices throughout the Common Market reasonably in line. The weight of the American surcharge had fallen on industry, but there are some agricultural groups which have been hit, medium priced wines and Dutch bulbs for examples.

There is also resentment about the Common Market's preferential trade agreements with countries like Spain, Morocco and Tunisia. These offer special rates for imports of oranges and limit American citrus exports.

The whole question was discussed in the early summer and eventually the Common Market agreed to halve the tariff on U S fruit, though the rates are still higher than for the Mediterranean countries.

There has also been some complaints about the Common Market's agreements with Turkey and Greece, which are based on the assumption that they will become full members when they are economically stronger and that Community concessions are due now.

The whole range of agreements with the EFTA neutrals which do not intend to follow Britain into the Common Market have not yet been concluded, but there could be American complaints of partiality there, too.

For the moment the main issues look very much bigger and will submerge the smaller American complaints.

But on trade, the core of the European argument will be that only $2 billions of the American balance of payments deficit this year will be caused by a deficit on trade, and $21 billions will be a matter of monetary movements. They complain of massive overkill on the trade front and the longer Mr. Nixon's surcharge remains, the more they will be inclined to retaliate.

As the monetary negotiations continued, it became increasingly evident that the major issues in dispute were, on the one side, the 10 per cent import surcharge and, on the other side, duties on agricultural imports and preferential arrangements between the enlarged EEC and other countries. The United States became especially anxious over what would be the tariff arrangements for industrial trade between the enlarged Common Market and the other members of EFTA who have not applied to join the Community. If the nonjoiners of EFTA are given associated status with the Common Market, then the new preferential arrangements—possibly even a new free trade arrangement—between the EFTA nonjoiners and the Common Market countries would cause more competition against the United States (and other third countries). In the old Common Market, the United States would have to compete with tariff-free products from both the EFTA joiners and the nonjoiners, as well as being faced with increased competition in the economies of the three joiners and the EFTA nonjoiners from tariff-free products from the old Common Market.

U. S. SCORES PLAN BY SIX ON TRADE [46]

A sharp dispute has arisen between the United States and the European Economic Community over the trading arrangements the enlarged bloc would make with the industrialized countries of Europe that do not intend to join.

The United States delivered a formal verbal protest of the contemplated arrangements to the six members of the Common Market and its Brussels executive authority last Friday.

While the governments have not yet drafted a reply, the chief of the E.E.C. executives, Franco Maria Malfatti, and the commissioner in charge of trade relations, Ralf Dahrendorf, took exception to the Ameri-

46. *New York Times*, Nov. 9, 1971.

can protest at a meeting of the foreign ministers of the E.E.C. member countries here today.

Mr. Dahrendorf said he took a "dim view" of Washington's move, calling it "direct interference with autonomous policies" of the community —a reference to the timing of the protest three days before the E.E.C. ministers were to deliberate again on the subject.

The E.E.C. foreign ministers apparently ignoring the protest tonight gave the Executive Commission a loosely framed mandate to negotiate an agreement with the European noncandidates. The aim is to set up a giant free-trade area.

The United States is worried about the probable loss of export markets, particularly in farm products, if anything like the arrangements now being discussed go through.

The Community argued that what it was doing was perfectly legal under the world trade charter known as the General Agreement on Tariffs and Trade, or GATT.

If this is so, then the United States reserves the right to get the rules changed. They were drawn up in 1947 when world trading patterns were much different than today. . . .

What has angered the United States, especially under the tough New Economic Program of the last three months, is that the Community wants to set up a giant preferential trading area within Europe, as it has already done with the Mediterranean states.

Specifically, the plans now being discussed involve the elimination of trade barriers on industrial goods (except for certain sensitive products) between the enlarged community and the following nations: Sweden, Switzerland, Austria, Finland, Portugal and Iceland.

In addition France, Italy and the Netherlands in the community councils, want agriculture side agreements to get rid of surplus grains, fruits and vegetables and dairy products.

The United States recognizes that there is a problem in the treatment of European countries that will not join the community. But it argues that such treatment must not be at the expense of American foreign trade.

According to some rough calculations from American sources, the United States stands to lose $200–300-million of foreign sales through the contemplated EFTA trade diversion. Countries like Sweden and Switzerland, for instance, might tend to replace present purchases from the United States with purchases from the E.E.C. bloc.

What the United States wants is the extension of the most-favored-nation principle so that whatever concessions are offered to the EFTA countries also become available to the United States. The Community has no intention of agreeing to this.

The United States is also expected to seek compensation for any trade losses it suffers. This it can do under the GATT rules.

But the heart of the matter is the Community's ever-greater impact in the world of commerce. The framers of the GATT charter did not envisage such a development back in 1947. As an illustration of the way one country after another is trying to come to terms with the Community, even mainland China has already had unofficial contacts, and according to sources here is believed to want diplomatic accreditation with the Community institutions.

The United States' demands for trade concessions from the EEC became even more pronounced when trade arrangements were interjected into the Group of Ten talks in December 1971, as part of the package settlement of the world monetary crisis. A report of these talks indicates some of the specific trade issues on which the United States wanted immediate redress of grievances, before settling other long-term trade questions.

U. S. TRADE GRIEVANCES [47]

The Indian summer of Richard Nixon's meeting with President Pompidou in the Azores last Tuesday was already over by the time the finance ministers of the Group of Ten met in Washington on Friday, to try to conclude the world monetary crisis.

The "concessions" by the U S, which Treasury Secretary John Connally promised at the time of the Azores meeting, and which were prompting such optimistic predictions by midweek, were not exactly abrogated; it is fairer to say they required careful interpretation. The hard fact of the matter is that Connally was fighting tooth and nail on Friday to squeeze every concession on trade, and every last point of strong currency revaluation (and dollar devaluation) that could possibly be achieved.

But the most remarkable difference between this and previous meetings was the emphasis on trade concessions which the U S wants its major partners to make. Separate talks were being held with the Canadians and the Japanese during the meetings, but the U S were disappointed to find that the Common Market members arrived with little more on trade than technical objections to the effect that only the Brussels Commission could negotiate trade issues for them, and that they could not provide a fresh mandate to the Commission. Connally remarked in exasperation to an aide, regarding the Market Six, "It's so damn hard to get all those 'coons up a tree at once."

The real problem about these trade issues, for the Six, is that France,

47. The *Sunday Times* (London), Dec. 19, 1971, p. 45. Report by Economics editor Malcolm Crawford.

for internal political reasons, refuses to agree to anything looking like blatant unilateral concessions to the United States. Nixon evidently agreed, in his meeting with Pompidou, to wrap up his demands so they appeared like a stage-by-stage negotiation, in which there would be both give and take. But, in reality, the U S required and still requires some immediate unilateral concessions on matters that are not politically important for the Community, but which are highly sensitive for the U S. Beyond that, there are to be negotiations on more difficult issues next year. And more important still, Connally is insisting on a commitment to continuing negotiations, on a more or less reciprocal and wide-ranging nature, from 1973 onward.

The issues which Washington regards as easy are citrus fruit exports (on which the U S wants Community duties abolished in the summer and early autumn months, which do not clash with the Italian marketing season) and storage of the Community's grain surpluses. The U S has asked the Six to stockpile up to 10% of its grain crop this year and next, instead of dumping it on world markets, depressing prices for traditional exporting countries.

In addition, the Americans also want something (they care not what) to provide easier access for American grain exports to Europe. They have suggested that the common agricultural policy cut feed-grain prices to slightly above world market prices, and provide deficiency payments to European grain farmers to make up part of the difference. These payments would be limited to a specified proportion of the crop.

There is no chance at all of the Six accepting this just now—though it would be in Britain's interests to press for something like it once she is a member. But meanwhile, the U S would still like to be assured that grain prices in Europe are not going to go up. They will go up, in some countries, because price supports in the Common Market are based on a unit of account, which will be raised in value as part of the currency revaluations. In addition to that, community farmers are pressing for general price increases in all member currencies.

The U S administration is adamant that these price rises should not be piled on top of each other so as to give total increases (in the case of France) of up to 13%.

The U S has also made some intriguing proposals on Community protection and taxation of tobacco. First, and simplest, they have asked for subsidies to tobacco manufacturers using Europe-grown tobacco to be stopped, or at least reduced. Also, they have proposed limits to the internal taxes on tobacco, of 75% in the form of specific duties, and 25% in *ad valorem* form. As the Community are just beginning harmonisation of their excise taxes, this is a delicate matter. It is also important politically to the U S, for not only does it export $150 million a year worth of tobacco to Western Europe (compared with $20 million of citrus fruit); all but one of the committees in Congress on trade and finance are chaired by men from tobacco-raising states.

There is no hope of the Six agreeing to such demands very quickly. For Britain, they entail the special problem that limiting excise duties on tobacco to 100% would cut Exchequer revenues from that source by about two-thirds. However, a big reduction is bound to ensue from harmonisation anyway.

The point of limiting *ad valorem* taxes to 25% is that specific excise taxes (like our present ones) favour more expensive grades of tobacco which the U S exports, and which British and German tobacco firms process. The French and Italian state monopolies, using cheap tobaccos, would benefit from an *ad valorem* system.

The U S has admitted defeat in its attempts to block the free trade area for EFTA nonapplicants. Instead it now proposes that all the 13 countries concerned agree with the U S on provisions to compensate the latter for any trade "distortions" that arise from the proposed free trade deal. In other words, the U S wants trade concessions to make up for any losses it sustains from Sweden, or Switzerland, or Finland, getting duty-free access to the expanded Common Market.

The Americans are also demanding a mutual standstill on preferential arrangements, other than those under the UNCTAD generalised preference scheme. Also, from next year, they want the Community to agree to examinations by the GATT of the effects of EEC trade arrangements on other countries, and to agree to negotiate compensation.

Finally, from 1973 onward, there should be continuing discussions aimed at trade liberalisation on agriculture, tariffs, non-tariff barriers—everything.

This would not be a Nixon round. It would be a never-ending series of little rounds. It is, on the whole, a very sensible programme. But just now it appears a very tough nut for those 'coons to swallow.

Although the monetary crisis accelerated discussions of the trade differences between the United States and EEC, it was clear that any resolution of differences would have to proceed in stages and that answers to the longer term—and more important—trade questions would still have to be sought after the monetary talks were concluded.

As "a background for the formulation of United States international economic policy in the 'seventies," President Nixon requested that Peter G. Peterson, his assistant for international economic affairs, prepare a report on trade policy. Parts of this report are relevant here in indicating the Nixon administration's opposition to the "trade-distorting practices" of the Common Market and to the formation of a discriminatory European trade system that threatens to split the world into rival blocs.

AMERICAN APPREHENSIONS [48]

The United States has long supported the multilateral, nondiscriminatory approach to the management of international economic relations, as opposed to bilateralism and discrimination. The United States has global economic interests: it thrives best in a world of nondiscrimination. The American interest is not solely economic, however. Nationalism is politically divisive, whether practiced militarily or economically. The United States has tried to encourage the development of an international system which would contain divisive economic nationalism and exclusive regionalism, so that political as well as economic relations might operate to the general benefit of all countries.

Some countries have looked at their own interests differently. Working from a smaller economic base, and heavily reliant on trade with their close neighbors, these countries have at times preferred to work outside the framework of nondiscrimination and multilateral negotiation. Sometimes, for historic and cultural reasons, they have used preferential commercial relations as a basis for continuing political ties and promoting exports. The countries of the European Community have been most active in practicing this kind of economic diplomacy, providing, for example, preferential access to the Community for certain exports of a large number of African and Mediterranean countries, and in return requiring preferred access for European exports *into* the markets of these countries. These latter preferences are known as *reverse* preferences and while they are presumed to be of value to European manufacturers, they are of little value to the developing countries which are required to provide them. These special trading arrangements between the Community and certain developing countries are often tied to aid flows, so that a broad, bilateral economic relationship is maintained.

It has also been argued that these special discriminatory arrangements are politically necessary—for example, with certain Mediterranean countries with "historic" ties to individual Member States. This may now be even more true since it is difficult to favor one such country over another. Moreover, it ensures favorable ties with countries which are primarily raw material suppliers, while at the same time restricting the manufactured products of Asia and Latin America.

The Community now is trying to make arrangements for the European countries which do not become full members of the Community, such as Switzerland, Sweden, Austria and Finland. It is proposing free access between the European Community and these EFTA countries on most, but not all, industrial products, and not agricultural products. One of the reasons why many Europeans give priority to regional relations is that Euro-

48. Peter G. Peterson, *A Foreign Economic Perspective, Report to the President,* Dec. 27, 1971 (U.S. Government Printing Office).

pean trade is heavily regional trade. The intra-European trade among EFTA and European Community countries accounts for about two thirds of their total trade. Thus, European countries are heavily dependent on trade and most dependent on trade with each other.

American apprehensions about this trend reflect more than a concern for the impact on certain American exports like citrus. In fact, the impact on potential American exports has not yet been great in the aggregate, though individual products or sectors may suffer. In the aggregate, European integration and growth has stimulated U. S. exports to the point where we sell more to Europe than they to us. However, discriminatory arrangements have proliferated in the last few years, and the forces that lead towards splitting up of the world into blocs of influence threaten both the basic foundations of the postwar trading system, and the nondiscriminatory basis of political-economic relations which has been of such great benefit. This trend threatens to leave as outcasts the Asian and Latin American countries, at a time when their trade needs are growing rapidly with their rising unemployment. The United States cannot for long be expected to adhere to the principle of non-discrimination when so large a breach in that principle has been made.

The trends in Europe recently have been unfavorable in other regards as well. For example, the Community has developed an agricultural policy which satisfied the political needs of their agrisectors at the expense of its own consumers and outsiders. This system, based upon very high support prices, is designed to limit other non-member nations to the role of residual suppliers. Since it is based upon high prices without production controls, the combination of high price incentives and technological progress has meant continued increase in domestic production and the generation of surpluses which are then exported. Since the domestic surpluses are priced too high for world competition, aggressive subsidization is used to push the surpluses into the traditional markets of other, more efficient suppliers. By any measure, the Community's policy has displaced imports, increased self-sufficiency, and forced exports onto world markets at distress prices. This system is the essence of mercantilism, forcing more efficient farmers in other countries to bear the costs which the Community itself ought to pay for internally. As a result, European consumers eat less well, and American and other farmers live less well.

All countries have protective mechanisms for agriculture, and we are certainly no exception. The political and social problems exist everywhere, as does the desire to avoid undue dependence on foreign suppliers for one's food. However, when other parts of the world could produce and sell far more efficiently, including some of the smaller trading countries like Australia and New Zealand, there is not real justification for continuation of a system like that of Europe's which passes so much of its adjustment costs on to other nations, distorting world production and trade.

The European system was not fully applied until the mid-1960's. It is from that date that the effects of the system must be measured. There is no doubt that for all the items covered by the Community's variable levy system, American trade and the trade of other countries has suffered. Some will say that Americans have done well in certain other agricultural exports, but that is no justification for the trade distorting practices which do exist, and even here it must be recalled that the Community has from time to time proposed new restrictions to cover these items as well.

Politically, these developments are tragic, given Labor's new trade policies and when farmers must become a main force in the political drive in the U. S. for internationally oriented policies. A mercantilist agricultural policy as aggressive in its actions and effects as European policy today must necessarily undermine support of American farmers for outward-looking U. S. policies. It is simply a matter of politics in one place causing political reactions in other places. Thus, the multilateral trading system is being seriously eroded by these new trends in agricultural trade. For these reasons we can no longer delay serious discussions on the future of agricultural trade.

These recent trends in Community policy toward internally-oriented problem-solving, and toward regionalism in external relations, seem to crop up in other areas of Community decisions. For example, in regard to certain elements of an emerging Common-Industrial policy, it appears to some that the Community has been trying to work out its technical standards and pollution control methods on a Community-wide basis, without any real effort to do this on a multilateral scale. The use of standards as a nontariff restriction to trade is easy when common standards are set for insiders and outsiders are excluded from deliberations. All countries sometimes sin in this regard, but the Community has recently shown what appears to me to be an excessive preoccupation with the evolution of its internal policies and has not exhibited adequate regard for the effects of these policies on outsiders.

Trade restrictions are a major problem in all countries, but, again, recent experience is disconcerting. The European Community's set of special restrictions, both formal and informal, against imports from Japan (and from Eastern Asia generally), and in turn, Japan's impressive variety of import restrictions are anachronistic survivals from the days before Japan became a member of GATT. But the EEC restrictions have been so effective, as have the Japanese restrictions, that Japan supplies only about 3 percent of the Community's outside imports, while Japan supplies 15 percent of the U. S. imports, thus unnaturally enlarging the external U. S. adjustment problem. Thus, the effects of the restrictions are triangular, and hurt more than the bilateral impact suggests.

Thus, there are some immediate problems with the European Community. But in the long run, of greater importance to us is the *future* orientation of an enlarged and strengthened Community. The Community stands today at one of the great crossroads of Western Europe's historic development. Presumably, it has now more or less defined the geographic extent of the nucleus of a new economic, and eventually political, union in Western Europe. It now has two options ahead of it: to proceed to consolidate or perhaps even enlarge that union as a kind of regional bloc concerned primarily with its own internal problems and its relations with its most immediate neighbors, or to build, from its new-found position of strength, a more open and constructive relationship with the world as a whole.

Underscoring some of the apprehensions expressed above, Western Europe's two trading blocs did formally merge in July 1972 when a treaty was signed providing for the lowering of trade barriers between the Common Market and EFTA countries. The key provision of the treaty was the agreement for mutual abolition of tariffs on industrial goods between the EEC and EFTA countries over five years—from April 1, 1973, to July 1, 1977—at the rate of 20 per cent reduction each year. A longer transitional period was introduced for "sensitive products," in which free trade could cause domestic injury.[49] The expanded European free-trade zone embraces countries whose foreign trade accounted in 1972 for nearly half the world total.

In ten years—from the Trade Expansion Act of 1962 to the enlargement of the EEC in 1972—the context of international trade policy has changed sharply. The United States now has to share its responsibilities and seek the co-operation of two other major trading entities—Japan and the EEC. And if the GATT has accommodated the trade problems of the 1960's, it has become questionable whether it can continue to do so in the 1970's. The momentum of trade liberalization has been lost; examples of a new mercantilism have increased; and trade policy has become even more complicated by international monetary disorder. The Bretton Woods system that has structured international economic order for the past quarter-century is being severely challenged. Complex trade and monetary problems and an altered international distribution of economic power are calling for a new second-generation Bretton Woods system for the last quarter of the century.

C. Questions

1. It has been stated that the "European Community is a political compromise which stems from strong differences of opinion about

49. For details, see *The New York Times,* July 23, 1972, p. 3.

just what form the European idea should take—and specifically over the place of the nation-state in an integrated Europe." [L. N. Lindberg and S. A. Scheingold, *Europe's Would-Be Polity* (1970), p. 3.]

a. Why did the European idea materialize mainly in the form of economic measures—which are, after all, a far cry from the grandiose visions of a single European state?

b. What compromises were initially made by the EEC members in order to launch the Community? How have conflicting forces been reconciled during the life of the Community? Or have they?

c. What compromises had to be made by the members and Britain in order to have Britain enter the EEC?

2. Central authority in the EEC is the Common Market Commission, a body of nine permanent officials, appointed by the governments of the member countries, and bound to carry out the provisions of the Rome Treaty. After considering the role of the Commission and the implications of other provisions of the Rome Treaty, one critic of the EEC concludes:

"It is a constitution which is illiberal and undemocratic not merely in legal form, but in basic philosophy. It is founded on the central belief that modern society ought really to be ruled by the expert, the technocrat, the super-bureaucrat, the scientifically equipped wise man, who can find the right answer by pure calculation, unaffected by the pressure of vested interests or politics. It is rooted in an essential distrust of the people." [Douglas Jay, *After the Common Market* (1968), p. 33.]

a. Do you believe that there is a real danger of creating a supranational bureaucracy, unchecked by a European parliament? Or do you think the immediate gains of political unity in Western Europe are worth the wait for the possible emergence eventually of a true political federation?

b. If the elitist or technocratic bias of the Economic Commission is a cause of considerable concern, how can it be corrected?

3. Recall that Article XXIV of GATT allows a departure from the General Agreement's basic principle of unconditional most-favored-nation treatment when the contracting parties form a customs union or free trade area, provided that trade barriers on substantially all of the trade within the region are eliminated, and that the duties applying to outside countries are not, on the whole,

higher than the general incidence which previously existed in the individual countries. This allows a regional integration arrangement that combines elements of free trade and protection.

a. Is it always beneficial to insist, as GATT does, that trade barriers on "substantially all of the trade" within a region be eliminated? In general, under what conditions would a customs union improve the international allocation of resources? Worsen the allocation? What do you think is now the situation for the European Common Market? What do you think would have been the situation if the United Kingdom had joined a North Atlantic Free Trade Area instead of the EEC?

b. Recognizing the possibility of injury to nonmember countries when a customs union is formed, Article XXIV (6) of the General Agreement provides that any contracting party changing its duties in the formation of such a union must provide for "compensatory adjustment." Should the United States be compensated for discriminatory trade arrangements as a result of enlargement of the EEC and arrangements between EFTA and EEC? If so, how can the amount of compensation be established?

c. It is clear that American direct investment in the European Common Market has increased significantly. Has this produced adverse "trade-diverting effects"?

d. What have been the effects of the EEC on the trade of less-developed countries? Distinguish the countries that are and are not associated with the EEC.

4. a. What do you consider to have been the strongest arguments presented by the proponents of Britain's application for membership in the EEC?

b. What do you consider to have been the strongest arguments presented by the anti-Marketeers?

c. Should the United States have supported Britain's entry, or should it instead have supported some alternative multilateral free trade area?

5. It has been observed that the Werner Plan for economic and monetary union had initially, at least, support from the informed public,

especially among the three elements most responsible for the creation, the success, and the now likely enlargement of the Community: the visionaries, the nationalists, and the pragmatists.

The visionaries tend to see a Europe united politically and economically with a European Parliament as the main legislative body in a European federation. To them, monetary union is vital to this United Europe to help end the divisions created by disparate fiscal and monetary policies among the member countries.

The European nationalists resent the dominance of the U. S. dollar in the Western economic system and, sometimes with more than a tinge of anti-Americanism, argue that until there is monetary union, Europe will not be in a position to negotiate on a basis of equality with Washington on monetary and other matters.

The pragmatists see considerable advantages of stability and simplicity arising from a stable monetary system in Europe, particularly in the execution of common farm policy and the coordination of capital markets.
[Anthony Thomas, "Does Europe Need a Common Currency?" *European Community*, September 1971, No. 148, p. 14.]

a. In what ways does the EEC confront different problems in seeking monetary integration from those which it encountered in creating a Common Market for industrial goods? In this connection, consider the effects on EEC monetary policies of the common agricultural policy; of the trade liberalization which has occurred in the Common Market; and of the habits of consultation and co-ordination that were established among the Six.

b. How much co-ordination of other policies is necessary to have a monetary union?

c. What is now left of the prospects for implementing the Werner Report? How is the emergence of an economic and monetary union as envisaged in the Werner Report related to the general problem of international monetary reform?

6. Commenting on the enlargement of the European Community, a *New York Times* economics analyst stated that "the Treasury, the Commerce Department and the White House are more worried about the negative impact on the American economy of European enlargement, trade preferences with third countries and agricul-

tural protectionism against the United States than they are impressed by Europe's contribution to Western security." (*New York Times*, Jan. 23, 1972, Sec. E, p. 5.)

a. Do you think that there are real grounds for worry about the negative impact on the American economy? Or are the concerns exaggerated?

b. Look to the future. When another President requests the preparation of a report as "a background for the formulation of U. S. international economic policy in the 'eighties," do you think it will express as severe criticism of the EEC as did the Peterson Report?